THE CAMBRIDGE COMPANION TO THE LITERATURE OF WORLD WAR II

The literature of the Second World War has emerged as an accomplished, moving, and challenging body of work, produced by writers as different as Norman Mailer and Virginia Woolf, Primo Levi and Ernest Hemingway, Jean-Paul Sartre and W. H. Auden. This Companion provides a comprehensive overview of the international literatures of the war: both those works that recorded or reflected experiences of the war as it happened, and those that tried to make sense of it afterwards. It surveys the writing produced in the major combatant nations (Britain and the Commonwealth, the USA, Japan, Germany, France, Italy, and the USSR), and explores its common themes. This book aims to supply the new reader with the essential knowledge and conceptual tools for reading the literature of World War II. With its chronology and guide to further reading, it will be an invaluable source of information and inspiration for students and scholars of modern literature and war studies.

THE CAMBRIDGE
COMPANION TO

THE LITERATURE OF
WORLD WAR II

EDITED BY
MARINA MACKAY
Washington University, St. Louis

CAMBRIDGE
UNIVERSITY PRESS

CAMBRIDGE UNIVERSITY PRESS
Cambridge, New York, Melbourne, Madrid, Cape Town, Singapore, São Paulo, Delhi

Cambridge University Press
The Edinburgh Building, Cambridge CB2 8RU, UK

Published in the United States of America by Cambridge University Press, New York

www.cambridge.org
Information on this title: www.cambridge.org/9780521715416

© Cambridge University Press 2009

First published 2009

Printed in the United Kingdom at the University Press, Cambridge

A catalogue record for this publication is available from the British Library

ISBN 978-0-521-88755-7 hardback
ISBN 978-0-521-71541-6 paperback

CONTENTS

CONTENTS

NOTES ON CONTRIBUTORS

DAGMAR BARNOUW taught intellectual and cultural history at the University of Southern California. Her American publications include *Weimar Intellectuals and the Threat of Modernity* (1988); *Visible Spaces: Hannah Arendt and the German-Jewish Experience* (1990); *Critical Realism* (1994); *Germany 1945: Views of War and Violence* (1997); *Naipaul's Strangers* (2003); and *The War in the Empty Air: Victims, Perpetrators, and Postwar Germans* (2005).

DONNA COATES is Associate Professor of English at the University of Calgary, where she teaches Australian and Canadian literatures, with an emphasis on women's war fiction and drama. She has published articles and book chapters on women's literary responses to the world wars and the Vietnam War. Her *Canada and the Theatre of War* (with Sherrill Grace) is forthcoming in 2008.

JAMES DAWES teaches American and Comparative Literature at Macalester College. He is the author of *That The World May Know: Bearing Witness to Atrocity* (2007) and *The Language of War* (2002) as well as numerous articles on topics including literary and language theory, international law and human rights, trauma, literature and medical studies, Shakespeare, aesthetic theory, and pedagogical technique.

ROBERT S. C. GORDON is Reader in Modern Italian Culture at the University of Cambridge. His books include *Primo Levi's Ordinary Virtues: From Testimony to Ethics* (2001), *An Introduction to Twentieth-Century Italian Literature: A Difficult Modernity* (2005), and (as co-editor) *Culture, Censorship and the State in Twentieth-Century Italy* (2005).

KATHARINE HODGSON is Senior Lecturer in Russian at the University of Exeter. She is the author of *Written with the Bayonet: Soviet Russian Poetry of World War Two* (1996), and of a monograph about Olga Berggolts, best known as the poet of the wartime siege of Leningrad.

PHYLLIS LASSNER teaches Holocaust Studies, Gender Studies, and Writing at Northwestern University. She is the author of two books on Elizabeth Bowen as well as of *British Women Writers of World War II* (1998), *Colonial Strangers: Women Writing the End of the British Empire* (2004), and many articles on interwar and wartime women writers. She has also published essays on Holocaust writing and her most recent book is *Anglo-Jewish Women Writing the Holocaust: Displaced Witnesses* (2008).

MARINA MACKAY teaches twentieth-century British writing at Washington University in St. Louis. She is the author of *Modernism and World War II* (2007) and editor (with Lyndsey Stonebridge) of *British Fiction After Modernism* (2007).

LEO GWILYM MELLOR is a Fellow of New Hall and a Newton Trust Lecturer at the University of Cambridge. He has written on Second World War literature, contemporary poetry, and Anglo-Welsh culture. His own poems have been published as *Marsh Fear/Fen Tiger* (2002) and *Things Settle* (2004). A book from his travels among the Welsh-speaking communities of Patagonia will appear in 2008. He is currently writing about the flowers of London's bombsites.

ROD MENGHAM is Reader in Modern English Literature at the University of Cambridge, where he is also Curator of Works of Art at Jesus College. He is the author of books on Charles Dickens, Emily Brontë, and Henry Green, as well as of *The Descent of Language* (1993). He has edited collections of essays on contemporary fiction, violence and avant-garde art, and the fiction of the 1940s. He is also editor of the Equipage series of poetry pamphlets, co-editor and co-translator of *Altered State: The New Polish Poetry* (2003), and co-editor of *Vanishing Points: New Modernist Poems* (2005). His most recent books are a dual-language *Selected Poems*, in English with Polish translations (2007), and, with Sophie Gilmartin, *Thomas Hardy's Shorter Fiction* (2007).

MARGOT NORRIS is Chancellor's Professor of English and Comparative Literature at the University of California, Irvine, where she teaches modern literature. She is the author of *Writing War in the Twentieth Century* (2000). She also has four books on James Joyce in print, as well as a study of the animal and anthropomorphism in nineteenth- and early twentieth-century intellectual history, *Beasts of the Modern Imagination* (1985).

ADAM PIETTE is Professor at the University of Sheffield. He is the author of *Remembering and the Sound of Words: Mallarmé, Proust, Joyce, Beckett* (1996) and *Imagination at War: British Fiction and Poetry, 1939–1945* (1995), is working on a monograph on Cold War writing and a book on close reading based on a series published in *The Reader*, and is also editing a companion to war writing.

GILL PLAIN is Professor of English Literature and Popular Culture at the University of St. Andrews. Her publications include *Women's Fiction of the Second World War: Gender, Power and Resistance* (1996), *Twentieth-Century Crime Fiction:*

Gender, Sexuality and the Body (2001), and *John Mills and British Cinema: Masculinity, Identity and Nation* (2006). She is currently working on a literary history of the 1940s.

PETRA RAU is Senior Lecturer in English and European Literature at the University of Portsmouth. She has published articles on fascist tourism, on contemporary and modernist war writing, and on the poetics of Freud's case studies. Her monograph *English Modernism, National Identity and the Germans, 1890–1950* is forthcoming.

DEBARATI SANYAL is Associate Professor of French at the University of California, Berkeley. She is the author of *The Violence of Modernity: Baudelaire, Irony, and the Politics of Form* (2006) and articles on Baudelaire, Holocaust studies, and French postwar commitment. She is currently writing a book on converging memories of the Occupation, the Shoah, and colonialism in postwar France.

LYNDSEY STONEBRIDGE is Professor of Literature and Critical Theory at the University of East Anglia, Norwich. She is the author of *The Writing of Anxiety: Imagining Wartime in Mid-Century British Culture* (2007) and *The Destructive Element: British Psychoanalysis and Modernism* (1998), and the editor (with Marina MacKay) of *British Fiction After Modernism* (2007) and (with John Phillips) of *Reading Melanie Klein* (1998). She is currently completing a book on writing about war-crime trials (*Law Writing: Fiction After Nuremberg*).

REIKO TACHIBANA is Associate Professor of Comparative Literature and Japanese at The Pennsylvania State University. Her research interests include East–West relations, contemporary Japanese fiction and culture, and transnational/diasporic writers of Japan. She is the author of *Narrative as Counter-Memory: A Half-Century of Postwar Writing in Germany and Japan* (1998) and is currently completing a book about transnational women writers of Japan.

ACKNOWLEDGMENTS

Warmest thanks are due to Ray Ryan at Cambridge University Press. This book was his idea, and at every stage he advanced the project with characteristic generosity and energy. Anna Zaranko copyedited the manuscript for the Press with insight as well as rigor. It is also a pleasure to acknowledge at least one of my debts to my friend and colleague Vincent Sherry, from whose work I have benefited all along. And to thank Dan Grausam for his indispensable contributions, intellectual and musical, to home-front morale.

The contributors to this volume have been a pleasure to work with, and I thank them sincerely for their patience, efficiency, and good will. Sadly Dagmar Barnouw did not live to see the project completed, and the death of this unshakably principled, passionate, and humane scholar is a loss to all of us who study the war and its aftermath.

MMK

CHRONOLOGY

1918   World War I Armistice
Murder of Tsar Nicholas II and family
Siegfried Sassoon, *Counter-Attack*
Oswald Spengler, *The Decline of the West*
Rebecca West, *The Return of the Soldier*

1919   Paris Peace Conference opens
League of Nations formed
Amritsar massacre
John Maynard Keynes, *The Economic Consequences of the Peace*

1921   Wilfred Owen, *Poems*

1922   Mussolini's march on Rome
Irish Civil War
E. E. Cummings, *The Enormous Room*
T. S. Eliot, *The Waste Land*
James Joyce, *Ulysses*
Virginia Woolf, *Jacob's Room*

1923   Nazi coup ("Beer Hall Putsch") fails
Jaroslav Hašek, *The Good Soldier Švejk*

1924   Death of Lenin; rise of Stalin

1925   Locarno Treaties reaffirm European peace
Sergei Eisenstein, *Battleship Potemkin*
F. Scott Fitzgerald, *The Great Gatsby*
Hitler, *Mein Kampf*
Virginia Woolf, *Mrs. Dalloway*

1926   General Strike
        Hirohito enthroned Emperor of Japan

1928   Kellogg–Briand Pact outlaws war as instrument of national policy
        British women fully enfranchised
        Edmund Blunden, *Undertones of War*
        Ford Madox Ford, *Parade's End* (tetralogy completed)
        Radclyffe Hall, *The Well of Loneliness*
        D. H. Lawrence, *Lady Chatterley's Lover*
        Robert Sherriff, *Journey's End*

1929   Wall Street Crash
        Richard Aldington, *Death of a Hero*
        Robert Graves, *Good-bye to All That*
        Ernest Hemingway, *A Farewell to Arms*
        Erich Maria Remarque, *All Quiet on the Western Front*

1930   Haile Selassie crowned Emperor of Ethiopia

1931   Statute of Westminster establishes equality of self-governing
        dominions

1932   Salazar establishes fascist regime in Portugal
        Nazis become largest party in Reichstag
        Roosevelt wins landslide presidential election
        British Union of Fascists founded
        W. H. Auden, *The Orators*
        Louis-Ferdinand Céline, *Journey to the End of the Night*
        Aldous Huxley, *Brave New World*

1933   Hitler becomes German Chancellor
        Gestapo and first Nazi concentration camp (Dachau) established
        Germany and Japan withdraw from League of Nations
        Roosevelt's "New Deal"
        Vera Brittain, *Testament of Youth*
        H. G. Wells, *The Shape of Things to Come*

1934   Austrian Civil War
        Japan invades Manchuria
        Nazi purge ("Night of the Long Knives")

1935   Italy invades Abyssinia
        Hitler announces rearmament
        Nuremberg Laws

1936   Berlin Olympics
Spanish Civil War starts
Germany remilitarizes Rhineland
Rome–Berlin Axis formed
Soviet show trials begin

1937   Chamberlain elected Prime Minister
Italy leaves League of Nations
Nanking Massacre
Picasso, *Guernica*
David Jones, *In Parenthesis*

1938   12 March: Germany annexes Austria ("*Anschluss*")
29–30 September: Munich Agreement partitions Czechoslovakia;
Chamberlain promises "peace for our time"
9–10 November: *Kristallnacht* pogrom
George Orwell, *Homage to Catalonia*
Virginia Woolf, *Three Guineas*

1939   15 March: Germans march into Prague
1 April: Fascists win Spanish Civil War
7 April: Italy invades Albania
23 August: Nazi–Soviet non-aggression pact
1 September: Germany invades Poland
3 September: Britain and France declare war on Germany
17 September: USSR invades Poland
30 November: USSR invades Finland
17 December: *Admiral Graf Spee* scuttled

Cyril Connolly founds *Horizon*
W. H. Auden and Christopher Isherwood, *Journey to a War*
Christopher Isherwood, *Goodbye to Berlin*

1940   9 April: Germany invades Denmark and Norway
10 May: Germany invades France and the Low
                      Countries
10 May: Churchill becomes Prime Minister
14 May: Netherlands surrender
20 May: Germans reach English Channel
27 May–4 June: BEF evacuated at Dunkirk
28 May: Belgium surrenders
10 June: Italy declares war on France and Britain

14 June:	Fall of Paris
22 June:	French sign armistice
28 June:	De Gaulle recognized as leader of Free French
3 July:	Britain sinks French fleet
10 July–15 September:	Battle of Britain
23 July:	USSR annexes Baltic States
7 September:	Blitz begins (until May 10, 1941)
27 September:	Germany, Japan, and Italy sign Tripartite Pact
28 October:	Italy invades Greece
11 November:	RAF attacks Italian fleet at Taranto
November:	Hungary, Romania, and Slovakia join Axis

The Great Dictator, dir. Charlie Chaplin
Ernest Hemingway, *For Whom the Bell Tolls*
Arthur Koestler, *Darkness at Noon*

1941	6 January:	Roosevelt's "Four Freedoms" speech
	1 March:	Bulgaria joins Axis
	11 March:	Lend-Lease Act
	29 March:	Battle of Cape Matapan
	6 April:	Germany invades Yugoslavia and Greece
	6 April:	Italy surrenders Ethiopia
	13 April:	Japan and USSR sign non-aggression pact
	17 April:	Yugoslavia surrenders
	21 April:	Greece surrenders
	10 May:	Hess undertakes unofficial peace mission
	20 May:	Germany invades Crete
	24 May:	German battleship *Bismarck* sinks *HMS Hood*
	27 May:	*Bismarck* sunk
	22 June:	Germany invades USSR
	12 July:	Anglo-Soviet Treaty of Mutual Assistance
	14 August:	Atlantic Charter outlines Anglo-American objectives
	17 August:	Fall of Kiev
	4 September:	Roosevelt authorizes naval "shoot on sight" policy
	8 September:	Siege of Leningrad begins (lifted January 27, 1944)
	2 October:	Final German offensive on Moscow begins
	17 October:	Tojo becomes Japanese Prime Minister
	14 November:	Germans sink *HMS Ark Royal*

5 December: Britain declares war on Finland, Hungary, Romania
7 December: Japan attacks Pearl Harbor
8 December: USA declares war on Japan
8 December: Japan invades Malaya, Hong Kong, Thailand, Philippines
11 December: Germany declares war on USA
11 December: Japan invades Burma
22 December: Japanese take Manila
25 December: Hong Kong surrenders

Bertolt Brecht, *Mother Courage and Her Children*
Virginia Woolf, *Between the Acts*

1942	11 January:	Fall of Kuala Lumpur
	20 January:	Wannsee Conference formulates "final solution"
	8 February:	Fall of Rangoon
	15 February:	Fall of Singapore
	19 February:	Japanese–American internment authorized
	19 February:	Japanese bomb Darwin, Australia
	22 February:	US leaves Philippines
	27–29 February:	Battle of the Java Sea
	2 March:	Fall of Batavia
	18 April:	US bombs Tokyo
	23 April:	"Baedcker raids" on historic English cities begin
	6–8 May:	Battle of the Coral Sea
	30 May:	"1000 bomber raid" on Cologne
	4 June:	Heydrich assassinated
	4–7 June:	Battle of Midway
	1–27 July:	First Battle of El Alamein
	7 August:	Battle of Guadalcanal begins (ends February 1943)
	19 August:	Allied Dieppe Raid fails
	13 August:	Battle for Stalingrad begins (ends February 2, 1943)
	23 October–4 November:	Second Battle of El Alamein
	11 November:	Germans occupy Vichy France
	31 December:	Battle of the Barents Sea

Manhattan Project established to build nuclear weapons
Beveridge Report outlines postwar British welfare state
Antoine de Saint-Exupéry, *Flight to Arras*
Casablanca, dir. Michael Curtiz
In Which We Serve, dir. Noel Coward and David Lean
Mrs. Miniver, dir. William Wyler
Prelude to War, dir. Frank Capra, first of seven "Why We Fight"
films

1943	23 January:	Allies take Tripoli
	2–4 March:	Battle of the Bismarck Sea
	19 April–16 May:	Uprising and extinction of Warsaw Ghetto
	13 May:	German and Italian forces surrender in Tunisia
	16 May:	Dambuster raids
	10 July:	Allied invasion of Sicily
	24 July:	Hamburg firestorm
	25 July:	Mussolini deposed
	3 September:	Italy surrenders
	15 September:	Mussolini founds Salò Republic
	23 September:	Italy signs armistice with Allies
	6 November:	USSR retakes Kiev
	28 November–1 December:	Churchill, Roosevelt, and Stalin meet in Tehran

T. S. Eliot, *Four Quartets*
Henry Green, *Caught*
Graham Greene, *The Ministry of Fear*
Fires Were Started, dir. Humphrey Jennings
Five Graves to Cairo, dir. Billy Wilder

1944	4 January–18 May:	Battle of Monte Cassino
	22 January:	US landings at Anzio
	22 February:	US takes Eniwetok
	4 June:	Fall of Rome
	6 June:	D-Day landings
	13 June:	Germans deploy V1 rocket against London
	9 July:	Allies take Caen
	20 July:	Assassination attempt against Hitler
	24 July:	Liberation of Majdanek
	1 August:	Warsaw Uprising (crushed October 2)

	23 August:	Romania surrenders
	24 August:	Liberation of Paris
	8 September:	German V2 rocket used against London
	11 September:	Allied troops enter Germany
	25 September:	Allies defeated at Arnhem
	28 October:	Bulgaria signs armistice
	16 December:	Germany begins Ardennes counteroffensive ("Battle of the Bulge")

Deaths of war poets Keith Douglas and Alun Lewis

1945	20 January:	Hungary signs armistice
	27 January:	Red Army liberates Auschwitz
	4–11 February:	Yalta Conference
	13–14 February:	Dresden firestorm
	19 February–16 March:	Battle of Iwo Jima
	9–10 March:	Tokyo firestorm
	April:	Liberation of Buchenwald, Bergen-Belsen, Dachau
	1 April–21 June:	Battle of Okinawa
	12 April:	Death of Roosevelt
	28 April:	Execution of Mussolini
	30 April:	Hitler commits suicide
	2 May:	Fall of Berlin
	7 May:	Germany signs unconditional surrender
	8 May:	V-E Day
	5 June:	Allied Control Council takes over Germany
	26 June:	UN Charter signed
	16 July:	Atomic bomb tested
	26 July:	Churchill loses election
	26 July:	Potsdam Declaration demands unconditional surrender of Japan
	6 August:	Atomic bomb dropped on Hiroshima
	9 August:	Atomic bomb dropped on Nagasaki
	15 August:	V-J Day
	2 September:	Japan signs instrument of surrender
	20 November:	Nuremberg Trials begin

George Orwell, *Animal Farm*
Karl Popper, *The Open Society and Its Enemies*
Rome, Open City, dir. Roberto Rossellini

1946   Churchill's "Iron Curtain" speech
Japanese war crimes trials begin
Italy becomes a republic
H. D., *Trilogy*
Keith Douglas, *Alamein to Zem Zem*
The Best Years of Our Lives, dir. William Wyler

1947   Truman Doctrine on Communist containment
European Recovery Program ("Marshall Plan")
Independence of India and Pakistan
Anne Frank's diary first published (in Dutch)
Theodor Adorno and Max Horkheimer, *Dialectic of Enlightenment*
W. H. Auden, *The Age of Anxiety*
Italo Calvino, *The Path to the Nest of Spiders*
Albert Camus, *The Plague*
Primo Levi, *If This Is a Man*
Thomas Mann, *Dr. Faustus*

1948   State of Israel proclaimed
Berlin Airlift begins
Tojo executed
Elizabeth Bowen, *The Heat of the Day*
James Gould Cozzens, *Guard of Honor*
Norman Mailer, *The Naked and the Dead*
Ezra Pound, *The Pisan Cantos*

1949   NATO formed
Partition of Germany
People's Republic of China proclaimed
USSR tests atomic weapons
Audie Murphy, *To Hell and Back*
George Orwell, *Nineteen Eighty-Four*
Jean-Paul Sartre, *The Roads to Freedom* (trilogy completed)
Sands of Iwo Jima, dir. Allan Dwan

1950   Truman authorizes development of hydrogen bomb
Korean War begins
The God that Failed, ed. Richard Crossman

1951   Hannah Arendt, *The Origins of Totalitarianism*
       James Jones, *From Here to Eternity*
       Herman Wouk, *The Caine Mutiny*

1952   US detonates hydrogen bomb
       Pierre Boulle, *The Bridge over the River Kwai*
       Evelyn Waugh, *Men at Arms*

1953   Death of Stalin
       Eisenhower becomes president
       Rosenberg execution
       Samuel Beckett, *Waiting for Godot*
       Arthur Miller, *The Crucible*
       From Here to Eternity, dir. Fred Zinnemann
       Stalag 17, dir. Billy Wilder
       The Desert Rats, dir. Robert Wise

1954   Algerian War of Independence begins
       US Senate censures McCarthy
       William Golding, *Lord of the Flies*

1955   Warsaw Pact signed
       The Dam Busters, dir. Michael Anderson
       Night and Fog, dir. Alain Resnais

1956   Soviet troops crush Hungarian uprising
       Kruschev denounces Stalin's excesses
       Britain and France forced to withdraw military response to Egyptian
       nationalization of Suez Canal ("Suez Crisis")

MARINA MACKAY

Introduction

"We in our haste can only see the small components of the scene," conceded one poet of the Second World War, writing about the predicament of Second World War poetry itself: "We cannot tell what incidents will focus on the final screen."[1] Seeing the big picture of a war that stretched across the globe was avowedly difficult at the time, and, notwithstanding the perspective supplied by our seventy years of distance, it remains so. What this book aims to do is to give a sense of those "components of the scene" directly witnessed by individual participants across the globe and reconstructed by onlookers who wrote after the event. All the same, and as many chapters of this book will demonstrate, what the poet calls "the final screen" necessarily remains elusive: as with any historical event and its representations, World War II and its literature are still subject to revision in the light of changing cultural priorities, needs, and interests. There is no definitive way of summing up for *all* time what the war meant for literature, although we hope to show in this volume at least how it looks in our own time.

"War's being global meant that it ran off the edges of maps," wrote the Anglo-Irish novelist Elizabeth Bowen in her novel of wartime espionage, *The Heat of the Day* (1948): "it was uncontainable."[2] Here Bowen is describing the impossibility of keeping in mind the multiple locations of a war on and around the Atlantic, Mediterranean, and Pacific Oceans, a war fought in deserts and jungles, on seas, fields, plains, and familiar city streets. "Where is the front?" Leo Mellor asks in his chapter on war reportage, responding to that contemporary sense that World War II had rendered inadequate, even entirely irrelevant, long-held assumptions about where – which is to say, how – wars are fought. The major challenge facing any synoptic account of World War II is how to convey the war's totally unprecedented geographical scope and the crushing totality with which it managed to turn into a battleground everything it touched. Devastating and deadly though it undoubtedly was, the Great War of 1914–18 can seem more like a European Civil War in comparison. The terrifying hints it gave of what total world war looks like would be realized in its successor.

World War II is "uncontainable," to use Bowen's word, for reasons of time as well as space. It perhaps gives some sense of the difficulty of generalizing about the war to note that even the seeming stability of its dates – 1939–45 – obscures as much as it contains. For the British, certainly, the war began in 1939, two days after Germany invaded Poland on September 1, and formally ended on September 2, 1945, when the Japanese signed the instrument of surrender three weeks after the United States used the atomic bomb against the cities of Hiroshima and Nagasaki. Having begun only when the Japanese attacked Pearl Harbor at the very end of 1941, the American war was substantially shorter than the one fought between Britain and Germany, although the war in the Far East began much earlier still, with Japanese aggression against China early in the 1930s. Back in Europe, Germany had already annexed Austria in 1938, and the war would begin that year also for Czechoslovakia, a small, prosperous democracy created after the Great War, when Hitler used the promise of peace to bribe and bully France and Britain into allowing Czechoslovakia to be partitioned (prefatory to a German take-over) in the Munich Agreement of September 1938. And, while 1945 brought the unconditional surrender of Germany and Japan, for many of the countries brutalized by the Axis powers, liberation would be the prelude to civil war. In many cases, too, five years of Nazi occupation would give way to almost five decades of Soviet domination, when two former Allies, the US and the USSR, dramatically parted company and the endings of World War II shaded into the beginnings of the Cold War. This sense that the war massively exceeded the parameters of its official dating was what the English novelist E. M. Forster implied when he wrote in 1951 of "the war which began for Great Britain in 1939, although earlier elsewhere, and which is still going on."[3]

And then there were the wars within the war. Robert Gordon begins his chapter on the Italian war by pointing out that Italy fought multiple wars, first with the Germans and then against them. France also had a very different war from those fought by Britain and America: the French entered the war with the British in September 1939 but laid down their arms in 1940, in that cataclysmic summer when the Germans conquered most of Europe. By the end of June 1940, France, Belgium, the Netherlands, Luxembourg, Denmark, and Norway had all fallen to the Germans, who were then poised to invade Britain (they had reached the English Channel in May). For those countries that made their coerced peace with Germany, the fighting war was short but the experience of occupation would be long and brutal. The different kinds of war that World War II encompassed affect its literature in profound ways. So, for example, Debarati Sanyal's chapter emphasizes the importance of questions of collaboration, engagement, and resistance in the French literature of the war – questions that the unoccupied British did not have to ask. They had questions of their own, though: as James Dawes, Margot Norris, Rod Mengham, and Adam Piette show in their discussions of British and American poetry and fiction, the Anglo-American experience of total war would give rise to vital questions about the nature of citizenship, democracy, and belonging, while, as Donna Coates shows in her discussion of war writing from Canada, New Zealand, and Australia, Britain's "war for democracy" looked substantially different again from the perspective of those former colonies that had joined the fight.

But this is not simply a book about the literary works that record the Allies' experiences of war. The chilling atrocities carried out by Nazi Germany and Imperial Japan made it easy for the war to slide into cultural memory in excessively simplified forms. Despite the fact that Britain and America have fought numerous wars since 1945, World War II remains a kind of gold standard for "just war" – an obvious contrast with World War I, which found its place in cultural memory as a tragic and obscene mess for everyone concerned. And although the Holocaust only accrued its current cultural importance decades after the war (because notwithstanding Churchill's undoubtedly sincere horror when news emerged of the Nazi genocide, saving the European Jews was not an Allied priority), it only reinforces the Anglo-American temptation to mythologize World War II as an epic struggle of good against evil. But the most important claim literature can make on our historical imaginations is to show how things felt at the time, and while I suspect it would take a criminally perverse form of historical revisionism to suggest that World War II was anything other than a war that the Allies had to win, looking beyond the trans-historical simplifications of "good against evil" offers us essential historical insight into the real experiences of the real people – British and American, French and Russian, German, Italian, and Japanese – who lived through it. That Germany and Japan surely had to be defeated scarcely means that their citizens did not suffer in wars waged on their behalf. Nor should history exact as unofficial reparations their enduring silence about their war experiences.

A recurring theme in the chapters that follow is the direct and indirect means by which literary witness is delayed – and many of the important works of World War II literature were in fact only written or published well after 1945 – or even silenced altogether. Katharine Hodgson's chapter on war writing from the USSR describes the gaping disparity between the lived experiences of Soviet soldiers and the Soviet party line, which required that all credit for the "great patriotic war" be attributed to the Soviet leadership. For war writers in the USSR, pushing hard at the boundaries of censorship in the effort to reflect conditions at the front to readers back home, the war fueled hopes of freedom of expression that were not to be realized in their own time. Of course censorship may be externally as well as internally imposed: Dagmar Barnouw's chapter on the German war experience opens in the stunned, wordless ruins of the bombed German cities of 1945; she and Reiko Tachibana emphasize the effects of censorship in the war's immediate aftermath, when a defeated Germany and Japan were under Allied occupation. At the very moment when American writers were starting to write and publish such future classics of modern war fiction as *The Naked and the Dead* and the other essential war novels James Dawes discusses in his chapter, German and Japanese writers found that their war experiences were both literally and figuratively unspeakable. In 1950, for example, the future Nobel Laureate Heinrich Böll could find no publisher for his tellingly titled first novel *The Silent Angel*, which would eventually be published only posthumously. This is a novel about a German soldier returned from war; he is a member of, in Böll's own words, "the generation which has 'come home,' a generation that knows there is no home for them on this earth."[4] German and Japanese war experiences were unspeakable not only in the familiar, colloquial sense that there seemed no words to describe destruction on such an unprecedented scale (Dresden, Hamburg, Berlin, Tokyo, Hiroshima, Nagasaki), but also politically unspeakable initially because their countries were occupied by the victorious Allied powers, and, in the longer run, because of the moral difficulty of saying anything that could be construed as "we suffered too" – which risks eliciting the response that, first, "they" brought it on themselves, and, second, that the crimes committed against them were dwarfed by those committed in their name.

Even writers in democracies, comparatively free to describe their war experiences both at the time and afterwards, worried about what could really be said, mindful as they were of the degrading effects of war on the integrity of descriptive language. In a famous essay published just after the war, and very clearly marked by the atrocities of the 1930s and 1940s, of the war and its grim aftermath in Europe, George Orwell protested the euphemisms, deceptions, and falsifications of public speech, singling out new phrasings formulated in order to avoid "calling up mental pictures" of the violent acts to which they refer:

> Defenceless villages are bombarded from the air, the inhabitants driven out into the countryside, the cattle machine-gunned, the huts set on fire with incendiary bullets: this is called *pacification*. Millions of peasants are robbed of their farms and sent trudging along the roads with no more than they can carry: this is called *transfer of population* or *rectification of frontiers*.[5]

No wonder wartime Europe should have provided the historical basis of Orwell's invention of "Newspeak" in *Nineteen Eighty-Four*, a totalitarian language that aims to reduce the possibilities of thought by minimizing and homogenizing the vocabulary available to its speakers. From Orwell's point of view, though, the problem for language was not solely a matter of totalitarianism's notorious euphemisms ("final solution," "liquidation," and so on), but the problem of what happens to speech everywhere in times of political crisis, at all moments when the unjustifiable has to be justified through a vocabulary that renders invisible the brutally violent phenomena it purports to name. The prosecution of war, infamously, depends on a referential minimalism akin to Newspeak – "casualties," "collateral damage," "strategic withdrawal," and "displaced persons" are among the many phrasings we use to name and avoid the unbearable. With this in mind, you could say that the strongest moral claim that the literature of World War II makes on our attention lies in its power to restore the devastating experiential realities that official languages conceal. Even so, it gives some indication of the extraordinary challenges that literary art faced – the trite "unspeakable" so often attached to the experience of war is sometimes more meaningful than its familiarity makes it sound – to mention here that the contributors in this collection will occasionally turn to film in an effort to convey those experiences of World War II that literature struggled to voice.

An important difficulty of expression unique to writers in democracies emerges in the tension between their general support for the war and their total unwillingness to submit to the uncritical, exclusionary, and blinkered forms of patriotism that war tends to elicit, in their time as in ours. As the British poet Cecil Day Lewis wrote in his "Where are the War Poets?" (1943), it was "no subject for immortal verse / that we who lived by honest dreams / defend the bad against the worse."[6] Nor could sensitive onlookers ignore such vicious ironies, not to say outright hypocrisies, as those World War II cast up: late imperial Britain newly casting itself as the guardian and champion of small nations' sovereignty; Allies deploying a racially segregated military to wage war on poisonously racist foreign regimes; Stalinist judges on the bench trying the Germans for particular crimes of which the Soviet regime was also notoriously guilty. The enduring legacy of literary responses to World War II is less a vindication of Allied righteousness than a demonstration of what it means to support a war in a genuinely clear-sighted and critical way.

Forster defined Orwell's patriotism as the belief that "all nations are odious but some are less odious than others."[7] Forster might have been describing himself as well as Orwell, and their move towards a highly critical patriotism during the war is entirely representative of a whole generation or two of writers. Passionate liberals though they were, both of them instinctively hostile to the idea that writers should ever become mouthpieces for the state, even Forster and Orwell would broadcast for the BBC during the war,

Forster writing and delivering anti-Nazi broadcasts that aimed to explain why, as he put it in 1940, "we have got to go on with this hideous fight,"[8] and Orwell trying to elicit support for Britain from an extremely restless (and soon to be independent) India. In "R.A.F.," a poem based on her experience of living in London during the Battle of Britain, even the American modernist poet H.D. turned – British – patriot: "I award myself / some inch of ribbon," she writes, in solidarity with the endangered pilots. It turns out that the courage for which she decorates herself is the courage needed to witness evil prosper while brave, good airmen fall.[9]

The American Allen Tate gently mocked this shift from the private ennui of interwar modernists to their public-spiritedness in wartime when he wrote in one of his own war poems of "[s]pirits grown Eliotic, / Now patriotic."[10] As Adam Piette points out in his chapter on British poetry of the war, one of the interesting, albeit potentially confusing, aspects of the material is that public feeling is often more resonant than the private feelings usually associated with lyric poetry.

Which is not to say, of course, that writers necessarily embraced the erosion of the private and the individual, the insidious infiltration of the war into all spheres of life during years when, in the words of one American war poet, "The private life is small; And individual men / Are counted not at all."[11] The hateful effects of enforced sociality, the exorbitant claims of the state, and the diminution of the private life were often noted, and by writers of all nationalities. In his autobiographical *WWII: A Chronicle of Soldiering*, the American novelist James Jones, author of *The Thin Red Line* and *From Here to Eternity*, described in detail how military life aimed systematically to erode individuality – through "the discipline, the daily humiliations, the privileges of 'brutish' sergeants" – in order to make the soldier feel that he is "as dispensable as the ships and guns and tanks and ammo he himself serves and dispenses," or "a nameless piece of expendable matériel."[12] These resentments at the demands of institutional life are described in Dawes's discussion of Jones and other American novelists of his generation, and what you absolutely don't find in the writing of soldiers and veterans is any self-righteous retrospective conviction about good clean wars that kill sixty million people; rather, only an ironic appraisal of what one war poet mordantly called "an approved early death / under the national aegis."[13] And although Germany's aggressive war aims obviously supplied an altogether different rationale for fighting from those given to Allied combatants, the war veteran Böll spoke for many of his generation, German and non-German, when at the very end of his life he wrote that "soldiers – and I was one – shouldn't complain about the people they've been sent to fight against, only about those who sent them there."[14] His early novella *The Train was on Time*

(1949) is a forceful indictment of nationalism rendered from the point of view of a terrified and unwilling young German conscript on his way to die on the brutal Eastern Front.

Still, with its awarding of "an inch of ribbon" to the civilian onlooker, H. D.'s "R.A.F." reminds us of the importance of inclusiveness in our definitions of the literature of World War II. The soldiers of the two world wars may have been largely conscripts, but they were soldiers nonetheless; World War II, on the other hand, was very substantially a civilian experience, and, in the eloquent words of the historian Tony Judt, "experienced not as a war of movement and battle but as a daily degradation, in the course of which men and women were betrayed and humiliated, forced into daily acts of petty crime and self-abasement, in which everyone lost something and many lost everything."[15] The writing discussed in this volume includes work by combatants and non-combatants, soldiers and civilians. World War II was a total war and, as the later chapters of this book insist, no literary imagination went unaffected. It is with this in mind that Gill Plain uses British women writers as a case study, surveying how this exemplary non-combatant group – British women constituting a representative group because they could not fight in the war but could certainly be killed by it – responded to the claims of state and nation during the war; while Lyndsey Stonebridge explains why the idea of trauma so central to discussions of World War II and its literature (and trauma theory itself largely arose out of considerations of mid-century writing) requires us to think more obliquely about whom war affects and how. Following on from Stonebridge's emphasis on questions of indirection and the disrupted chronologies of "latency," the final chapter of this collection explains how and why the war continues to affect the literary imagination; in this concluding chapter Petra Rau surveys fictional accounts of the war written in the last thirty years, novels produced by those who did not experience the war at first hand. This is the trajectory of the book, then: we begin with surveys of the British and American materials likely to be most familiar to students of Anglophone war writing, and then go on to encompass international perspectives on the war; this last section of the book invites us to think more inclusively about what constitutes the literature of World War II.

"Composition on the subject of decomposition?" asked the Ukrainian Holocaust survivor Piotr Rawicz in his *Blood from the Sky* (1961), a powerful experimental novel about the round up of the Eastern European Jews in the early years of the war.[16] This question is at the heart of our collective enterprise. What does composition on the subject of decomposition really look like? What form could be adequate to the task of representing a world destroyed? Rawicz's novel is one of the many texts the war produced that test the limits of representation; many others are discussed in this book. Thus, for example, Phyllis Lassner's chapter on life writing and the Holocaust describes how Holocaust literature confounds our familiar reading conventions and expectations; Leo Mellor describes the literariness and studied anti-literariness of Anglo-American reportage; and James Dawes's discussion of the American war novel describes the formal transformations that war generates when it turns the world upside down.

And war is nothing if not an overturning of collective and humanistic hopes and values. "Courage smashes a cathedral," Graham Greene marveled in his novel of the London Blitz, *The Ministry of Fear* (1943), and "endurance lets a city starve."[17] "Observe in what an original world we are living," wrote the Polish wartime political prisoner Tadeusz Borowski: "how many men can you find in Europe who have never killed; or whom somebody does not wish to kill?"[18] These writers were compelled to give voice to the unprecedentedly violent and the often senselessly cruel, and, although the literature of World War II can be resistant to generalization, it would be true to say that one of its widely shared tendencies is a questioning of the adequacy of literature to convey the magnitude of what it records. "Less said the better," is the diffident opening line of John Pudney's wartime elegy, "Missing": "Words will not fill the post / Of Smith, the ghost."[19] In this poem about an airman shot down over the ocean, what is "missing" is not simply the much-missed Smith, but also the writer's faith in the capacity of poetic language to describe and acknowledge that loss adequately.

So the eloquence of World War II writing is essentially a kind of anti-eloquence, and it is no less powerful and moving for all that. Although it is impossible to agree with Pudney that "the less said the better," especially in view of the vast and extraordinary archive his contemporaries have bequeathed us, any claim for the redeeming and compensatory power of literary art has to be humble and hesitant in the face of a war that spanned the globe, destroyed a continent, and killed sixty million people; a war whose consequences Europe had to live out so painfully and visibly for half a century, and which are, we rather suspect, still part of our own lives. The deservedly admired American war correspondent Martha Gellhorn supplies words that could serve as the epigraph to any account of this war's literature when she introduces her World War II journalism with an admission of failure: "These articles are in no way adequate descriptions of the indescribable misery of war. War was always worse than I knew how to say – always."[20]

NOTES

1. Donald Bain, "War Poet," *Penguin New Writing* 21 (1944), 150.
2. Elizabeth Bowen, *The Heat of the Day* (New York: Anchor, 2002), p. 347.
3. E. M. Forster, "Prefatory Note," *Two Cheers for Democracy* (San Diego, New York, and London: Harcourt, 1966), p. xi.
4. Heinrich Böll, *The Silent Angel*, trans. Breon Mitchell (New York: Picador, 1995), p. vii.
5. George Orwell, "Politics and the English Language," *A Collection of Essays* (San Diego, New York, and London: Harcourt, 1981), pp. 166–7.
6. Cecil Day Lewis, "Where are the War Poets?" *Word Over All* (London: Jonathan Cape, 1946), p. 30.
7. Forster, "George Orwell," *Two Cheers for Democracy*, p. 62.
8. Forster, "Three Anti-Nazi Broadcasts," *Two Cheers for Democracy*, p. 43.
9. H. D., "R.A.F.," in *Poets of World War II* ed. Harvey Shapiro (New York: The Library of America, 2003), p. 11.
10. Allen Tate, "Ode to Our Young Pro-consuls of the Air," in *Poets of World War II*, ed. Shapiro, p. 24.
11. Yvor Winters, "To a Military Rifle," in *Poets of World War II*, ed. Shapiro, p. 26.
12. James Jones, *WWII: A Chronicle of Soldiering* (New York: Grosset and Dunlap, 1975), pp. 54, 55, 31.
13. Alan Dugan, "Stentor and Mourning," in *Poets of World War II*, ed. Shapiro, p. 167.
14. Heinrich Böll, "A Letter to my Sons," in *The Norton Book of Modern War*, ed. Paul Fussell (New York and London: Norton, 1991), p. 629.
15. Tony Judt, *Postwar: A History of Europe Since 1945* (New York: Penguin, 2005), p. 41.
16. Piotr Rawicz, *Blood From the Sky*, trans. Peter Wiles (New Haven and London: Yale University Press, 2003), p. 11.
17. Graham Greene, *The Ministry of Fear* (London: Penguin, 2005), p. 62.
18. Tadeusz Borowski, "Auschwitz, Our Home (A Letter)," *This Way for the Gas, Ladies and Gentlemen* (London: Penguin, 1976), p. 122.
19. John Pudney, "Missing," *Beyond This Disregard: Poems* (London: John Lane, 1943), p. 12.
20. Martha Gellhorn, "The Second World War," *The Face of War* (New York: Atlantic Monthly, 1988), p. 86.

PART I

Anglo-American texts and contexts

I

ADAM PIETTE

War poetry in Britain

The Second World War is now recognized as a watershed for British poetry, breaking the dominance of high modernist orthodoxies (signaled by the death of Yeats), transforming the openly political poetics of the Auden group into a war poetry of symptom and reportage (inaugurated by the emigration of Auden and Isherwood to the US), releasing a contained and self-censored British surrealism in the form of the New Apocalypse, and seeing the redefinition of formal genres such as the religious ode, sonnet sequence, elegy, and ballad within a range of new registers, from Rilkean-Jungian (Sidney Keyes) to psychoanalytic-demotic (G. S. Fraser).

The changes were masked for some time by the enormous power and shock of the conflict itself, and by the restrictions on poetry publishing consequent on paper rationing and the general business of wartime. The Ministry of Supply cut quotas to publishers down a third by 1943, their Paper Control stipulating page limits, words per page, and minimizing unnecessary design. Literary periodicals suffered badly under the new regime, including the closure of Geoffrey Grigson's *New Verse* and T. S. Eliot's *Criterion*. In those that remained, it became something of a cliché to run "Where are the War Poets?" featurettes, especially in the protracted silly season of the Phoney War, with dispiriting results, especially when real poets responded to the challenge. Stephen Spender and Alun Lewis signed a manifesto published in *Horizon* in 1941 asking the government to employ war writers, since "[writers'] propaganda was deeper, more humanly appealing and more imaginative than newspaper men had space or time for."[1] Cecil Day Lewis went further and, agreeing to disavow communism, became specialist editor in the Publications Division of the Ministry of Information. This was a confusing war in that public feeling was in many ways more powerful than stunned and detached private emotions (in poetry, those feelings associated with the lyric) – and in wartime such public feelings were being controlled by propaganda machines like the Ministry of Information, modeled in opposition to Goebbels's *Propagandaministerium*.

The search for trench poetry in the early years of war also betrayed false expectations. Most of the British army was holed up in supply lines and camps, safely tucked away from bombed cities. The early war poetry was by observers in the blitzed cities themselves. The poets ranged from established 1930s figures such as Louis MacNeice, whose "Brother Fire" is one of the best Blitz poems ("O delicate walker, babbler, dialectician Fire"),[2] through Apocalyptic poets like J. F. Hendry, whose collection, *The Bombed Happiness*, is a superb prospectus of the horrors and unconscious dreamwork among Blitz survivors (Hendry's wife was killed in one of the raids) to ordinary citizens, like Margery Lea, commenting on the Manchester Blitz with troubling good humor as a "strategy of detachment," in Gill Plain's words:[3]

> Our neighbour's garden had a crater that would hold two buses.
> He said the rich soil thrown up was most productive,
> And round the perimeter he grew excellent lettuces
> The next spring of the war.[4]

The detachment is echoed in Hendry's fine sequence, the response to the Blitz collapsing into symptomatic indifference, even admiration for the formal properties of war's power over cities and bodies, reveling in molten metal and the naturalized war machine in the skies:

> artist and scientist concur to admire
> A formal pattern of battle, where herring-bone squadrons
> Elude the swaying bars of light, and white fire
> From London's living furnace, flung up like a tilted cauldron,
> Splits the atom of doom[5]

In the immediate run-up to the war, as James Keery has shown,[6] Henry Treece and J. F. Hendry had launched the Apocalyptic school of poetry, with Dylan Thomas as inspiration, and following the lead of David Gascoyne's *A Short Survey of Surrealism*. The group aimed in the first instance to establish a mythopoeic resistance to what Hendry was to call the "object-machine," a figure for the mechanization and indoctrination of the industrial complex. As the war broke, and under the influence of fellow editors such as G. S. Fraser, the Apocalyptics (baptized by Herbert Read the "New Romantics") developed a force and style of writing that sought to combine social realist concerns with Freudian emphases. Much of the writing produced by the school is vapid and overwrought, but it was a response that struck a chord, voicing the extraordinary power of events, the dark fears and obsessions of a terrified populace and death-entranced army, as well as anarchist-communitarian resistance to war technology and bureaucracies. The best of the neo-Romantics gravitated towards the *Poetry London* anthologies, with a poetry of myth-making, strong allegory, a language of natural organic forms, a vibrant twisting rhythm, and high violent rhetoric. Their undisputed leader was Dylan Thomas – his collection *Deaths and Entrances* is most interesting for its lush elegiac poems "Among those Killed in the Dawn Raid" and "Ceremony after a Fire Raid." Angry at the cheap idea that war generates poems,[7] and himself a pacifist who evaded conscription, Thomas's poems chant hymns to the dead child victims of the war as sacrifices offered to war's violence, but refuse to mourn them as such (as in "A Refusal to Mourn the Death, by Fire, of a Child in London").

Related to, but politically distinct from, the Apocalyptic school were the Oxford poets emerging from the colleges and moving into the army. A similar neo-Romantic strain is legible in the combatant poets from Oxford, but with a marked Christian-mystical content, particularly after the arrival of poet-theologian and novelist Charles Williams of Amen House. Sidney Keyes combined Williams's rhetoric of sacrifice and love substitution with the 1940s Rilke craze, a Yeatsian symbolic language, and the doctrine of Jungian archetypes. Coded by the medievalism of Williams's fellow "Inklings," C. S. Lewis and J. R. R. Tolkien, Keyes's poetry managed to articulate some of the dark melancholia of wartime culture, as here, imitating an ancient bard:

> How ten men fell by one heroic sword
> And of fierce foray by the unwatched ford,
> Sing, blinded face; quick hands in darkness groping
> Pluck the sad harp[8]

Decrypted, these lines sing of the difficulties of expression at a heartbreaking time, whilst translating wartime conditions into other times, other places: note the discreet references to mass civilian deaths ("ten men fell"), to the innumerable struggles around the globe ("unwatched"), to the blackout ("in darkness groping"). More sinister was Keyes's fear of the brutalizing effects of war's violence on the combatant's imagination, as in his extraordinary poem "Gilles de Retz." Gilles de Retz not only fought with Joan of Arc but later became the infamous Bluebeard, serial torturer, abuser, and killer of children snatched from peasant families on his demesne. Keyes's poem, based on a reading of Charles Williams's contrast in his 1941 *Witchcraft* between Joan of Arc and de Retz and C. S. Lewis's meditation on evil in the world in *The Problem of Pain*, is a dramatic monologue in which Gilles betrays his abandonment to evil in his cherishing of pain in wartime after the death of Joan of Arc: "never / Since Christ has any man made pain so glorious / As I."[9] Similarly wracked by guilt at the imagination's succumbing to the temptations of violence are the voices in Keyes's long poem, "The Foreign Gate," specifically the spectacle of the suffering of the Jews in Europe: "beyond / Live death's great enemies, the undefeated. / These are a stronger nation. /... Look in those eyes and learn the speech of pain."[10] Such a gaze into the eyes, such learning moves perilously close to a relishing, intensified by the very distances set up by the neo-Christian frame.

The neo-Christian revival was being spearheaded by T. S. Eliot – "Little Gidding" staging Eliot's fire-watching duties in London, controversially crossing the Luftwaffe's bombers with the dove of the Holy Ghost ("the dark dove with the flickering tongue")[11] – and by Auden in America ("no nightmare / Of hostile objects could be as terrible as this Void. / This is the Abomination. This is the wrath of God"),[12] both explicitly under Charles Williams's influence. The intensity of this revival cannot be underestimated: this was the age of imaginary martyrdoms, Freudian damnation, and Simone Weil.

In London, the poetry scene was dominated by three literary magazines: Cyril Connolly's *Horizon*, John Lehmann's *New Writing*, and Tambimuttu's *Poetry London*. With the closure of so many literary journals, this dominance was artificially sustained, giving the editors powers undreamt of – as a result, much of the poetry of the wartime 1940s existed in more ephemeral form: small-scale little magazines launched for tiny readerships, service-specific publications, or as unpublished manuscript, to be recuperated, if at all, after the war. Despite this, there was an extraordinary poetry boom during the war years. Much of the renewed interest in poetry was being boosted by the power of unexpressed feeling wartime generates, especially in a superheated propagandized and censored environment. It was also true that the brevity and concentration of poetry suited the intensities and fractured experiences of wartime during the long hours of waiting in shelter, camp, hospital, and transport.

More specifically, the war gave sudden new vitality to the political and aesthetic concerns of the 1930s poets. The Spanish Civil War and Nazi–Soviet Pact had scuttled many of the revolutionary expectations associated with wartime, but these returned with the entry into the war of the Soviet Union as an ally in 1941. The shift to the left was fueled also by hopes of radical reconstruction, the Beveridge report, the perceived end of Empire in the loss of the colonies in the Far East, and the influence of the anti-imperialist United States in the run-up to their entry into the war, as well by as the renewed energy of separatist movements in Wales and Scotland. Consequently many of the predictions and political animus of the 1930s bore significant fruit in the lyrics and ballads of the new conscript army.

The army recruit, as Alun Lewis saw it in "Lance-Jack," was "a migrant, an Arab taking his belongings with him, needing surprisingly little of the world's goods," liberated in the "sudden *levelling down*," the "possibility for change" involved in the democratic environment of the new army.[13] Government initiatives fostered this political camaraderie, in particular the work of the Army Bureau of Current Affairs (ABCA) whose fortnightly *Current Affairs* bulletins sent to army units popularized the idea of the citizen soldier, encouraging discussion of radical post-war reforms, "the first gesture towards politicizing a British army since Cromwell's day."[14] The move to North Africa, the first significant front after the defeats in Greece and the Far East, coincided with the entry of the Soviet Union into the war, an event which finally released the anti-fascist radicalism implicit but repressed in the real Dunkirk spirit. The army became a radical force. As Edward Thompson remembered in 1978: "I recall a resolute and ingenious civilian army, increasingly hostile to the conventional military virtues, which became ... an anti-fascist and conspicuously anti-imperialist army."[15]

Something of the leveling was due to the desert itself, forcing combatants down to bare essentials, life in common, men having to rely on each other for their very lives. As Dan Billany wrote of his desert campaign:

> You love yourself and your fellow-man better when you are constantly reminded, by proximity, that you and he are subject to the same necessities ... our lives were common property. Similarities and the droppings of protective reserve endeared man to man. So many of our old, complicated sophisticated reactions were not needed, and fell away.[16]

It was in Egypt that the socialist energies of the Popular Front first reemerged, in the form of the "new model army" of the Eighth Army, typified by the Music for All Parliament that took place in Cairo in September 1943: "akin," Neil Grant has argued, "to a soviet, romantic and mutinous in character," a soldiers' parliament which had, "rather like the Putney Debates in the English Civil War, involved soldiers debating the purposes of the war and nature of the post-war world."[17] And, significantly, the Parliament took place in a former cinema, base for the poets of the Salamander Society, run by Keith Bullen and John Cromer, which issued the influential Oasis anthologies. Georgian and Kiplingesque in spirit, the group sought, in Roger Bowen's words, "to memorialize the soldier as amateur poet and oral historian," to counter what Cromer identified as "obscurantist modernism," and to celebrate the common purpose and camaraderie of the troops.[18]

Many writers attempting to represent the international theatres of the war were dogged by a sense of repetition of the tropes of First World War writing, confused about History, subject to war's mechanical forces, haunted by local and individual incapacity, tempted by extreme faith and private mythologies, fearful of overheated melodrama, torn between cynicism about and passion for the People's War. Donald Bain's "War Poet" acknowledges the pressure to restrict representation to the narrow experiences quickly jotted down within the confines of individual theaters: "We in our haste can only see the small components of the scene; / We cannot tell what incidents will focus on the final screen. / ... We only watch, and indicate and make our scribbled pencil notes. / We do not wish to moralize, only to ease our dusty throats."[19] At the same time, writers in the armed forces felt it as part of the fact of their participation that they respond to the global scale of the war: "although [the position I'm in is] only a tiny one," wrote Alun Lewis in the army, "it's on a world scale, war being a sum of countless units."[20]

Lewis's own poetry and prose is caught between twin responsibilities: to graph the small components of the scene – his individual emotional experience as he traveled towards India and Burma and the Japanese enemy – and to interpret those experiences on a world scale. The act of global interpretation is uneasily mixed up with his role as an officer: he had to lecture his men about the war. At times, in his letters, he attempts to disengage his poetry from the international politics of warfare, yet the entanglement of the personal and the superpolitical forms part of the creative/self-destructive energy of his war work, a systolic fluctuation between morbidly absorbed inwardness and charged collective significance. His best work is about this dual energy: his letters to Gweno Lewis, *Letters to My Wife*; the poems "All Day it has Rained," "To Edward Thomas," "Water Music," and "The Jungle"; and the short stories "Lance-Jack," "Night Journey," "The Earth is a Syllable," and "Ward 'O' 3 (b)." The writing interrogates the international political engagements of the citizen, the obstacles to democratic change in the military, the ambiguities of fighting an anti-fascist war from imperial bases, and the range of commitments and voices fighting the war, at the same time as it courts a Rilkean drift towards deep solipsistic release, mystical love, and darkness. Lewis died of a self-inflicted gunshot wound, in Burma, hours before engagement with the enemy.

More cold-hearted and chillingly gifted, Keith Douglas wrote poetry and prose about the war in the desert that stage the soldier's boyish cruelty and technological power as dual deranged forces within the arrogantly trained mind. Playing with war tropes, Douglas reads the tank commander as the new cavalry officer, gallantry become bantering mastery of machine and wireless technology, the speed and efficiency and long-range killing giving the officer a William-like boisterousness, as well as an anesthetizing cynical energy that disinvests the infliction of death of any of the normal range of human responses. The much-anthologized poems about the German dead in the desert, "Vergissmeinnicht," "How to Kill," and "Cairo Jag," need to be placed alongside the prose memoir *Alamein to Zem-Zem* to get a real sense of the audacity of Douglas's achievement.

To write Second World War poetry, for Douglas, was to write second-rate, second-hand verse belatedly in styles borrowed from the trench poets, sons imitating fathers. Douglas implies as much in "Desert Flowers" where he admits that any poem about flowers feeding off the blood of dead men must lamely follow Rosenberg's lines on poppies in "Break of Day in the Trenches": "Rosenberg I only repeat what you were saying."[21] The repetition is more endemic than repetition of trope, however. As Douglas argued in an essay on war poetry, "Poets of This War," the Great War hung over everything any combatant poet might care to say:

> there is nothing new, from a soldier's point of view, about this war except its mobile character. There are two reasons: hell cannot be let loose twice: it was let loose in the Great War and it is the same old hell now. The hardships, pain, and boredom; the behaviour of the living and the appearance of the dead, were so accurately described by the poets of the Great War that every day on the battlefields of the western desert – and no doubt on the Russian battlefields as well – their poems are illustrated. Almost all that a modern poet on active service would be inspired to write, would be tautological.[22]

The two reasons – continuation of mass industrial warfare and repetition of descriptions of conditions and appearances – are troubled by tiny concessions to difference: the desert war's mobile character, and the fact that poets are "modern" now. Modernity and mobility are key vectors in the cold-blooded and symptomatic writing Douglas produced late in the war. It nevertheless remains the case that the tautological nature of writing shapes and conditions the scope of individual responses to the war, if only in some twisted (and psychoanalyzable) act of difficult acknowledgment of debt to the father's superior knowledge, as in Roy Fuller's "Another War": "Our fathers felt these things before / In another half-forgotten war."[23] On June 9, 1944, Keith Douglas was killed near St. Pierre in Normandy.

The reputations of Lewis, Douglas, and Keyes obscured the collective contribution of the service poets during the war. "By 1941," Brian Gardner has argued, "a remarkable thing had happened. From poetry being the almost private game of a literary set ... there came something like a people's poetry."[24] The huge influx of service poems was characterized by a new style, "nonchalant, cool, laconic," in Gardner's words.[25] The poems are, in the main, in accord with the spirit animating Douglas's poems: they make observations in the detached-demotic idiom of barrack and military code, sentimentalities and high rhetoric repressed by male bluster and comedy, service business, the rare stunning shocks and drawn out boredom of a long and technical war. The Australian poet John Manifold, for instance, wrote a clear, fresh poetry of commitment to the common man soldier. His poem

"Camouflage" looks beneath the "skinny false / Mask" of fake camaraderie in the army to the real "iron skeleton of constraint" forcing recruits to their deaths – preferring the cruel honesty of the "tommy-gun, the clean, functional thing."[26]

The talented poets to emerge from the services and combat units managed to voice this people's poetry idiom by crossing it with the plainer styles that had emerged in the 1930s. In a useful review of war poetry in 1943, Peter de Vries described the styles as issuing from Eliot's "refrigerated understatement" and Auden's redefinition of the poem as "a clinical instrument," Freudian–Marxist, "a curiously cross-grained verse evolving an increasingly private language even as it turned to more public concerns."[27]

The combatant poets committed to a modified Auden–Eliot plain style clearly include Douglas given his insistence on a new version of 1930s reportage as necessary witness: "réportage and extrospective (if the word exists) poetry ... seems to me the sort that has to be written just now," Douglas advised fellow-poet J. C. Hall in 1943.[28] Non-introspective reportage was demanded not only by the logic of his own poetic gift, but by the ordinary ways of feeling amongst the ranks, a modernized Sassoonese, cynical, unadorned, without bullshit, as developed *by the soldiers themselves*. As Douglas explained to Hall:

> if you come across the word Bullshit – it is an army word and signifies humbug and unnecessary detail. It symbolizes what I think must be got rid of – the mass of irrelevancies, of "attitudes", "approaches", propaganda, ivory towers, etc., that stands between us and our problems and what we have to do about them.[29]

Other poets practicing the plain style include Alan Ross who served in the Navy: his wartime poems attend finely to the exiled torpor and menace of life on destroyers, bringing the warships' lethal, unreal technologies of radar and deception into strange relationship with the living companionship of the bodies of the crew. He went on in 1950 to write one of the great narrative poems about the war, "J. W. 51B: A Convoy," a searching and affectionate account of the 1942 Battle of the Barents Sea.

Bernard Gutteridge, who served in Burma, wrote one of the best long poems of the war, "Burma Diary" (1948) collected in *Old Damson-Face: Poems 1934 to 1974*,[30] which is a moving testament to the culture and landscape being destroyed: the Arakan section interrogates the anti-Japanese propaganda necessary for morale in the context of the deaths of Alun Lewis and a Japanese poet his unit has captured.

Roy Fuller was a lieutenant with the Royal Navy, first as radar mechanic in Kenya, then as radio and radar officer at the Admiralty. His is a brave and serious public poetry, probing the relations between the enormous abstractions of violent history ("the formidable expression of time and destiny") and the seemingly futile mind's engagement with the "escaping seconds, terrible and real / Through which I live."[31] The African poems, though a pure interlude where the war is merely news, manage to create passionate accounts of the associations between empire, anthropology, natural and European history, and a confessedly bourgeois observer. Fuller sustains the political commitments of Audenesque travel writing into the war, as an act of desperate and fearful rationality: "Now man must be political or die."[32] His war poems (sections II and III of the *Collected Poems 1936–1961*) are his major achievement.

John Jarmain, who fought at El Alamein and Normandy as an anti-tank gunner for the 51st Highland Division, killed by shrapnel in 1944, wrote two of the most direct poems of the war about a soldier's mental confusion ("Fear") and the innocent dead of the war ("The Innocent Shall Suffer").[33] South African R. N. Currey's poems "Unseen Fire" and "Boy with a Rifle" from the collection *This Other Planet* (1945) are sharp and discerning about the technology of warfare in the mind. Geoffrey Matthews, who served in Cairo and Haifa, manages a fine marriage of history and emotional detail, holding true to the values of the Spanish Civil War.

Related to the Auden–Eliot group of plain style demotic poets were the poets who gathered round the *Personal Landscape* journal in Cairo during the desert war run by Lawrence Durrell, Robin Fedden, Terence Tiller, and Bernard Spencer. Their stance was apolitical, anarchist-individualist, standing back from the war effort to examine the deep histories of precisely "personal" experiences in wartime. Their representative poem, Fedden's "Personal Landscape," insists on the importance of personal life and values (here figured as a Donne-like aubade) at the same time as it acknowledges that love cannot be disengaged from the ways the human body is being broken by wartime, the military inhabiting the loved one's body (the pun on "arms"): "I cannot disentangle your arms / From the body of the day that is breaking."[34] The *Landscape* group was contemptuous of the war poet anthologies, particularly the *Oasis* project, and looked askance at the whole idea of war poetry as a genre. Durrell wrote to John Waller with typical disdain: "I think all this war-poet stuff is bogus and vulgar really ... the only kind of work worth while is work that wears no uniform but its own merits."[35]

Ranged against the plain-style poets typified by Douglas were combatant poets influenced by the Apocalyptic school and Dylan Thomas, drawn to Tambimuttu's *Poetry London* and subscribing to what Peter de Vries described as (in contrast to the "astringent" idiom of the Audenesque war poets) "a looser, freer diction, a more expressionistic style often brightly dyed with surrealism."[36] Francis Berry, who served in the Mediterranean, wrote the powerful New Romantic fable "Murdock" about two demon brothers at war in a wood above a terrified town. G. S. Fraser served in the Middle East: his war poems, collected in *Home Town Elegy* (1944) and *The Traveller has Regrets* (1948), are urgent attempts to clear space for the poet's clairvoyant senses under the technological and myth-making power of war's managers ("Mappers of nerves, who graph our play and trial").[37]

Fraser's poem should be read alongside Hamish Henderson's astonishing sequence, *Elegies for the Dead in Cyrenaica* (1948), which reads the desert war as a human civil war distorted by the war's "effect of mirage and looking-glass illusion": the poems de-create all "blah about their sacrifice" and attend to the common humanity of the dead on both sides.[38] Henderson also experienced the war in Italy, working closely with the communist partisans – much of his postwar work, such as the ballads, the Gramsci translation, and the elegies for the victims of fascism, is indebted to this time.

The South African poet F. T. Prince did not experience combat, but served in the Intelligence Corps of the British Army in the Middle East and Italy. His poems are a vital, complex, and subtle questioning of the animal flesh, mechanical utility, and criminal conscience implicit in every soldier's move in wartime, as the poems "At a Parade" and "Soldiers Bathing" show.[39]

Other service poets we should attempt to recuperate include: Emanuel Litvinoff, who served in West Africa, and whose three collections, *Conscripts* (1941), *The Untried Soldier* (1942), and *Crown for Cain* (1948), are a powerful expression of Jewish anger and denunciation. Herbert Mallalieu, who served in Africa and Italy, wrote some of the best love poetry of the war, and the elegy to war-ravaged Greece, "Greece 1945."[40] Sorley MacLean, who was severely wounded at El Alamein, wrote the finest Gaelic poetry of the war, notably *Dàin do Eimhir* (translated by both Iain Crichton Smith and Christopher Whyte), which puts its faith in both the face of the loved one and the sweet sounds of his "dying tongue" despite the fact that "Europe, raped and torn, / moans behind my song."[41] His desert war poems are collected and translated in the *Blar/Battlefield* section of *Spring Tide and Neap Tide: Selected Poems 1932–72*. Henry Reed, working for Naval Intelligence, wrote the justly celebrated poems about military technology, "Judging Distances" and "The Naming of Parts" – the effect, as Walter Allen remarked in a 1946 review, was "as though Jules Laforgue had suddenly appeared in a conscript army."[42]

Looking closely at these poems as a congeries of statements and states of being generated by wartime, the distinction between surrealist and plain style engagements begins to fall away. All the poets responded to the democratization of the army, to the "death-image-haunted" nature of wartime imaginings,[43] to the servo-mechanical entrancement brought about by the fabulous new killing technologies of warfare – "war, its terrible pressure that begets / A machinery of death and slavery," F. T. Prince had sung.[44] The war had the curious effect of draining out the passionate commitments of the public voice, privatizing them within neurotic displays of symptoms, whilst isolating the private poets, forcing them to defend their introspective territories with public declamations. Spender had noted the strain, in particular, on 1930s poetry of political commitment:

> The violence of the times we are living in, the necessity of sweeping and general immediate action, tend to dwarf the experience of the individual, and to make his immediate environment and occupations something that he is even ashamed of. For this reason, in my own most recent poems, I have deliberately turned back to a kind of writing which is more personal, and I have included within my subjects weakness and fantasy and illusion.[45]

The individual's "weakness and fantasy and illusion" meshes in with wartime violence in either extreme and mythopoeic ways, as with the Apocalyptic school, or as coded within neurotic cross-grained plain style, "increasingly private ... even as it turned to more public concerns."

The result is a body of work, collective, shocking, death-haunted, that succeeds, even though failing to follow through the ABCA army solidarities, in representing symptomatically and diagnostically the impact on the minds of contemporaries of mass death on an industrial scale. The dead speak fitfully, brokenly, enigmatically, hopelessly, in the Rilkean poems of Lewis, in Henderson's elegies, in Douglas's reportage. The dead speak as fellow soldiers gone into a common dark – as in James Walker's tour of a cemetery in Tobruk, sensing how the astringent idiom of reportage might be colluding in the technologizing impersonality of death in the Second World War: "in the sunlight / Their identities oppressed, as all things did / In that meticulous vivisecting light."[46] Or they speak through unbearable guilty witness, as the European dead the Allies failed to save. As Robert Conquest wrote, in terrible despair: "there is too much. / Too much confusion! Too much metal! / They have gazed too long into a mirror of Europe / And seen the Minotaur reflections gnash their teeth."[47] Those oppressions, that gaze, empty the war poems of political power just as they make them invaluable as documents of confusion, weakness, fantasy, and illusion attempting to track the dead across the wastelands of technological warfare.

NOTES

1. "Why Not War Writers? A Manifesto," *Horizon* 5, 22 (Oct. 1941), 238.
2. Louis MacNeice, "Brother Fire," *Collected Poems*, ed. E. R. Dodds (London: Faber, 1979), p. 196.

3. Gill Plain, *Women's Fiction of the Second World War: Gender, Power and Resistance* (Edinburgh University Press, 1996), p. 4.
4. Quoted in Plain, *Women's Fiction*, p. 5.
5. J. F. Hendry, "Midnight Air-Raid," *The Bombed Happiness* (London: Routledge, 1942), pp. 15–16.
6. See James Keery's series of articles on the Apocalypse group, "The Burning Baby and the Bathwater," in *PN Review* 29, 4 (July–Aug. 2003) to 31, 1 (Sept.–Oct. 2004).
7. "War can't produce poetry, only poets can," letter to Oscar Williams dated July 30, 1945. Dylan Thomas, *The Collected Letters*, ed. Paul Ferris (London: Paladin, 1987), p. 561.
8. Sidney Keyes, "The Bards," *The Collected Poems of Sidney Keyes*, ed. Michael Meyer (London: Routledge, 1988), p. 48.
9. Keyes, "Gilles de Retz," *Collected Poems*, p. 24.
10. Keyes, "The Foreign Gate," *Collected Poems*, pp. 74–5.
11. T. S. Eliot, "Little Gidding," *Collected Poems 1909–1962* (London: Faber, 1985), p. 217.
12. W. H. Auden, "For the Time Being: A Christmas Oratorio," *Collected Longer Poems* (London: Faber, 1988), p. 137.
13. Alun Lewis, "Lance-Jack," *Collected Stories*, ed. Cary Archard (Bridgend: Seren Books, 1990), p. 64.
14. Max Beloff, *Wars and Welfare* (London: Arnold, 1984), p. 264.
15. Quoted in the introduction to David Edgar and Neil Grant's dramatization of the Music for All Parliament, *Vote for Them* (London: BBC Books, 1989), p. 5.
16. Dan Billany, *The Trap* (London: Faber, 1986), p. 254.
17. Grant, *Vote for Them*, p. 6.
18. Roger Bowen, *"Many Histories Deep": The Personal Landscape Poets in Egypt, 1940–45* (London: Associated University Presses, 1995), p. 47.
19. Donald Bain, "War Poet," *Penguin New Writing* 21 (1944), 150.
20. Letter to Gweno Lewis dated May 21, 1942. Alun Lewis, *Letters to My Wife*, ed. Gweno Lewis (Cardiff: Seren Books, 1989), p. 219.
21. Keith Douglas, "Desert Flowers," *Collected Poems*, ed. John Waller, G. S. Fraser, and J. C. Hall (London: Faber, 1966), p. 129.
22. "Poets in This War" was written in May 1943 and first published in 1971. Quoted in Sebastian Knowles, *A Purgatorial Flame: Seven British Writers in the Second World War* (Bristol: The Bristol Press, 1990), p. xviii.
23. Roy Fuller, "Another War," *Collected Poems* (London: Faber, 1966), p. 55.
24. Brian Gardner, "Introductory Note," *The Terrible Rain: The War Poets 1939–1945* (London: Methuen, 1993), p. xviii.
25. Gardner, "Introductory Note," p. xix.
26. John Manifold, "Camouflage," in *More Poems of the Second World War*, ed. Erik de Mauny, Victor Selwyn, and Ian Fletcher (London: J. M. Dent & the Salamander Oasis Society, 1989), p. 79.
27. Peter de Vries, "Poetry and the War," *College English* 5, 3 (Dec. 1943), 114.
28. Letter to J. C. Hall dated June 10, 1943. Keith Douglas, *The Letters*, ed. Desmond Graham (Manchester: Carcanet, 2000), p. 287.
29. Douglas, *Letters*, p. 294.
30. See also Bernard Gutteridge, *Traveller's Eye* (London: Routledge, 1947).

31. Roy Fuller, "Autumn 1941" and "The Bay," *Collected Poems 1936–1961* (London: André Deutsch, 1962), pp. 50, 49.
32. Fuller, "Winter Camp," *Collected Poems*, p. xx.
33. John Jarmain, "Fear" and "The Innocent Shall Suffer," *Poems* (London: Collins, 1945), pp. 29, 39–40.
34. Robin Fedden, "Personal Landscape" in Bowen, "*Many Histories Deep*," pp. 46–7.
35. Quoted in Roger Bowen, "'The Artist at his Papers': Durrell, Egypt and the Poetry of Exile," *Twentieth Century Literature* 33, 4 (Winter 1987), 468.
36. De Vries, "Poetry and the War," p. 117.
37. G. S. Fraser, "Journey," *Scottish Arts and Letters* 1 (1944), 37.
38. Hamish Henderson, *Elegies for the Dead in Cyrenaica* (London: John Lehmann, 1948), pp. 11–12, 36.
39. F. T. Prince, "At a Parade," in *The War Poets*, ed. Oscar Williams (New York: John Day, 1945), pp. 209–10; "Soldiers Bathing," *Collected Poems 1935–1992* (Manchester: Carcanet, 1993), pp. 55–7.
40. Herbert Mallalieu, "Greece 1945," *Poems from New Writing 1936–1946*, ed. John Lehmann (London: John Lehmann, 1946), pp. 188–9.
41. Sorley Maclean, *Eimhir*, trans. Iain Crichton Smith (Stornoway: Acair, 1999), p. 101.
42. Walter Allen, "Poetry," *Time and Tide* 27, 21 (May 25, 1946), 499.
43. Keidrych Rhys, "Victoria Leave Train" in *The Terrible Rain*, ed. Gardner, p. 180.
44. Prince, "Soldiers Bathing," p. 55.
45. Spender's foreword to *Ruins and Visions* (London: Faber, 1943), quoted in de Vries, "Poetry and the War," p. 115.
46. James Walker, "Portrait and Background," in *The Terrible Rain*, ed. Gardner, p. 101.
47. Robert Conquest, "A Minor Front," in *The Terrible Rain*, ed. Gardner, pp. 176–7.

2

ROD MENGHAM

British fiction of the war

It is not an overstatement to say that the writing and reading of fiction was seriously disorientated by the events of the Second World War. The paper shortage meant a reduction in the total number of books published, but as a proportion of that total, there was in any case a considerable drop in the number of novels published. Conversely, there was a proportional increase in the number of short story titles.[1] The short story enabled rapid response to the constantly changing conditions of Phoney War, conscription, Blitz, blackout, evacuation, the housing crisis, and the reorganization of the workforce. Its brevity and capacity for sharp focus made it more suitable as a means of reflecting disruptions in the rhythm of everyday life and a profound sense of historical discontinuity. Both in form and content, the short story was the medium of choice for conveying a shared experience of fragmentation, unpredictability, and the psychological stress of having to live from moment to moment. Elizabeth Bowen was quite clear about the historical role of short fiction at this time and of the necessity to defer the writing of novels until after the war had finished: "When today has become yesterday, it will have integrated."[2] Those novels that were written and published during the war often gravitated towards the problem of integration, often specifically towards the challenge of grasping the imaginative, if not the practical, means of maintaining the continuity of British traditions, customs, and ideas about identity, at a time of historical irresolution.

The shock of disorientation – spatial, temporal, historical – is captured most powerfully in representations of the Blitz: in the opening strangeness of James Hanley's novel *No Directions* (1943), where a drunken sailor stumbles over broken glass in a London street, imagining himself to be stranded on pack-ice in the course of breaking up; in the firefighting stories of William Sansom, that react to the Blitz as a bombardment of the senses too intense to be assimilated by conventional methods of perception and representation; and in the writings of Henry Green, in the novel *Caught* (1943) and in the stories "Mr. Jonas" and "A Rescue," that express, in their tentative negotiation of the new spatial experiences of wartime London, a sharpened awareness of new conditions of thought, of a mentality seemingly unrelated to previous historical episodes, as if the present moment existed in a kind of historical parenthesis:

> What I saw, a pile of wreckage like vast blocks of slate, the slabs of wet masonry piled high across this passage, was hidden by a fresh cloud of steam and smoke, warm, limitless dirty cotton wool, disabling in that it tight bandaged the eyes. Each billow, and steam rolls unevenly in air, islanding a man in the way that he can, to others, be isolated asleep in blankets. Nor did the light of a torch do more than make my sudden blindness visible to me in a white shine below the waist. There was nothing for it but to go on towards voices out in front, but climbing, slipping up, while unrolling the hose, I felt that I was not a participant, that all this must have been imagined, until, in another instant, a puff of wind, perhaps something in the wreckage which was alight below the surface, left me out in the clear as though in, and among, the wet indigo reflecting planes of shattered tombs deep in a tumulus the men coughing ahead had just finished blasting.[3]

At this point in the story, which concerns the rescue of a man who has been blown down a hole in the ground, the writing slows right down, becomes especially intricate and involved precisely in order to emphasize feelings of isolation and abandonment. Syntactically and imagistically, it obscures the threshold between interior and exterior, most succinctly in the clause that "left me out in the clear as though in." The anecdotal destination of the story is the deep interior of the hole beneath ground level, but the metaphorical interior on which it is simultaneously focused is that of a tomb, a tumulus, as if it is concerned to retrieve something buried deep in the past. In the work of many writers and film-makers of the time, the urgency for excavation, for recovery, is part of an attempt to assert continuity with the past and to project a credible future, but in Green's fiction it is more often a reflection of being "caught" or trapped in an impasse, in a circularity, able to see only that things are hidden, constrained, to be uncertain whether the present is intelligibly connected to, or disconnected from, the movement of history.

Few texts are more severe in insisting on the ellipses between memories of the past and a desire for the future than Bowen's "The Happy Autumn Fields," a short story collected in *The Demon Lover and Other Stories* (1945). The four sections of the story are divided between two settings: a bombed house in the Blitz, and the country home and surrounding fields owned by a late Victorian or Edwardian family. There is no direct connection between the characters and events of these two scenarios, or none that can be given a rational basis. The character Sarah, seen in the autumn landscape of the turn of the century, seems to be a figure dreamed of by Mary in wartime London, and it is implied that Mary is dreamed of by Sarah. The barrier of realism that keeps them separate is obscured in the vividness of their individual reveries. As Mary regains consciousness, it seems possible just for a moment that she might wake up not as herself but as Sarah:

> A shock of striking pain in the knuckles of the outflung hand – Sarah's? The eyes, opening, saw that the hand had struck not been struck: there was a corner of a table. Dust, whitish and gritty, lay on the top of the table and on the telephone. Dull but piercing white light filled the room and what was left of the ceiling; her first thought was that it must have snowed. If so, it was winter now.[4]

Bowen makes neither character simply the creature of the other's imagination, and hesitates in the allocation of active and passive roles. As Mary emerges from dream to reality, she emerges into a dramatically altered reality, an obdurate, material environment that is stranger than any dream. As she takes her bearings by familiar objects, the aftermath of the bombing turns this experience into one of defamiliarization. The imaginative leap into her own past reaches after a condition that is now as divorced from the present as the turn-of-the-century tableaux. This story is one of several in the same volume that locates the center of shared experience during the Blitz in the intensity of dreams, fantasies, hallucinations; in an imaginative surplus that cannot be housed satisfactorily in a realist aesthetic, and that is motivated by a compulsion to see beyond the temporal hiatus of the present.

The pressure exerted on this imaginative project gives some measure of the psychological strain involved in trying to sustain the possibility of integrating past and present selves. In Patrick Hamilton's novel of 1941, *Hangover Square*, the protagonist is betrayed by a lover who transfers her affections to a vicious fascist. This act of emotional sabotage weakens further the protagonist's ability to withstand the mental deterioration set in train already by the worsening political situation of 1939. His deepening schizophrenia takes the form of an obsession with the need to kill the lover, named Netta, as a necessary step towards recovery of the past, idealized in the image of a dead sister with whom he expects to be reunited. The narrative culminates with his return to the childhood setting of Maidenhead, aptly associated with the virginal figure of the sister, where he gasses himself, after the declaration of a war whose entangling net he will not be caught up in. Extreme psychological measures are also called for in the situation of Arthur Rowe, the protagonist of Graham Greene's *The Ministry of Fear* (1943). He is forced into a condition of amnesia as a means of suppressing the mercy-killing of his own wife, but also in order to shed all memory of his silence in the face of appeasement; his effective acquiescence in the growth of fascism. This rejection of his recent past allows Rowe to construct an alternative self, based on the desires and ambitions of his childhood: "the kind of man the boy he remembered would have become."[5]

The overwhelming desire to restore the coherence of relations between past, present, and future draws a large number of wartime writers towards the figure of the child, both as a literal embodiment of the future and as a vehicle for meditating on the past, on the lost world of the writer's own childhood. Henry Reed, in the earliest authoritative survey of British fiction during the 1940s, notes the widespread enthusiasm for childhood themes.[6] The value of childhood, both as social resource and as incentive for family life, is enhanced dramatically by the national crisis of evacuation, which separates millions of parents from their children and requires a corresponding number of adults to act as surrogates. Representations of evacuees in film tend not to dwell on the trauma of separation, and emphasize instead socialization through the juvenile gang, which plays a symbolic role in building the future; evacuees in fiction, on the other hand, are more ambivalent figures. At the end of the war, the very first Ealing comedy, *Hue and Cry* (1945), directed by Charles Crichton, centers on the activities of a juvenile gang that is perceived as the source of moral renewal in a postwar settlement where nearly all the adults are corrupt. The children are seen meeting in bombed houses rather than in their own homes, emphasizing their construction of a collective identity outside the family structure, in a society of equals where the rivalries are good-natured and superficial, and where everyone is united by a common purpose.

But despite the writer's and director's clear endorsement of a communitarian ethos, there is one short but memorable scene in the film that presents a very different image of childhood, that of a solitary boy sitting among the bomb-damage, locked into an obsessive routine of fantasizing the violence of the Blitz. The public-spirited protagonist of the film, played by the young Harry Fowler, expresses facially and gesturally a certain amount of distance from, a certain disapproval of, the young boy's behavior. And yet that behavior has a certain power and fascination, a weird intensity. The mimicry of the sounds of aircraft engines and gunfire is uncanny, and the boy's complete absorption in his fantasy of violence is extremely unsettling. What is especially disturbing is the enthusiasm with which the child imagines the kind of aerial conflict that has produced the huge pile of rubble on which he is seated. The camera angle, which sees him from below, enhances the illusion of power and control that he is reaching for.

And it is precisely this paradox that characterizes the behavior of children in Henry Green's novel *Caught*: particularly the key figure of Christopher, son of the protagonist, the middle-class auxiliary fireman Richard Roe; but also the stray boy that the working-class regular fireman Pye keeps in his room overnight, having found him wandering the streets of the city in his eagerness to witness destruction. The boy's parents reveal that "the boy was so mad to see a raid he often stopped out all night in case there was one at last."[7] What is peculiar about Christopher is not the avidity with which he fantasizes scenarios of violence but the relish with which he mimics not British servicemen, but German soldiers, airmen, policemen. In the final section of the novel, he rushes around the garden constantly "slashing" and "laying about him": "'Look,' Christopher said, another snowball in his hand, 'I'm a German airman, I'm bombing'."[8] And somewhat more chilling is the exchange that takes place between Christopher and Richard:

> "Look," his father interrupted, "haven't you knocked those branches about enough? There's hardly a bird left in the garden since you've been out. You'd do better to put food for them. They starve in this weather you know."
> "They're Polish people," Christopher said, "and I'm a German policeman, rootling them about."[9]

The roots of this behavior are almost certainly in Christopher's experience of abduction at the hands of Pye's sister. His constant imaginative resort to the roles of bully and tyrant are effectively a refusal of the role of victim that has so traumatized him. Children in *Caught* do not so much represent a resource for the future – as they are supposed to in *Hue and Cry* – as a generation that is "caught" or trapped in its fears of separation, isolation, loss. In this respect, the centrality of abduction in the novel represents a dramatizing of the much more widespread phenomenon of evacuation, as Lyndsey Stonebridge has pointed out: "in Britain the evacuation of children away from the city centres was felt by many to be at least as violent as an abduction."[10]

What is extraordinary about the abduction scene in *Caught* is that it is made to correspond directly to Richard Roe's experience of the first night of the Blitz. Roe himself enforces the comparison. The two passages are distinguished typographically from the rest of the text by being set in parentheses. What they share most obviously is an intense chromaticism with vivid effects of chiaroscuro. The flames of the Blitz are anticipated in these melodramatic fireside flames, as are the conditions of the blackout, dispelled only by conflagration or by the sudden bursts of light provided by incendiaries. The correspondence is already provided for in the initial paragraph of the abduction episode:

> (The lady took Christopher into a room. It was very hot. It had a coal fire. He was surprised that she did not take off his things. She crouched by the fire. Looking back over her shoulder, she poked it, saying, "the darling, the darling." She did not turn on the light, so that he could see her eyes only by their glitter, a gyrating round sprawling rosy walls. "I've done right haven't I, the darling," she murmured. "My tea," he announced, surprised to find none.)[11]

Christopher's peremptory announcement, like an order to a servant, does not establish a connection, but pushes it away in the act of trying to assert control over a situation in which he feels suddenly alone and helpless. Amy Pye's self-communing, seeking reassurance from herself, since she will receive it from no one else, is conditioned by her inability to connect with Christopher. Her yearning for him is deflected into a third-person construction – "the darling" – rather than the vocative and possessive alternative – "my darling" – that would be natural in a genuinely intimate relationship.

What the passage shares quite profoundly with Roe's later account of the Blitz is an emphasis on abandonment, separation anxiety, and isolation. Throughout the long night of the first bombardment, Roe is constantly troubled by the loss of communications, by the lack of clear orders, by the fear of separation from his unit, and by the guilt that goes along with this. His bewilderment culminates in the encounter with another fireman who has been abandoned by his unit, clutching the branch of a hose-pipe, waiting for water, completely unaware that the hose has been uncoupled from the pump that has long since driven off. This image encapsulates Roe's own fear of abandonment. There is also a decisive parallel in the attention given to the imagery of boats. Christopher is lured away by Pye's sister when she buys him a toy boat; after the incident, he never plays with boats again, "hurling away from him" the model of a tanker when it is presented to him a few weeks later. Roe's barely subdued panic threatens to overwhelm him when his unit is given the task of putting out the fire on a liner moored at the docks. Luckily for them, the order is superseded.

In one way, it seems odd that the highly specific anxieties of evacuee children should be merged textually with the corresponding feelings of loss endured by adults, although identification with one's childhood self is not uncommon in the fiction of the period and is of course much more blatantly present in the many urgent projects of autobiographical writing, not least in Green's own *Pack My Bag* (1940). Elsewhere in Green's writing about the Blitz, firemen imagine themselves in the position of children, as in "The Lull," where a cultivated middle-class fireman called "Henry" surprises the young woman he is flirting with by making just such an imaginative leap: "She wondered that he could see himself as a child with her, when he was old enough to be her father."[12] In *Caught*, what binds together father and son most effectively is the contradictory image of the hearth at the center of the abduction scene. This symbolic focus for the domestic interior is of course present in the form of a charade in Pye's household, where the possibility of incest hovers over the figures of brother and sister who echo and displace the parental roles. Just as the flames of the hearth represent what will overtake the physical fabric of British society, so the symbolic meanings of the "home fires kept burning" are imbued with the means of their own destruction.

Green provides a structural parallel between the hearth and the fires of the Blitz, while William Sansom embeds one directly within the other, in his story "Fireman Flower." As Jeremy Treglown has pointed out in his biography of Green, both writers were auxiliary firemen stationed in Westminster at the same time.[13] Their practical experience of the Blitz would have been closely similar. The significance of the hearth in "Fireman Flower" is even more shockingly anomalous than in *Caught*. In a surrealistic turn of events, the isolated fireman battling a huge warehouse fire stumbles, without warning, into a magically protected domestic interior:

> It was a still room. Dark plush curtains hung from a brass curtain rod over the window. On heavy wooden rings they had been drawn across to drown all sound from outside. The wallpaper seemed to be flowered, perhaps in red on a background of deep brown. In the centre of the room stood a wide round table covered with a green plush cloth. Books, a microscope, rulers, a tea-cosy and a Toby jug littered the inkstained plush. At each side of the fire waited black leather armchairs, leaning a little on tired castors. A single light, shaded green, hung down over the table, illuminating it brightly like the light over a billiards cloth. Beyond the firelight, beyond the armchairs and the turkey rug, the room lay back in shadow. Flower could see dimly that there were bookcases, and somewhere a white plaster head. The firelight flickered, but that one electric light shone steadily. He could almost hear the steadiness with which it shone. His old friend continued to rustle the leaves of the grammar. A beetle ticked somewhere behind the wainscot. No other sound.[14]

Part of the comfort offered by this room comes from the details that anchor it in a world of measurement, calibration, regulation: microscopes, rulers, grammars, tea-cosies. Teatime is perhaps the most stereotypical way in which the British household maintains an ordered temporal rhythm. It is precisely what is appealed to so desperately at the end of the paragraph from *Caught*. What makes this particular room anachronistic, deliberately so, is its impermeability – its ability to shut everything out that does not belong there.

For much of the war, the threat of invasion was not limited to the dread of seeing German troops on British soil, but touched off various kinds of alarm over the increasing frequency with which people and objects were transposed from familiar to unfamiliar surroundings, often with a sense of being uprooted, out of place, and sometimes made to feel, or look, unwelcome or intrusive in their new setting. The new scope of the question of belonging, which has both a local and a national dimension, often interfused during wartime, is broached with unusual concentration in Rumer Godden's *Gypsy, Gypsy* (1940), which is effectively a Great House novel transposed to a French setting, or, more precisely, to Normandy. The protagonist is an

English-born eighteen-year-old girl named Henrietta Castle. The house she comes to at the start of the narrative is run by the English widow of Henrietta's Norman uncle Louis. Louis is in a direct line of inheritance that stretches back to the time of the eleventh-century Duke Robert, predating even the Norman conquest of England. The English widow, Aunt Barbe, is resented by her tenants as intensely as the eleventh-century Saxon inhabitants of England would have resented the arrival of William the Conqueror; she has the character almost of an occupying power. However, this national antagonism is defused in some degree by stress on the friction between Norman and French culture, which means that the degree of identification with place that is of immense significance for the protagonist Henrietta must be disengaged from a territorial brand of nationalism and focused on the attachment formed by personal history alone.

Individual attachment, however, is complicated by questions of property and inheritance. The owners of the chateau control the use of the land all round the neighboring village, and many of the villagers are their tenants. Moreover, those at the chateau are in a position to buy up the land of smallholders when these are forced to sell it after bad harvests. An atmosphere of oppression gathers around the concept of ownership in the text, to an extent that makes it seem the equivalent of expropriation. Differences of nationality, therefore, only accentuate the hostility generated by other factors.

The first half of the novel establishes the complex basis for the protagonist's commitment to place – her childhood memories preserve an image of its relations that she cannot square with her eighteen-year-old's awareness of class and national antagonisms. The second half of the novel shifts onto other ground by introducing a fundamental challenge to the idea of property and possession in the arrival of a gypsy family in the field below the chateau. This distinctive social group takes the place of evacuees, soldiers, or patients billeted at the Great House in English novels of the Second World War that contrast an insular mentality with an outsider's perspective, often associated with the urban environment or with public concerns or affairs of state. The presence of the gypsy in such a setting is only ever temporary, yet recursive. Gypsy nomadism is fundamentally opposed to concepts of settlement and land ownership; it mounts a challenge that relativizes the rival territorial claims of different nation states that in the 1930s and 1940s were often associated with the idea of a homeland. Gypsies together with Jews were the only groups routinely and systematically interned in wartime concentration camps on the basis of ethnicity rather than politics or sexuality. The main difference between them was that Jews retained the cultural memory of a homeland to which they aimed to return, while gypsies were and are more radically itinerant, definitively unsettled. Theirs is a culture not of belonging to a particular place but a culture based on traditional practices, on customs held in common.

The second half of Godden's novel unfolds the ever deepening and inevitable catastrophe that is the outcome of the English widow's attempt to tame the gypsies by various forms of inducement, bribes, and temptations that will corrupt them through assimilation to the values of property ownership. A crisis is reached when Henrietta and Aunt Barbe discover the gypsy in the act of taking two birds from the estate dovecot. Barbe's response is both appalled and jubilant:

> Her hand tightened on Henrietta's wrist and her look went out like the whisper to reach him and touch him, piercing him, flooding him with guilt. "Thief. You thief!"
>
> There was a long pause, oddly silent; then as if he answered, a tide began to well up in the gypsy; it grew stronger in his shamed dark face and guilty eyes, something strong and fierce and powerful that rose and swamped that look of Aunt Barbe's and flooded it down. Under the curve of his hat, his eyes moved quickly and his ear-rings glittered as he breathed. They were utterly alone with him in the courtyard, he was between them and the house; his lips parted and drew back, his body changed as if he were going to spring and Henrietta cried out, tearing the stillness, "Aunt Barbe! Let go! You're hurting me!"[15]

With this breaking of the silence, the gypsy drops the two birds and leaves. Barbe's paralyzed and paralyzing grip on Henrietta's arm during this timeless interval fixes the relations between gypsy and landowner and draws Henrietta into complicity with the project of contamination. Barbe and Henrietta then cooperate in an act that is strangely more furtive than the behavior of the gypsy had been; Barbe asks Henrietta to take the two birds and throw them over the headland into the sea:

> When she took the doves they were still warm and their bodies were heavy and soft and limp; she held them bundled on the peak of her saddle and rode quickly up through the orchard and along the road, avoiding the field and the short cut through the waste ground; the wind blew cold on her hands and parted the white feathers into dark patches between her fingers. She had to dismount to throw the doves over the cliff, and with a rush of fear that she could not explain, she hurtled back into the saddle and turning Bellairs almost on his hocks, she sent him back to the road at a gallop; the sounds of his hooves clattering on the road made her ashamed and she pulled him up and rode quietly down to the house; but she could not rid herself of the thought of those warm soft bodies, turning over and over through the air till they hit the cold sea with a splash that was lost in the sound of the waves.[16]

The two women are effectively conspiring to dispose of evidence, the evidence of a failed experiment in domestication, except that failure in this instance is the equivalent of success, since the gypsy's manifestation of shame and guilt indicates the degree of his adaptation to the values of Aunt Barbe. Henrietta's corresponding impulses of fear and shame advertise her awareness of complicity in the process of instilling these values. After this confrontation, the gypsies attempt to leave the estate and the forms of entrapment it represents, but in the momentary confusion of a quarrel, the gypsy knifes one of Barbe's houseguests, resulting in a charge of murder being brought against him. During the ensuing trial, the gypsy's behavior both does and does not conform to the stereotype of "the essence of every servant tale and superstition, of thievery and cunning."[17] It appears to conform in terms of outwardly observable behavior, but appears not to conform in terms of the insight gained by the heroine into the gypsies' total independence from the priorities and values of settled culture.

It is striking that the most vehement opposition to the idea that gypsy culture can be justified in any way is that of the Church. The local curé acts humanely towards the defendant's wife and children but insists that gypsies as a rule are morally unreclaimable. Their lives cannot be administered by a Church that relies on the geography of settlement, on the division of the population into parishes, in order to exert its influence. The heroine is the only character who endorses gypsy culture, even though she is poised, at the end of the novel, to inherit (through marriage to the English widow's nephew) the chateau and all its responsibilities and entanglements of class relations. There is a potentially tragic irony in the circumstance that the character most sympathetic to the gypsy perspective is the least well placed to accommodate its values in any practical way. Gypsy culture remains at the end of the text the most important means of exposing the venality and avidity for power of European society at the beginning of the Second World War, while also remaining totally unassimilable.

There is a very similar understanding of the structural value of this perspective in Rosamond Lehmann's story "The Gypsy's Baby," collected in the 1946 book of the same title. The baby of the title is supposed to be dead and left unburied in a gravel pit for three days, but the denouement of the story reveals it to be wholly imaginary, the product of the imagination of the most alienated and impoverished child in the village where the story is set. The story does not specify the historical time at which it is set, but reflects the historical conditions of its time of composition; there are no evacuees in this village, although there is nevertheless an extraordinary clash of cultures between the two neighboring houses that are at the center of the story's attention: the prosperous middle-class home of the child narrator and the hovel next door that contains the local shepherd's nine children. The shepherd's wife dies in childbirth, and it is the simultaneous death of her newborn child that implicitly motivates the fantasy of Chrissie, the second daughter, who projects onto the gypsies the responsibility for neglecting the imagined dead baby, and perhaps even the responsibility for murdering it. The scenario she imagines is one in which the unfathomable gypsies can ride away from the death of a child unmoved, emotionally untouched, but is also one in which the shame attached to her own condition as guilty survivor can be transferred to a social group even more despised than her own family in the scapegoat culture of an ordinary English village. The deaths of mother and child stimulate various charitable benefactions, but this only makes the surviving children feel more stigmatized than before, and the rapidity with which the state moves in to split the family up reflects perhaps the contemporary trauma of evacuation, the nationwide separation of families as an official policy, as well as Lehmann's political nervousness over state intervention in the domestic sphere.

In Agatha Christie's detective story of 1941, *N or M?*, it is the spectacle of parental indifference that leads to the exposure of an enemy agent. The N and M of the title are the male and female organizers of a Fifth Column whose infiltration of the British Establishment is phenomenally successful. Their converts include rear-admirals, air vice-marshals, cabinet ministers, police chiefs, and members of the intelligence service: precisely those whose situations will enable them to direct all the relevant command structures after an enemy invasion. If the extent of the conspiracy seems fantastic from a twenty-first-century perspective, it is important to remember the intensity with which the cultural imagination projected its fear of betrayal during the first few years of the war. Films such as *Cottage to Let* (1941) and *Went the Day Well?* (1942) took for granted the facility with which German agents could blend into the British social environment. In the first of these two films and in *N or M?*, it is precisely in respect of attitudes towards children that a distinctly alien sensibility emerges. The female agent M betrays herself through the indifference she shows to the potential suffering of the child she has cynically adopted to provide her with cover. When the child's real mother, a Polish refugee, regrets her decision to give the child up for adoption, she tries to reclaim her in what appears to the other characters to be a kidnapping attempt. In the critical scene, she stands by the edge of a cliff clutching the child, and is promptly shot through the head by the enemy agent posing as the child's mother. This confrontation is a clear echo of the Judgment of Solomon, in which the authentic mother shrinks from an act that would risk harming her child, while the impostor has no such qualms. The death of the mother who allows her child to be taken by strangers speaks to the guilt and anxiety of British parents who accede to the government policy of evacuation. The extent of enemy infiltration into branches of government suggests the depth of distrust the British have in their own culture and institutions. However, this intimation of the possibility that the real enemy is to be found within is superseded by the generically conservative ending of the detective story, with its defusing of all ambiguities. In an almost Dickensian gesture of reparation, the orphaned child is adopted at the end of the novel by the middle-aged amateur sleuths who manage to break the spy-ring.

Despite the suspense injected into many of the scenes in Christie's narrative, her representation of the dynamics of intimate betrayal is remarkably unpressurized, and even insouciant. The child is passed from one character to another without the reader being given any sense of the impact on her of this emotional relay-system. In the wartime stories of Anna Kavan, there is hardly any sentence that does not bear the weight of anxiety over the anticipation or the effects of betrayal. The protagonist narrator of her two volumes *I Am Lazarus* (1943) and *Asylum Piece* (1945) is betrayed by her lover, the person she trusts most, to whom she is most attached, and whose loss means more than anything else. In fact, his loss means a general loss of meaning for the protagonist, who enters a world of paranoid alertness to the possibility of betrayal at every turn, and by everyone she encounters:

> Whenever I speak to anyone I catch myself scrutinizing him with secret attention, searching for some sign that would betray the traitor who is determined to ruin me. I cannot concentrate on my work because I am always debating in my mind the question of my enemy's identity and the cause of his hate. What act of mine can possibly have given rise to such a relentless persecution? I go over and over my past life without finding any clue.[18]

The desperate project of "secret attention," intended to provide the means of "betraying the traitor," requires a level of dissimulation on the part of the protagonist herself that results in a profound dissociation of character. Her entry into a mental asylum represents the ultimate cost of the kind of psychological struggle endured by several fictional characters during wartime, in their failed attempts to find clues in their past lives that will account for their present condition and provide connection and continuity with it. Elizabeth Bowen's postwar novel *The Heat of the Day* (1948) circles around a similar set of dilemmas, although the female protagonist's deception by her lover is more overtly politicized; his activities as a Nazi agent, set within an environment of English traditions and myths of behavior, heighten his breach of trust into a betrayal not just of key individuals but of an entire way of life.

Julian Maclaren-Ross's 1945 story "The Swag, the Spy and the Soldier" identifies the true Fifth Columnist as the writer himself. The character in question, named Sandy O'Connor, is an amateur writer, assigned by the narrator to the "proletarian school of literature."[19] An ex-thief, whose illegal activities are detailed in the first part of the story, Sandy escapes detection as a regular criminal, but is court-martialed after conscription into the army on the much more serious charge of contravening the Official Secrets Act. The supposed evidence for this offense comes from the discovery among Sandy's belongings of "notebooks, sketches, maps, and a German dictionary."[20] On this basis, the narrator (also a writer) recognizes that he himself would be equally liable to prosecution: "Suppose my own kit was searched? They might even court-martial *me* as a Fifth Columnist."[21] Sandy's own account of his incriminating behavior explains it away as research conducted in preparation for the writing of a novel. The textuality of the resulting notes and drawings bears a remarkable resemblance to the documentary criteria for wartime writing endorsed so consistently by *Penguin New Writing* itself. In response to the narrator's question whether they are "really notes for a novel," Sandy evokes the delayed-response methodology prescribed by Elizabeth Bowen:

> "Sure. I was going to write it when the war's over, see? I took notes on every-thing I seen. Realism; atmosphere; same's you always told me. Bits in the paper too I copied out. All this stuff about factories they're kicking up a caper about, it's all bin printed; there're the dates written down, proof plain. But would they believe that? Not a word. No, they was dead set on me being a spy."[22]

The collecting of materials that are left in a relatively raw state, unedited and uninterpreted, ought to guarantee a degree of authorial disengagement. But the structural flaw in the writer's long-term project of assembling material without placing any construction on it until after the war is over, is that its very neutrality, its ownerless condition, leaves it open to construction by others. The decision not to narrate wartime events, not to subject them to authorial arrangement, but simply to record their occurrence, runs the risk of fostering a passive attitude to history. Maclaren-Ross himself practices a very different aesthetic, in the tradition of the well-made story, strongly anecdotal and conventionally plotted. His character Sandy is acquitted of treachery, of writing as an act of deception, and yet the final section of the story reopens the possibility that he has been guilty all along. In a letter sent to the narrator two years later, he makes it clear that there is more to tell: "*You must wonder even now how I got myself mixed up in that espial. I only hope we meet again so I can tell you.*"[23] The conspicuously deliberate use of the archaic word "espial" draws together the alternative meanings of neutral observation on the one hand, and of espionage on the other, proposing the essential ambivalence of the documentary aesthetic. Maclaren-Ross waits until the last page of the story to give point to a detail recorded in passing on its first page, the fact that Sandy speaks in a "Scotch-Irish accent"; his ambivalent national status reflects the possibility, at least, of a compromised neutrality. The narrator is careful to note that the intriguing letter has been passed by the censor, a reminder of the passive condition of all writing during the war, its exposure to radical reinterpretation, its paradoxical liability to being authored by others.

Censorship affected particularly the literary productions of servicemen. Both of Arthur Gwynn-Browne's wartime texts, *F.S.P.* and *Gone for a Burton*, were refused publication for lengthy periods of time. *F.S.P.*, a brilliantly eccentric memoir of Dunkirk, written in the style of Gertrude Stein, was delayed for almost a year, on the grounds that no accounts by private soldiers of the sequence of events at Dunkirk could be released into the public domain before the publication of official dispatches early in 1942.[24] This amounted to suppression by a technicality, but when the remarkable novel *Gone for a Burton* was completed in 1943, it was held back for an indefinite period of time, and not finally released until 1945, when the end of the war was in sight. It was felt to be too much of a threat to morale while the outcome of the fighting was still in the balance. The subject matter of the book was virtually identical to that of the popular Powell and Pressburger film, *One of Our Aircraft is Missing* (1942), but its narrative development was almost contrary to that of the determinedly optimistic screenplay. Both concern the shooting down of a British bomber and the subsequent attempts of the aircrew to escape capture while making their way across enemy-occupied territory. In the film, the British servicemen are looked after by an efficiently organized Resistance cell, in a Dutch community that is almost entirely united against the Germans. The crew are spirited away to freedom with a renewed faith in their allies. But in Gwynn-Browne's novel, the aircraft comes down in Vichy France, in a divided community where the British feel increasingly unable to trust anyone, and where they even begin to turn against one another. The representation of the French as unreliable allies, and of British forces as incapable of withstanding the stress of operations behind enemy lines, was clearly judged an affront to the war effort, the more so because Gwynn-Browne's abandonment of the avant-garde experimentalism of *F.S.P.* made the conceptual plan of his novel more transparent.

But more lethal forms of censorship were experienced with regard to the operations of the unconscious, especially in the case of returning servicemen for whom the suspension of life on the Home Front meant the freezing of memories of a way of life, and of personal relationships, that were sometimes violently dislocated from the reality of the postwar world. Demobilization could wreck lives. The protagonist of Henry Green's novel *Back* (1946), Charley Summers, clings tenaciously to the memory of his dead sweetheart, Rose, with an obsession that is systematic; his psychological tunnel-vision homes in on rosy iconography at every step, and his ear detects any elements of language that brush up against the sound of Rose's name, especially overheard uses of the past tense of the verb "rise." Everything in his physical and linguistic environment is colonized by the need to keep going a fantasy of Rose's survival. Summers has returned not just from active service overseas, but from several years in a prisoner-of-war camp, which increases dramatically the pitch of his alienation. But a steady investment in the illusion that historical time can be cheated somehow, its motion brought to rest in the mind, was a condition of resort for many less troubled servicemen on extended – sometimes greatly extended – tours of duty, such as those in John Sommerfield's stories about itinerant aircrews:

> An insidious falsification of the past was our drug, and under its influence we gave ourselves up to dreams of future deliverance, of a time of "after the war," a certain date when suddenly all the lights would blaze out again, the doors of our prisons spring open, and we'd be able to go to bed with our wives whenever we wanted – and each time it would be quite special, like the romantic dream of a honeymoon night.
>
> It's true that there could not have been one of us who did not, at some time or other, realize that he was deceiving himself; but that only made it worse; frustration caused us to lie to ourselves and knowledge or even a blind semi-conscious awareness of the lies increased the sense of frustration. We were not sustained by any sense of taking part in a war upon whose outcome would depend the future of most things we loved, hated, and feared, the true substance of our hope's dreams. History, that pushed us about the map, hid its face from us.[25]

The title of the volume from which this extract is taken is *The Survivors*, a reference not only to those still alive at the end of the war but to the imaginative strategies required for psychological survival. The notorious inactivity of service life for much of the time is in fact the pretext for its most important form of activity: reverie.

This is a war that requires a significant concentration on daydreaming. If the emphasis on the Home Front is one of the defining differences between the cultures of the two world wars, the remoteness from home of many combatants is equally significant. Distance sponsors fiction as an everyday habit of mind. Sommerfield's published stories are in fact indistinguishable from memoirs, and their generic proximity is owing partly to their fascination with memory as a resource that expands to fill the space opened up by ignorance at a time of disrupted, censored, and coded communications.

Sommerfield's dream of the future centers on the imagery of a house returning to normal, when the blackout is no longer needed and divided families can be reunited. After the destruction of the Blitz, with the ensuing housing shortage, the crowding of available domestic space, the necessity to share that space with strangers, the suspicion and distrust of the stranger in the house, and the dispersal of families through mobilization and evacuation, it is unsurprising that the house is made synecdochic of British culture and society in general. And throughout the war, the dependence on memory, which inevitably means the gradual alteration of memory – what Sommerfield refers to as the "falsification of the past" – enshrines certain images of the house as epitomes of English culture and history. There is a series of novels and memoirs in which the war becomes what Marina MacKay has referred to memorably as a "fight for the preservation of a sanitised past."[26] Her case in point is supplied by the great estate in Evelyn Waugh's *Brideshead Revisited* (1945). But there is equally a series of texts in which the same tropes become the focus of a de-sanitizing project. Virginia Woolf's *Between the Acts* (1941) turns the Great House into a stage for the presentation of a village pageant that functions as a popular equivalent of the modernist engagement with tradition, altering the perception of tradition – intervening in cultural memory – in the process of adding to it. Henry Green's *Loving* (1945) satirizes the mutual deceptions and self-deceptions of an aristocracy whose control over the running of their own house is exposed as illusory. Their surname, Tennant, implies the spuriousness of their hold over a cultural legacy whose lease is running out. One of the most distinguished examples of literary writing at the end of the war, Elizabeth Taylor's *At Mrs Lippincote's* (1945) indicates by its title the centrality of the idea of homelessness as a condition of the British cultural imagination. The protagonist, Julia Davenant, is more at home in the settings of English literature than in the house she lives in, which is owned by the absent Mrs. Lippincote. A survivor of the successive futures the British dreamed for themselves, she is forced to exist among a collection of mementos of someone else's past. The spatial imagination of this text is motivated by the experience of temporal displacement.

In Henry James's conceit of the House of Fiction, the author is a watcher at the window, reviewing life outside from one of several apertures. In the fiction of the Second World War, the house itself is the principal object of attention, architecturally and socially, in a period of disorientation between parents and children, hosts and guests; between what is routine and what is unpredictable, what is revealed and what is hidden, what is brought inside and what is kept out; and the House of Fiction itself is variously rebuilt, or discovered to have rooms that were previously unseen, rooms with secrets; or it might just be blown to bits.

NOTES

1. For further details, see my essay "Broken Glass," in *The Fiction of the 1940s: Stories of Survival*, ed. Rod Mengham and Neil Reeve (Basingstoke: Palgrave, 2001), pp. 124–33.
2. Elizabeth Bowen, "Contemporary," review of *In My Good Books* by V.S. Pritchett, *New Statesman*, May 23, 1942.

3. Henry Green, "Mr Jonas," *Surviving: The Uncollected Writings of Henry Green* (London: Chatto & Windus, 1992), pp. 85–6.
4. Elizabeth Bowen, "The Happy Autumn Fields," *The Demon Lover and Other Stories* (London: Jonathan Cape, 1945), p. 100.
5. Graham Greene, *The Ministry of Fear* (London: Heinemann, 1943), p. 114.
6. Henry Reed, *The Novel Since 1939* (London: British Council, 1949).
7. Henry Green, *Caught* (London: Hogarth, 1943), p. 196.
8. Green, *Caught*, p. 173.
9. *Ibid.*, p. 188.
10. Lyndsey Stonebridge, *The Writing of Anxiety: Imagining Wartime in Mid-Century British Culture* (Basingstoke: Palgrave MacMillan, 2007), p. 69.
11. Green, *Caught*, p. 15.
12. Green, "The Lull," *Surviving*, p. 108.
13. Jeremy Treglown, *Romancing: the Life and Work of Henry Green* (London: Faber, 2000), p. 124.
14. William Sansom, "Fireman Flower," *Fireman Flower and Other Stories* (London: Hogarth, 1944), p. 148.
15. Rumer Godden, *Gypsy, Gypsy* (London: Peter Davies, 1940), pp. 205–6.
16. *Ibid.*, pp. 206–7.
17. *Ibid.*, p. 247.
18. Anna Kavan, "The Enemy," in *Asylum Piece* (Garden City, NY: Doubleday, 1946), p. 18.
19. Julian Maclaren-Ross, "The Swag, the Spy and the Soldier," *Penguin New Writing*, no. 26 (Harmondsworth: Penguin, 1945), p. 57.
20. *Ibid.*, p. 54.
21. *Ibid.*, p. 46.
22. *Ibid.*, p. 55.
23. *Ibid.*, p. 59.
24. See Neil Reeve's introduction to Arthur Gwynn-Browne, *F.S.P.* (Bridgend: Seren, 2004), p. xix.
25. John Sommerfield, "Worm's-Eye View," *The Survivors* (London: John Lehmann, 1947), p. 13.
26. Marina MacKay, *Modernism and World War II* (Cambridge University Press, 2007), p. 127.

3

MARGOT NORRIS

War poetry in the USA

In 2003, Harvey Shapiro edited an anthology called *Poets of World War II* as part of the American Poets Project published by The Library of America.[1] In his introduction he expresses his regret that "common wisdom has it that the poets of World War I – Wilfred Owen, Robert Graves, Siegfried Sassoon, Edmund Blunden, Isaac Rosenberg – left us a monument and the poets of World War II did not" (p. xx). Given America's late entry into the war in 1917, little of the monumental poetry of the Great War was written by Americans. Shapiro writes, "The American poets of World War I – John Peale Bishop, E. E. Cummings, Archibald MacLeish, Alan Seeger – were too few to constitute a group" (p. xx). This imbalance in the poetic production of war poetry should have been redressed in World War II, although here a different set of impediments intervened. Paul Fussell suggests two reasons why the war produced more silence than poetic expression. The first was the sheer magnitude of violence and the level of cruelty produced by the war. "Faced with events so unprecedented and so inaccessible to normal models of humane understanding, literature spent a lot of time standing silent and aghast."[2] The second was that redemptive notions of patriotism, heroism, and even elegiac sentiment had been effectively exhausted by World War I. "It is demoralizing to be called on to fight the same enemy twice in the space of twenty-one years, and what is there to say except what has been said the first time?" Fussell writes.[3] And yet poetry *was* produced in response to World War II, including a wide range of American poetry, as Shapiro's anthology demonstrates. Taken as a whole, these poems exemplify another reason why their response to World War II has not achieved the same public visibility and cultural significance as the poetry of the Great War. Unlike British World War I trench poetry, whose pastoralism allied it to the Georgian poetry movement to give it a specific aesthetic profile, the American poetry of World War II is extremely diverse both formally and thematically. As a result it defies ready classification and frustrates any sense of coherence.

This lack of coherence is itself symptomatic of the fragmented historical and ethical configuration of the war. The US certainly saw itself as responding defensively both to European totalitarianism and Japanese militarism, a posture that made pacifist responses and anti-war protest in poetry far more difficult than in World War I. At the same time, soldiers in the field could express anti-military sentiments and complaints of national hypocrisy without an overall compromise of their patriotism. The role of African-American soldiers in defending a nation that continued to abuse them represents an emotional pole countered by Jewish soldiers thankful to be fighting Nazi brutality against European Jews. Combat experience created another arena of diversity representing disparate technological and strategic exigencies. The bomber pilot and the infantryman experienced different genres of warfare with differing ethical dimensions. Formally, the American poetry of this period represents virtually every innovation produced in the immense range of Anglo-American modernism, from local specificity and realism to classical allusion and referential obliquity, from the primness of regular meter and rhyme to the idiom of slang and the vernacular of obscenity.

Given its formal and thematic diversity, how does one discuss this historically specific body of work? One plausible strategy is to analyze a series of poems relationally, aligning them in clusters that highlight their differences as divergent perspectives on the same historical phenomenon and on its challenges to poetic expression. By letting the poems converse with each other, the reductive sense of World War II as a comparatively "good war" from an American vantage is exploded to produce a poetically contentious and contested terrain. The pairings and clusters offered here will address thematic, formal, and ethical divergences produced by the complex character of this monumental mid-twentieth-century conflict. Three formally disparate poems of combat experience that are connected by a surprising evocation of *innocence* may usefully launch this exploration: Louis Simpson's "Carentan O Carentan," Richard Hugo's "Where We Crashed," and Randall Jarrell's famous "The Death of the Ball Turret Gunner." Three poems that express *knowing* born of experience – by Harvey Shapiro, Howard Nemerov, and Gwendolyn Brooks – will respond to this first set. The discussion will conclude with the work of three canonical American poets – W. H. Auden, Robert Lowell, and Marianne Moore – whose poems mark specific dates in the course of the war yet nonetheless draw back to offer universalizing observations.

I. Poems of innocence

Louis Simpson, an émigré of Scottish and Russian parentage from Jamaica, spent the years from 1943 to 1945 as a member of the 101st Airborne Division in Europe, after attending Columbia University. His division played a role in one of the most famous American assaults of the war – "Operation

Overlord" which required taking the Normandy town of Carentan before 150,000 American troops could land on the beaches called Utah and Omaha on June 6, 1944, D-Day.[4] The highly dramatic and historically significant character of the battle in and around Carentan has been celebrated in such popular productions as Stephen Ambrose's *Band of Brothers*, the basis of an HBO mini-series, and the video and strategy games "Call of Duty" and "Company of Heroes." The quiet opening of Simpson's "Carentan O Carentan" – pastoral, romantic, and idyllic – is remarkable in contrast:

> Trees in the old days used to stand
> And shape a shady lane
> Where lovers wandered hand in hand
> Who came from Carentan. (p. 183)

Soldiers, guns, and D-Day appear almost surreptitiously, creating barely a sound or a ripple in the simple rhymed quatrains sounding "the singsong quality consistent with the childlike comprehension" that characterizes several of Simpson's war poems according to Ronald Moran.[5] Men appear "two by two / Walking at combat-interval," and the time is "early June" when "the ground / Was soft and bright with dew. / Far away the guns did sound, / But here the sky was blue" (p. 183). The simplicity of the rhymed verse reflects the soldier's childlike wonder and inexperience on his first encounter with combat. The mood is never disrupted even by the shooting – until the "watchers in their leopard suits" aim "between belt and boot" (p. 184). The speaker, forced to lie down by the action of a "hammer" at his knee, reacts like a hurt child surprisingly wounded in a game gone awry; he first reassures his mother – "Everything's all right, Mother ... It's all in the game" (p. 184) – before turning to his officers to beg their counsel. Their deathly silence is construed in the uncomprehending idiom of the child. The Captain, asked to show the troop's position on a map, fails to respond – "But the Captain's sickly / And taking a long nap" (p. 185). The Lieutenant's silence is similarly construed as the faux death of fairy tale:

> Lieutenant, what's my duty,
> My place in the platoon?
> He too's a sleeping beauty
> Charmed by that strange tune. (p. 185)

Moran calls "Carentan O Carentan" Simpson's "most successful war poem," offering in its "balladlike way" a situation "so real that it is archetypal."[6]

Richard Hugo, an American poet born in Seattle, Washington, served in the Army Air Corps as a bombardier in the Mediterranean between 1943 and 1945. He flew thirty-five missions and was awarded the Distinguished Flying Cross

45

among other awards.[7] His poem "Where We Crashed" was inspired by the crash landing of the B-24 in which Hugo flew. Hugo himself says little about the crash in his essay "*Ci Vediamo*" in which he reminisces about his war experiences, his memories triggered by a 1963 return to Italy. "We had crashed only a week before – miraculously the full load of gas and bombs hadn't ignited."[8] It is unclear whether Hugo was familiar with the avant-garde productions of the German World War I poet August Stramm, but Hugo's imitative form – having the lines of the poem arranged in simulation of a rapid vertical descent – resembles some of Stramm's battlefield poems.[9] The poem's speaker appears to narrate the event as it occurs, as the plane is in the process of crashing, reducing his thoughts to fragments and terrified expletives – "nothing / fuckass / nothing / shithead / nothing / moldy / cunteyed / bastard" (p. 176). The poem begins in the first person, "I was calling airspeed / christ /one-thirty-five and / pancake bam / glass going first," when the voice quickly registers danger:

> now
> here
> explode
> damn
> damn
> Steinberg
> pilot
> should
> have found
> more sky
> you end
> here
> boom
> now
> boom
> gone   (pp. 174–5)

Like Simpson's, Hugo's speaker also exhibits a strange innocence – but of the adolescent rather than the child. The crash is a group experience of a youngster and his pals finding themselves in real danger and responding with the blunt curses of their shared idiom. The pals in the poem are real, however. The "Steinberg / pilot" is identified as "our pilot, Lt. Howard (NMI) Steinberg," and "O'Brien / L. A. / broken foot / limping / away / all away / from gas / from bombs" (p. 177) is identified in "*Catch* 22, Addendum" as his crew's navigator, Ryan O'Brien. Mercifully, the group is described as surviving the crash in the poem:

> Knapp
> ball turret
> joking

```
farmer
yelling
Steinberg
staring gray
and in this grass
I didn't die                                    (p. 177)
```

But this lucky outcome could not have been predicted by the poem's beginning. As readers learned from Erich Maria Remarque's *All Quiet on the
Western Front*, and as we will see in Randall Jarrell's "The Death of the
Ball Turret Gunner," the first-person voice does not guarantee the survival of
the speaker. In the end, the survival in the poem does little to mitigate the
terror of the hellish descent of the words because it nonetheless simulates for
us the sensation of the thousands of US Air Force flyers killed or missing in
World War II. The poem's panic shares the innocence of Simpson's speaker at
Carentan by producing an immediate, visceral, and uncomprehending
response to violence and endangerment that resorts to conspicuous *form* for
its expression.

The reference to "Knapp / ball turret" in Hugo's poem reminds us immediately of Jarrell's famous five-line poem, "The Death of the Ball Turret
Gunner." Like Hugo, Jarrell enlisted in the United States Army Air Corps,
but unlike Simpson and Hugo, he did not qualify to fly and as a result worked
as a tower operator and as an instructor in Tucson, Arizona, for navigators
serving on bombing missions. Jarrell himself explained clearly what a "ball
turret" was in his note to the poem. "A ball turret was a plexiglass sphere set
into the belly of a B-17 or B-24, and inhabited by two .50 caliber machine-
guns and one man, a short small man."[10] It is his further explanation,
however, that provides a clue to his poem's enigmatic first line. "From my
mother's sleep I fell into the State, / And I hunched in its belly till my wet fur
froze" (p. 88). Only a very small man can fit into the acrylic sphere attached to
the underside of the plane, and the spherical shape of the turret forces his
posture to curl. Jarrell goes on to note that "When this gunner tracked with
his machine-guns a fighter attacking his bomber from below, he revolved with
the turret; hunched upside-down in his little sphere, he looked like the foetus
in the womb."[11] Like the poems of Simpson and Hugo, the soldier in Jarrell's
poem is transformed from a fighter into a figure whose vulnerability and
helplessness are rendered *in extremis* as a small animal trapped in a lethal lair
or a fetus violently aborted by the flush of a steam hose.[12] The visceral effect
of violated innocence is further intensified by the first-person speaker's invocation of the trope of sleep: "From my mother's sleep I fell . . . I woke to black flak
and the nightmare fighters" (p. 88). Aerial warfare is here evoked as a cruel
awakening into a horrific alien universe "[s]ix miles from earth, loosed from

its dream of life" (p. 88). The figure of Jarrell's ball turret gunner is eerily resonant of the strange image of Stanley Kubrick's astronaut in the film *2001*, morphing into an orphaned fetus separated from the maternal body and isolated in outer space. In the last line, the speaker is identified as a voice of the dead whose living body was horrifically disintegrated – "When I died they washed me out of the turret with a hose" (p. 88).[13] J. A. Bryant, Jr., grounds Jarrell's later reputation as a writer of children's stories in a peculiar empathy already exhibited in his early war poems: "he had a set of sensibilities finely tuned to respond to all orders of living creation – plants, animals wild and domestic, men, women, and children; for all these he had compassion, disdaining nothing and respecting everything."[14] It is the innocence of childlike perception that makes the brutal last line of his most famous war poem one of the most shocking of the genre.[15]

II. Poems of knowing

These poems of innocence – representing war as a violation of the soldier's innocence – are countered by a different cluster of American poems in which speakers cannot disavow what they know of the war's larger historical and political context and its ethical stakes. The diverse voices of Harvey Shapiro, Howard Nemerov, and Gwendolyn Brooks offer striking illustrations of the burden of knowing, in reflections of the American soldier in World War II. Loss of innocence precedes war experience in Harvey Shapiro's "War Stories" with its opening of a scene of childhood. The speaker's father buys the *Sunday Journal American* "because I was a kid and needed the colored comics – / Maggie and Jiggs, Popeye and Dick Tracy," but puberty erodes the purity of those youthful comics as in high school they resurface "in their porno resurrection, strips / in which even Dagwood had a big erection" (p. 206). However, full adulthood is deferred a bit longer, as the radio gunners at Sioux Falls in South Dakota burst into radio serial theme songs on their way to training classes, singing of "that little chatterbox," little Orphan Annie (p. 207). The second section of the poem opens in the Italian city of Foggia, which was reduced to rubble by Allied bombing in July and August of 1943, and conquered on October 1 of that year. The speaker is in a bar – "this is 1944" – on the verge of tipping the barmaid when a British sergeant tries to stay his hand by explaining that the Italians are "a conquered people": "I liked the phrase / because it had the ring of history, / suggested dynasty policy, put / the British empire with the Roman / down the long reach of time" (p. 207). But he quickly deconstructs the grandiose phrase by breaking it anecdotally into individual Italians, kids who "trade eggs for cigarettes" in his tent, the old lady who teaches him Italian, the girl in Capri he fell in love with: "They were hardly a people, much less conquered" (p. 207). Then, just before the beginning of the third part, the speaker is obliged to concede his own implication:

> But high above their cities
> on my way to Germany to kill the enemy
> I was part of the sergeant's fictive world,
> part of the bloody story of our century. (p. 208)

The third part of the poem takes place in the air, on an approach to Berlin at "23,000 feet, our usual / altitude for bombing" (p. 208). The scene is described with a combination of technical precision and aesthetic imagery – "P38s," "P51s," and "Flying Fortresses" producing a sky-full of "big-assed birds," silver baubles, white contrails, colored tracers, and "black flak ... a deadly fungus": "Planes would blossom into flame / in that bewildering sky" (p. 208). The scene is utterly vivid but curiously silent, like a film played without sound. And that is how it is remembered. "How to believe all that happened, / as in a movie, a tv drama, or some other life" (p. 208). The end of the poem, with its evocation of modern media, returns to the beginning with its newspapers, comics, and radio programs. A double reversal has occurred. The media of childhood and youth were never innocent, the conservative Hearst papers swallowing up the liberal outlets, Daddy Warbucks politicizing the little orphan's adventures. The fighting, in turn, would be seemingly restored to the innocence of media representations, the movies and television of civilian life, and the grandiose rhetoric of postwar history books. But the scene that is never described in the poem, in exploded buildings on the ground, in the cockpits of the planes that blossomed into flames, constitutes that which is not-innocent, that which is perpetrated and suffered, that which is the bloody inside or underbelly or antithesis of "war stories."

While Shapiro wrote a poem called "War Stories," Howard Nemerov published an entire volume called *War Stories: Poems About Long Ago and Now* (1987). Like Simpson, Hugo, and Shapiro, Nemerov too served as a pilot in World War II, although a circuitous route took him to aerial combat. Having failed the rigorous pilot training program of the US Army, Nemerov enlisted in the Royal Canadian Air Force, which qualified him as a fighter pilot, and allowed him to transfer to the American Air Force in early 1944. His missions chiefly patrolled shipping in the North Sea and attacked German coastal defense lines. Nemerov's war poems aim to deflate the retroactive and synthetic innocence produced long after the war and given a name in the title of Studs Terkel's Pulitzer Prize-winning 1985 oral history, *The Good War*.[16] "That was the good war, the war we won / As if there were no death, for goodness' sake," Nemerov writes in "The War in the Air" (p. 142).

Nemerov's poems deflate both the myth of military prowess and heroism, and the myth of common purpose and moral superiority as the keys to Allied victory. "Night Operations, Coastal Command RAF" tells of casualties produced not in aerial combat – "We didn't need the enemy" – but by aviator "folly and misfortune":

> Some hit our own barrage balloons, and some
> Tripped over power lines, coming in low;
> Some swung on takeoff, others overshot,
> And two or three forgot to lower the wheels. (p. 141)

Nemerov's poem "IFF" ("Identification Friend or Foe") further challenges one of the most enduring war myths, forged as early as World War I – the idealization of comradeship and solidarity among soldiers fighting the good war. "Hate Hitler? No, I spared him hardly a thought," Nemerov writes, and then names officers who "were objects fit to hate": "Hitler a moustache and a little curl / In the middle of his forehead, whereas these / Bastards were bastards in your daily life" (p. 142). Nemerov gives them names and ranks – "Corporal Irmin, first, and later on / The O.C. (Flying), Wing Commander Briggs" (p. 142). Friends and foes are complicated to identify in the military setting, he suggests, particularly if you were yourself a Jew:

> Not to forget my navigator Bert,
> Who shyly explained to me that the Jews
> Were ruining England and Hitler might be wrong
> But he had the right idea . . . (pp. 142–3)

Deborah Dash Moore argues that anti-Semitism in the World War II military was not abstract but deeply personal. And she cites a Jewish recruit who complained that "The primary objective of our war is to defeat the Jap – not Hitler, and certainly not Nazism."[17]

Gwendolyn Brooks also glosses the confusion attending "IFF" in her poem "Negro Hero *to suggest Dorie Miller*." Doris ("Dorie") Miller was an African American mess attendant aboard the USS *West Virginia*, and was collecting laundry when Pearl Harbor was attacked on December 7, 1941. The Naval Historical Center gives this account of what happened:

> He headed for his battle station, the anti-aircraft battery magazine amidship, only to discover that torpedo damage had wrecked it, so he went on deck. Because of his physical prowess, he was assigned to carry wounded fellow Sailors to places of greater safety. Then an officer ordered him to the bridge to aid the mortally wounded Captain of the ship. He subsequently manned a 50 caliber Browning anti-aircraft machine gun until he ran out of ammunition and was ordered to abandon ship.[18]

Dorie Miller was awarded the Navy Cross by Admiral Chester Nimitz in May 1942. A year later he was aboard the *USS Liscome Bay* when it was sunk by a Japanese torpedo. Miller was missing and declared dead in 1944.

Brooks gives Miller a voice and a perspective that modulates the gap between his appreciation of his own heroism ("For I am a gem" [p. 115]) and the demeaning treatment accorded African Americans not only in the Navy, but also in the nation at large. Echoing Nemerov's speaker in "IFF," Miller's persona offers a sardonic aside: "(They are not concerned that it was hardly The Enemy my fight was against / But them)" (p. 115). The poem digs deep into the ironies and paradoxes of the African American enlisted man consigned to the kitchen rather than taught to use arms, who fights and dies for a democracy that dishonors and demeans him. The question he asks himself – "am I good enough to die for them, is my blood bright enough to be spilled" – is given a stunningly cruel reply:

> (In a southern city, a white man said
> Indeed, I'd rather be dead;
> Indeed, I'd rather be shot in the head
> Or ridden to waste on the back of a flood
> Than saved by the drop of a black man's blood.)   (pp. 116–17)

The rhyme marks the comment more as stock formulation or folk saying than as reported anecdote. But the poem's opening line – "I had to kick their law into their teeth in order to save them" (p. 115) – expresses how bitterly democracy has withheld itself from the black soldier who is disenfranchised from, and by, his nation's law. Brooks modulates the voice carefully to keep it on the offensive rather than the defensive, to ensure that the hero prevails over the victim by virtue of his patriotic idealism. "I loved. And a man will guard when he loves. / Their white-gowned democracy was my fair lady" – he says, knowing, and at times forgetting, that she has a knife up her sleeve (p. 116).[19]

III. Specific dates – large overviews

Turning to poems that address different moments in time, we fail to find a simple trajectory from innocence to experience marking perceptions of the course of the war. The three notable poets selected for this address were all non-combatants, although it is not certain that their distance from the front was solely responsible for their wide vision. W. H. Auden was born in England, came to the United States in 1939, and became a US citizen in 1946. Although he did not see combat, he served in the Morale Division of the US Strategic Bombing Survey after the war, and from May to August of 1945, "interviewed civilians in Germany about their reactions to Allied bombing" (p. 223). His poem titled "September 1, 1939" begins locally – "I sit in one of the dives / On Fifty-Second Street / Uncertain and afraid / As the clever hopes expire / Of a low dishonest decade" (p. 41) – but moves quickly to a universal historical perspective. Innocence has been preempted by history. The poet looks past the impending war to the "[a]ccurate scholarship" that will follow and predicts its failure (p. 41). Neither classical historical analysis ("Exiled Thucydides knew / All that a speech can say / About Democracy") nor modern psychoanalytic theories of Hitler's personality ("What huge imago made / A psychopathic god") can provide insights to prevent future wars. "Mismanagement and grief: / We must suffer them all again" (pp. 41–2) As a poet he can do no more than Wilfred Owen did – "All I have is a voice / To undo the folded lie" – but with as little hope of success. "Defenceless under the night / Our world in stupor lies" – although he pledges to join the "[i]ronic points of light" emitted by "the Just" to "[s]how an affirming flame" (pp. 43–4).

Robert Lowell's poem, marked by the date of 1942, takes an equally universal and perhaps even more aggressively pacifist view of the war in progress. Lowell's stance as a conscientious objector earned him five months in prison after he refused to be inducted in 1943. He acted in protest of "the Allied bombing of German cities, the policy of unconditional surrender, and the US alliance with the Soviet Union" (p. 233). "On the Eve of the Feast of the Immaculate Conception: 1942" takes the form of a blasphemous prayer invoking the Virgin Mary to triumph over the gods of war. "Mother of God, whose burly love / Turns swords to plowshares, come, improve / On the big wars" (p. 118). The poet's allusive voice pits the Christian and classical tropes of the high modernists against topical historical references to elevate the agon of the war from national conflict to the more elemental battle between the spirits of war and peace: "Freedom and Eisenhower have won / Significant laurels where the Hun / And Roman kneel / To lick the dust from Mars' bootheel" (p. 118). Like Auden, Lowell acknowledges war as a millennial fact of earthly life: "Six thousand years / Cain's blood has drummed into my ears" (p. 118). Mary is then evoked in her various iconic guises as Virgin, *pietà*, and Victorix. As "Celestial Hoyden" she is wooed and ingested by devout soldiers – "Oh, if soldiers mind you well / They shall find you are their belle / And belly too; / Christ's bread and beauty came by you" (p. 119). As *pietà* she performs disarmament – "when our Lord / Gave up the weary Ghost and died, / You took a sword / From his torn side" (p. 119). As Victorix she tramples the head of the serpent – "Jesus' Mother, like another / Nimrod danced on Satan's head" (p. 119). Yet in the end "Man eats the Dead" in a dreadful communion that appears to require bloody sacrifice for redemption. "Shall I wring plums from Plato's bush / When Burma's and Bizerte's dead / Must puff and push / Blood into bread" (pp. 118–19).

Finally, Marianne Moore's poem "'Keeping their World Large'" amplifies a cited catchphrase by keeping a large view of not only the war, but also the way we speak about war. Her epigram, taken from the *New York Times* of June 7, 1944, quotes the words "*All too literally, their flesh and their spirit are our shield*" (p. 15). Moore takes words of appreciation for the soldiers fighting the war and meditates on how such words could be made meaningful. Her answer is delivered formally, in sentences that are broken, that fail to work entirely logically or grammatically, and thereby render fractured and contradictory sentiments.[20] The poet's voice begins with a wish – "I should like to see that country's tiles, bedrooms, stone patios / and ancient wells: Rinaldo / Caramonica's the cobbler's, Frank Sblendorio's / and Dominick Angelastro's country" (p. 15). The names imply that the country is Italy, and that it "belongs" to the American immigrants who hailed from there. Moore offers here another variant of IFF, by drawing deep national linkages between the Old World and the New World to confound "us" and "them." But other confusions follow. "A noiseless piano, an / innocent war, the heart that can act against itself" – these items do not function cleanly as analogies (p. 15). Does a heart that acts against itself – for example, a socialized man forced to kill – produce an oxymoronic "innocent war"?

> Here,
> each unlike and all alike, could
> so many – stumbling, falling, multiplied
> till bodies lay as ground to walk on –
>
> "If Christ and the apostles died in vain,
> I'll die in vain with them"
> against this way of victory.   (p. 15)

Without negating heroism, Moore transforms it into sacrifice, partly by shifting the shield from a vertical to a horizontal surface, a "forest of white crosses," an altar: "All laid like animals for sacrifice – like Isaac on the mount, / were their own sacrifice" (pp. 15–16). Ethically, too, the shield is transformed from protection against violence to protection against smug self-satisfaction or sentimental indulgence. "They fought the enemy, / we fight fat living and self-pity. / Shine, o shine, / unfalsifying sun, on this sick scene" (p. 16). As in her other famous war poem, "In Distrust of Merits," Moore turns the terrain of writing about a topic as huge and complex as World War II into an internal battlefield of the heart, the brain, and the ethical soul.

NOTES

1. Harvey Shapiro, ed., *Poets of World War II* (New York: The Library of America, 2003). Unless noted otherwise, all subsequent citations refer to this text and are given in parentheses.

2. Paul Fussell, ed., *The Norton Book of Modern War* (New York: Norton, 1991), p. 311. Anthony Hecht's "Rites and Ceremonies" addresses this difficulty most explicitly. Hecht belonged to the force that liberated the Flossenberg concentration camp. Peter Sacks writes of this poem, "Like Adorno [though of course more positively, since this is after all a poem], Hecht now implicitly questions the adequacy of poetry in the wake of the Holocaust." Peter Sacks, "Anthony Hecht's 'Rites and Ceremonies': Reading *The Hard Hours*," in *The Burdens of Formality: Essays on the Poetry of Anthony Hecht*, ed. Sydney Lea (Athens: University of Georgia Press, 1989), p. 81.

3. Fussell, *Norton Book of Modern War*, p. 311.

4. "I was on the beach at Normandy on D Day ... I can see every detail of the scene as clearly as if it were present: the lane with trees among which we were pinned down by German machine guns and mortars ... the tree a few feet away being raked by bullets." Louis Simpson, *The Character of the Poet* (Ann Arbor: University of Michigan Press, 1986), pp. 35–6.

5. Ronald Moran, *Louis Simpson* (New York: Twayne, 1972), p. 50.

6. *Ibid.*, p. 37.

7. Hugo's essay "*Catch 22*, Addendum" offers a demythification of the "Innsbruck nuisance raid" that earned him the Distinguished Flying Cross. He remembers how he was unable to drop the bombs because "The bomb racks are frozen and my throat mike has malfunctioned," and as he was ready to release them manually the "bombs fell, where there were no towns, no farms, no roads ... And so the officers (enlisted men were given few citations) of Lt. Howard (NMI) Steinberg's crew were given the DFC for bombing some remote mountains, maybe in Switzerland." Richard Hugo, *The Real West Marginal Way: A Poet's Autobiography*, ed. Ripley S. Hugo, Lois M. Welch, and James Welch (New York: Norton, 1986), pp. 103–5.

8. Hugo, *Real West Marginal*, p. 124.

9. For example, August Stramm's "Guard-Duty" contains the lines:

> mists spread
> fears
> staring shivering
> shivering
> cajoling
> whispering
> You!

A. Stramm, "Guard Duty," *The Penguin Book of First World War Poetry*, 2nd edn., ed. Jon Silkin (New York, Penguin, 1971), p. 239.

10. Randall Jarrell, *The Complete Poems* (New York: Farrar, Straus, & Giroux, 1969), p. 8.

11. *Ibid.*

12. Stephen Burt offers a psychoanalytic reference to the gunner's experience as evoking a Freudian "birth trauma": "the gestation and birth, or abortion, of a fetus (nine months or less); the gestation, birth, and death of a human being old enough to serve in a war; and even (if ontogeny recapitulates phylogeny) the (painful or futile) evolution of the human species" (*Randall Jarrell and His Age* [New York: Columbia University Press, 2002], p. 95).

13. Shapiro remembers an instructor telling the men, "Sometimes when they return from a mission, they have to wash him out of the turret with a hose"; he speculates that Jarrell may also have heard the line (p. xxiv). Bryant also discusses Jarrell's experiences as an instructor – "he learned by training men who would fight what it was like to fight." J. A. Bryant, Jr., *Understanding Randall Jarrell* (Columbia: University of South Carolina Press, 1986), p. 50.
14. *Ibid.*, p. 49.
15. The poem has not lacked critics, as William H. Pritchard points out. Donald Hall objected to its "'tough' tone of voice that is really sentimental and that titillates the sensationalistically minded reader with a shocking image." William H. Pritchard, *Randall Jarrell: A Literary Life* (New York: Farrar, Straus, & Giroux, 1990), p. 120.
16. Steven Gould Axelrod discusses how the "American victory narrative" has "been reified into myth and used as a paradigm for American conduct in the world" ("Counter-Memory in American Poetry," in *Tales of the Great American Victory*, ed. Diederik Oostdijk and Markha G. Valenta [Amsterdam: VU University Press, 2006], p. 20).
17. Deborah Dash Moore, *GI Jews: How World War II Changed a Generation* (Cambridge, MA: The Belknap Press of Harvard University Press, 2004), p. 26.
18. Naval Historical Center FAQ: www.history.navy.mil/faqs/faq57-4.htm
19. Witter Bynner's poem "Defeat" also addresses racial discrimination in the Armed Forces: "On a train in Texas German prisoners eat / With white American soldiers, seat by seat, / While black American soldiers sit apart" (p. 1).
20. Moore's "In Distrust of Merits" (1943) has been retroactively criticized for its support of war. However, Axelrod argues that "[t]his poem seems tempted to tell war's big story, but the story breaks down under the weight of conflicting elements … Moore steps back from the war's particulars, evoking its physical and mental pain, its moral perplexity, and its cathected relation to the poetic project." Axelrod, "Counter-Memory," pp. 22–3.

4

JAMES DAWES

The American war novel

The United States entered the war late, but its cost in blood and treasure for the nation was staggering: over 400,000 dead and more than 600,000 wounded. Marching into the appalling bloodletting of Europe, Asia, and Africa – many put total world fatalities at 60 million or higher – the United States would be radically transformed. The astonishing breadth of these changes is best symbolized in the distance between two of its most important war-related creations: the atomic bomb and, through the sponsorship of Eleanor Roosevelt, the Universal Declaration of Human Rights.

The immediate fictional response to the war, however, was not the watershed that might have been expected from such tumult. A great deal of readable, competent work was produced and lavishly celebrated – like Irwin Shaw's engaging if formulaic *The Young Lions* (1948) or Herman Wouk's prim but somehow irresistible *The Caine Mutiny* (1951) – but few of these novels marked new directions for literature and fewer still are given extended attention by literary critics today. It is a much smaller subset of works that is now widely taken as the most important art coming out of the conflict, all of it published after the war ended, including Norman Mailer's punishing *The Naked and the Dead* (a first novel so successful as to almost ruin the 25-year-old, by making what came after seem a failure), Joseph Heller's hilarious and grim *Catch-22* (panned by the *New York Times* in 1961 "for want of craft and sensibility"),[1] and the absurdist pair of Kurt Vonnegut's *Slaughterhouse-Five* and Thomas Pynchon's *Gravity's Rainbow*.

There are a handful of basic characterizations that can be made about the World War II novel. Of course, any group that includes writers as different as James Jones and Kurt Vonnegut will be resistant to generalizations, but let me offer a few as starting points. Most broadly, the fiction of World War II looks back not to its immediate precursors, Hemingway, Faulkner, and the modernists, but rather to an earlier literary patrimony represented in the work of writers like Theodore Dreiser. The World War II novel recalls the naturalist novel in its narrative sprawl and sheer bulk, its sociological fascination with

56

exposing society's hidden spaces (brothels, gambling dens, prisons), and its anthropological commitment to preserving for posterity the small details of subcultures that were felt to be fading fast (samples of slang and clothing, values and customs). It also shares many of the same alienating attitudes toward race, gender, and sexuality, the same stylistic unevenness, and, ultimately, the same unexpectedly powerful accumulation of narrative force. Its philosophy is now generally existential rather than social Darwinist, but it is just as often obtrusive and ham-fisted – a structural risk in war representation, it must be said, since the heart-sickening content demands at least some speculation about the meaning of recklessly shattered lives. Finally, these novels are less often taught than the novels of World War I, if only because their length makes them inconvenient for undergraduate education, and there is as a result a generally unspoken but nonetheless palpable sense that the work is a lesser part of the American literary canon.

The most perfect embodiments of this characterization are James Jones's *From Here to Eternity* (1951) and *The Thin Red Line* (1962) – highly acclaimed works that were both turned into movies (the former won eight Academy Awards and achieved cinematic immortality with the image of Burt Lancaster and Deborah Kerr in a lovers' embrace beneath crashing waves). *From Here to Eternity* tells the story of life at the Schofield Barracks near Honolulu in the months before Pearl Harbor. It is peopled with a range of lively characters and subplots, but it gives special focus to a pair of romantic affairs: between Sergeant Milt Warden and Karen Holmes, the wife of his superior officer, and between Private Robert E. Lee Prewitt and the prostitute Alma Schmidt. While fleshed out in convincing and idiosyncratic detail, these characters are ultimately types: the tough, no-nonsense Army men; the beautiful, hysterical housewife; the flinty prostitute with a heart of gold. The painfully achieved intimacy and mutual vulnerability in these unlikely pairs is the novel's poignant counterpoint to the alternating sadism and dehumanizing indifference of the Army bureaucracy. In one of the most stressful subplots, for instance, Prewitt is relentlessly and brutally hazed for refusing to box for the company: he will either surrender and box (breaking a deathbed promise to his mother), or break and lash out at those giving him "The Treatment" (ending up in the Stockade). But he will be given no mercy, because the Captain needs to win the Division championship to retain his status in the bureaucratic hierarchy, and the life of a man is not an important price to pay. At the same time, however, Prewitt and Alma are stumbling into love, alternating between recklessly giving themselves to each other and skittishly retreating from intimacy and commitment, all the while slowly turning her home and their shared bed into one of the novel's only safe spaces. "Without this sanctuary they would have cracked him with The Treatment long ago."[2]

The hazing of Prewitt is only one of Jones's many tableaux of organizational brutality and coercion. The novel continually asks, with the didactic sincerity typical of a culture newly concerned with the petty bureaucratization of daily life, what is the price a person must pay for trying to live free? In *From Here to Eternity* it is, ultimately, "the System" that is the main character, the system that, as one character puts it, leaves you "feeling you're locked up in a box thats two sizes too small for you and theres no air in it and you're suffocatin, and all the time outside the box you hear the whole world walkin around and laughin and havin a big, big time."[3] Such anxiety over "systems" was pervasive in postwar society. Sociological works like David Riesman's *The Lonely Crowd* (1950) and William Whyte's *The Organization Man* (1956) testified to widespread fears about the increasing power large organizations were claiming over individual lives. "We have entered a period of accelerating bigness in all aspects of American life," Eric Johnston, former president of the American Chamber of Commerce, said in 1957: "We have big business, big labor, big farming and big government."[4] Postwar corporate consolidation was particularly rapid. From 1940 to 1950 the labor force increased by over 10 million, but the number of self-employed workers remained roughly constant: 85 percent were now employees, and 9 million of these worked for the 500 largest industrial corporations.[5] "The bureaucratic model," Robert Presthus wrote by 1962, is the "major organizational form in our society."[6] *From Here to Eternity* offers blunt commentary on these developments: "Would you say a man in a Nazi concentration camp had the right to commit suicide?" "Hell yes." "Then why not a man in an American corporation?"[7]

The flipside of the organizational alienation that troubles Jones is the intense attachment to organizational subunits that he examines more fully in *The Thin Red Line*. In an emblematic moment at the end of the novel, Buck Sergeant Big Queen – wounded and prepped to be shipped back to the States – decides instead to go AWOL so that he can fight (and perhaps die) at the front alongside his friends in C-for-Charlie Company, where he feels he finally belongs. Earlier, Private Witt discovers in the emotional whiplash of combat feelings of belonging and care "he had never known existed in him," feelings strong enough to make him repeatedly risk death: "The truth was, Witt loved them all, passionately, with an almost sexual ecstasy of comradeship."[8] Importantly, this is for Witt not just a matter of loving individuals, but of loving individuals because they are part of a greater organizational whole: he loves "everybody else in *the company*."[9] In fact, Witt loves the company itself – it gives him a kind of meaning – and throughout the novel he will follow it anywhere.

It should be noted, however, that Jones does not romanticize combat brotherhood – it is presented more as an anthropological fact – and above all he does not use visions of brotherhood to romanticize war. "Modern war," one character thinks, "[y]ou couldn't even *pretend* it was human."[10] Soldiers pull rotting corpses out of mass graves to loot them, beat the enemy to death with their hands, and help friends commit suicide to end their pain. A psychiatric report about Jones reveals how pitiless he could be about writing: "He has disturbed dreams and is bothered by memories of combat, blood, stench of dead and hardships. Feels it was valuable to him tho as background for his writing."[11] Jones's powerful realism makes painfully vivid for the reader the grim details of the invasion of Guadalcanal; it pulls few punches. Nonetheless, for the war writing that is truly most pitiless to the sentiments of its readers, one must turn to Mailer.

In one typical scene from *The Naked and the Dead* (1948), he describes a group of dead Japanese soldiers: "His head was crushed from his ear to his jaw and it lay sodden on the runningboard of the vehicle as if it were a beanbag...Another Japanese lay on his back a short distance away. He had a great hole in his intestines, which bunched out in a thick white cluster like the congested petals of a sea flower...The singed cloth of his uniform had rotted away and exposed his scorched genitals. They had burned down to tiny stumps but the ash of his pubic hair still remained like a tight clump of steel wool."[12] What's most remarkable about this scene is not the brute fact of injury, but rather how Mailer attempts to slam the injuries of war right up against our domestic contentment, forcing us to hold together in our mind images that we, unlike combat survivors, can typically keep separate: your daughter's beanbag and a crushed skull, the pans you are scrubbing and a burned penis. "It will probably offend many," a review in the *Library Journal* declared, "and may create problems in handling."[13]

What is most pitiless about *The Naked and the Dead*, however, is not necessarily its grisly injuries. As in Jones, organizational domination is what defines the novel. General Cummings is Mailer's personification of "the system," a commander who sees in fascism the consolidation of power that is America's great destiny. "When there are little surges of resistance," he explains, "it merely calls for more power to be directed downward."[14] Private Red Valsen is, by contrast, Mailer's model of the strong-willed, working-class man who refuses to surrender to the coercion of the "system," who (like Jones's Prewitt) would rather get busted than get along. But toward the end of the novel, during an exhausting and pointless reconnaissance mission – or, rather, an exhausting and pointless forced march that becomes the novel's most powerful symbol of unrelenting coercion – Red is finally broken. When the narrative of the ascent of Mount Anaka finally approaches its cruelly delayed conclusion, with men collapsing and weeping for rest, Red loses the will to fight: "He was licked. That was all there was to it. At the base of his shame was an added guilt. He was glad it was over, glad the long contest with Croft was finished, and he could obey orders with submission, without feeling that he must resist. This was the extra humiliation, the crushing one. Could that be all, was that the end of all he had done in his life?"[15]

The Naked and the Dead is a book of constant humiliations, a book deeply concerned with the gap between our fierce ambitions and our essential meaninglessness. "[Mailer's] heroes," writes Richard Poirier, "are isolated, ineffectual, with merely a rhetoric of engagement."[16] As the novel closes, two soldiers labor to bring a comrade's body down from the mountain so they can properly bury him, but they lose him in a river. One of the soldiers, Ridges, begins to weep, experiencing the loss as a failure representative of his entire life, indeed, of all lives. "He wept from exhaustion and failure and the shattering naked conviction that nothing mattered."[17] But the crushing quality of this realization is hard to sustain, for Ridges as for Mailer. The book ends shortly after this moment in what is, essentially, comedy, with the foolish exclamation "Hot dog!" (Daft Major Dalleson is clenching his fists in excitement over his plan, sure to make him famous, to teach map-reading classes to soldiers using a photograph of Betty Grable with a coordinate grid system laid over it.) As the book wishes to reveal, the meaninglessness that breaks us also makes us cling ever more bitterly and joyfully to our petty hopes, to our secretly cherished gambles for meaning.

Kurt Vonnegut's *Slaughterhouse-Five* (1969) is built around this existential contradiction, but in every other way it is entirely different from the work of both Mailer and Jones. It is short, more funny than gruesome, closer to science fiction than realism, and is concerned primarily with harm to noncombatants, not soldiers (it is about the deliberate killing of tens of thousands of civilians in Dresden during the Allied bombing campaign). *Slaughterhouse-Five* thus commemorates a transformation not only in war writing but in war itself: in World War I, approximately 95 percent of all casualties in war were combatants; in World War II, 50 percent were civilians; by the end of the century the ratio had nearly reversed, with 90 percent civilian casualties.[18]

Like the novels already discussed, *Slaughterhouse-Five* is a book by a veteran reflective of his personal experiences during World War II – up to a point, that is. Here's the plot: Billy Pilgrim comes unstuck in time, traveling back and forth between his war experience (a dazed soldier who is captured by the Germans and shipped to Dresden, where he survives the firebombing) and his postwar life as an optometrist and the prisoner of a race of aliens – the Tralfamadorians – who mate him with a voluptuous Hollywood star in an intergalactic zoo. Billy is throughout the novel feeble, nonreactive, preposterous. Whenever he hears that somebody has died, he explains, "I simply shrug and say what the Tralfamadorians say about dead people, which is 'So it goes.'"[19] All of life is reduced to a trifling gag; even Apocalypse, suddenly a very practical concern after the bombing of Hiroshima and Nagasaki, is a punch-line: when Billy warns the Tralfamadorians about the danger humans pose to the universe ("If other planets aren't now in danger from Earth, they soon will be") they point out that, because they can see the future, they already know they will themselves blow up the universe while experimenting with new fuels for flying saucers: "A Tralfamadorian test pilot presses a starter button, and the whole Universe disappears" – and then the rimshot – "So it goes."[20] But the absurdity of the characterizations and plot is not finally comedy; it is the disengaged stance of deep shock, the broken soul's retreat into quietism and fantasy. "Conscience simply cannot cope with events like the concentration camps and the Dresden air-raid," Tony Tanner explains of Billy. "Even to try to begin to care adequately would lead to an instant and irrevocable collapse of consciousness."[21] By the end, however, this self-protective quashing of affect begins to fail. Vonnegut and Billy's distancing catchphrase – "So it goes" – becomes in the last two pages the verbal equivalent of a facial tic, revealing both the emptiness of language in the face of atrocity and a deep, repressed, rageful disgust.

In Joseph Heller's *Catch-22* (1961), disgust – though strong – loses out to slapstick. Heller tells the story of the war from the opposite perspective of Vonnegut: *Catch-22* is about the Allied bombers. Suffused with anger (an anger much like that of Mailer and Jones, focused on army bureaucracy as the enemy), and structured by tragedy (it concludes with the protagonist, Yossarian, haunted by the traumatic memory of a young soldier dying in his arms), it is also, simultaneously, a laugh-out-loud novel. Heller jokes about lost faith in God – "the God I don't believe in is a good God, a just God, a merciful God" – about the way security hawks justify curtailing civil liberties – you jeopardize your traditional freedoms by exercising them – and about arbitrary military detention: "That's a very serious crime you've committed." "What crime?" "We don't know yet ... But we're going to find out. And we sure know it's very serious."[22] The following passage reads like a sketch from Abbott and Costello; it's a representative example of the novel's humor as well as the bitterness beneath it. In one of the many arbitrary exercises in domination that define the novel, a colonel is punishing a soldier for breaking ranks while in formation (stumbling, actually) and for reportedly denying they had the right to punish him.

"I didn't say you couldn't punish me, sir."
"When?" asked the Colonel.
"When what, sir?"
"Now you're asking me questions again."
"I'm sorry, sir. I'm afraid I don't understand your question."
"When didn't you say we couldn't punish you? Don't you understand my question?"

"No, sir. I don't understand."

"You've just told us that. Now suppose you answer my question."

"But how can I answer it?"

"That's another question you're asking me."

"I'm sorry, sir. But I don't know how to answer it. I never said you couldn't punish me."

"Now you're telling us when you did say it. I'm asking you to tell us when you didn't say it."

Clevinger took a deep breath. "I always didn't say you couldn't punish me, sir."

"That's much better . . ."[23]

Catch-22 shares with *Slaughterhouse-Five* not only an absurdist manner but also shame over the fate of civilians in modern war. Among its vignettes in cruelty is an account of a useless bombing raid on an undefended Italian village: the airmen protest the plans, but when their superiors threaten to send them instead on a bombing run over a fortified city they give in, abjectly surrendering one more piece of themselves. Harm to civilians has always figured prominently in American war literature, from General Sherman's autobiographical account of the shelling of Atlanta during the Civil War ("War is cruelty, and you cannot refine it," he wrote in defense of his actions)[24] to Hemingway's retreat from Caporetto in *A Farewell to Arms* (soldiers laughing at the terror of two sisters expecting to be raped is one of the book's casual cruelties).[25] But the literature of World War II represents a decided shift in intensity – or rather, the literature of World War II published after 1960 does, including *Slaughterhouse-Five*, Jerzy Kosinski's *The Painted Bird* (1965), and Thomas Pynchon's *Gravity's Rainbow* (1973). Earlier work, like that of Jones and Mailer, was able to be what it was in part because of a collective cultural refusal either to understand the Holocaust or to make it a central part of war memory. The *New York Times*, for instance, did not use the word "holocaust" until 1959; and, in a galling act of censorship that speaks volumes about cultural attitudes, the American Gas Association was able to force CBS to eliminate references to gas chambers in the 1961 film *Judgment at Nuremberg*.[26] But as the decade progressed, and in particular as the daily horrors of the Vietnam War were publicly revealed, attitudes changed dramatically.

The replacement of the soldier by the civilian in fiction of this later period was anticipated in the earlier work of Martha Gellhorn. Now seriously neglected – introductory descriptions of her always begin by describing her as blonde, leggy, and Hemingway's third wife – Gellhorn was an indefatigable war correspondent who, barred from covering combat zones, stowed away on a hospital ship to cover the invasion of Normandy and remained through the liberation of Dachau. (Hemingway could never recover from an exchange with the younger woman in which, as one of her biographers writes, "he had tried to compliment her by saying she had seen almost as much war as he had, and she had claimed to have seen more – unless he was counting World War I.")[27] In any case, her World War II fiction, including *Point of No Return* (1948) and *A Stricken Field* (1940), remains overshadowed by her personal life. As the journalist John Pilger commented of one of her biographies: "The problem Martha Gellhorn still presents to the jealous, envious and scandalmongers is that she was brave, beautiful and clever, and had passionately held political principles. Worse, she was a woman who was decades ahead of her time in pushing the boundaries of her gender. Salacious demolition jobs on remarkable human beings after their death are not new; and they are as craven as ever."[28]

Gellhorn's fiction dramatizes the way civilians become war's afterthought. A soldier passing through a flattened village comments idly in *Point of No Return*: "I wonder where the civilians get to? Does anybody look out for them?"[29] Gellhorn's worry over civilians is comprehensive, extending beyond the battlefield to female support staff and even veterans as civilians. Dotty is a Red Cross volunteer who, brought to feeling that it is her job to support the war effort by providing sex to officers, is continually characterized as diseased and on the verge of cracking up. Across the gender divide, one of her lovers, Lt. Colonel Smithers, is struck with the startling realization that he can no longer endure the war but dreads as much becoming a civilian in the approaching peace. "He had commanded nine hundred men from the English Channel to the Bavarian Alps ... How would they know, in La Harpe, that an American officer, a Lieutenant Colonel, lived in a world where ... [he] was treated with respect as an officer and a gentleman? He was Johnny, was all, he'd started as Johnny and if he came home wearing his uniform and his ribbons and anything else, they wouldn't forget that his father was a retired post office clerk and his mother said Ma'am to people like Mrs. Cotterell and Mrs. Merrill and Mrs. Rathbone, and he didn't go to college, he studied at a filling station."[30]

The heart of Gellhorn's fiction, however, is for the victims of Nazi atrocities, from the refugees and tortured detainees of *A Stricken Field* to the living and dead of Dachau in *Point of No Return*. Gellhorn described Dachau as her own "lifelong point of no return" (a technical term designating the point in an air mission when a plane's fuel load would not allow the pilot to return home). Indeed, writing about the concentration camp at the end of *Point of No Return*, Gellhorn begins in places to lose authorial control: one can feel her barely contained fury in the concluding sequence in which a soldier who has seen Dachau deliberately runs over three Germans. "Three Germans, who had laughed a mile from that merciless death, would not laugh again. It was all I could do, he thought."[31] In *A Stricken Field*, Gellhorn incorporated even more specifically autobiographical elements into the story, fictionalizing her unsuccessful attempts to get the League High Commissioner for Refugees to pressure the Prime Minister of Czechoslovakia into delaying general deportation orders (orders that would send thousands to the concentration camps). Later she wrote that she felt "shame" for writing like that: "It was not my tragedy and I disliked myself for taking a fictionalized share." But, she would also characterize her writing as an act of faith, "believing still in telling the truth," and would explain that she was proud to remember the history for those who had no choice "except to live through it or die from it."[32] The narrative of *A Stricken Field*, as one critic points out, is structured by this ethical challenge: troubled by the process of *taking* somebody's story, of turning atrocities into "commodities," Gellhorn struggles, and shows her characters struggling, to represent victims "not only as objects of a sympathetic American observer's site but *subjects* of sight."[33]

If Gellhorn's work is an example of fiction where the author continues to emerge for the reader, Thomas Pynchon's *Gravity's Rainbow* is a repudiation of the idea that there is a self that can emerge in the first place. The ostensible main character, Tyrone Slothrop, for instance, disappears by the end of the novel ("He is being broken down instead, and scattered"), or rather, is revealed never to have been (few see him "as any sort of integral creature," refusing to try "to hold him together, even as a concept").[34] *Gravity's Rainbow* develops many of the same themes as the other books discussed in this essay – meaninglessness, the plight of civilians, organizational anxiety (blooming here into conspiracy theories and paranoia), and the retreat into intimacy ("They are in love. Fuck the war.")[35] – but it is as different from what precedes it as Vietnam was from World War II. The most memorably gruesome scene in this book is not a depiction of battlefield carnage; it is the description of Slothrop climbing down into the pipes of a toilet to recover a lost harmonica. As for detainees, Byron the immortal light bulb stands out (guilty of extending the mean operating life of bulbs, he's held in one of many "control points" for monitoring).[36] And the invidious bureaucracies of Jones have now metastasized unimaginably, growing beyond nations, beyond even *functions*, becoming things "like Shell, with no real country, no side in any war, no specific face or heritage: tapping instead out of that global stratum, most deeply laid, from which all the appearances of corporate ownership really spring."[37] As one critic writes, "Pynchon urges us to think of the war not as a conflict that was terminated in 1945 but as a key point of transition to, and perhaps the agency of, a new global order," a "transnational 'war-State'" comprised of "Rocket-cartels."[38]

Gravity's Rainbow is a sprawling book that is either a unique and masterful literary achievement (if you agree with the judgment of the National Book

Award) or "unreadable," "turgid," "overwritten," and "obscene" (if you agree with the Pulitzer Prize advisory committee, which denied Pynchon the prize in 1974 despite a unanimous jury recommendation).[39] The book's plot, insofar as it has one with its 700-plus pages and 400-plus characters, is about the German bombardment of London with V2 rockets – which, as it turns out, proceeds according to a particular pattern: shortly after Slothrop has an erection, a rocket will fall in the same spot. To come to Pynchon from Jones and Mailer is, then, to make a series of startling and sometimes disorienting leaps: from naturalism to postmodernism, from cocky defiance to insecure paranoia, from work culture to consumer culture, and from individualism to the post-human. Perhaps most fundamentally, it is to move from despair over meaninglessness (the world lacks meaning: our lives do not matter) to anxiety over indeterminacy (the world lacks meaning: our words have no secure referents). "The full significance of Pynchon's fiction," George Levine explains, "is in its styles, in its language, since the language is called upon to sustain the uncertainty it is structured to deny, to imply what cannot be articulated in language ... This is only possible if language does not protect us with the comfort of its structure, if the word can somehow put us in the presence of 'whatever it is the word is there, buffering, to protect us from'."[40]

Gravity's Rainbow is From Here to Eternity through the looking glass. Of course, the literature of earlier wars saw stylistic and conceptual transformations of their own: in the Civil War, from the romance of Sidney Lanier's Tiger-Lilies (1867) to the realism of Stephen Crane's The Red Badge of Courage (1895); and, in World War I, from the sentimentalism of Edith Wharton's A Son at the Front (1923) to the modernism of William Faulkner's A Fable (1954). But even these sharp contrasts do little to prepare us for the remarkable literary changes seen in the arc of the World War II literary canon in the US.

NOTES

1. Richard G. Stern, "Bombers Away," New York Times, October 22, 1961.
2. James Jones, From Here to Eternity (New York: Scribner, 1951), p. 432.
3. Ibid., p. 363.
4. Quoted in James Gilbert, Another Chance: Postwar America, 1945–1968 (Philadelphia: Temple University Press, 1981), p. 186.
5. Robert Presthus, The Organizational Society: An Analysis and a Theory (New York: Knopf, 1962), pp. 69, 79.
6. Ibid., p. 91. As Heller commented in a 1962 interview about Catch-22: "I think anybody today feels, for example, that he is at the mercy of superiors – who don't know his job as well as he does, who don't know their own jobs as well as he knows their jobs and who, he feels, hamstring him or limit him in the execution of his duty ... I cannot imagine ... anybody of any real intelligence, choosing to place

himself within a large organization." See "An Impolite Interview with Joseph Heller," in *Conversations with Joseph Heller*, ed. Adam Sorkin (Jackson: University Press of Mississippi), pp. 7–8, 26.

7. Jones, *From Here to Eternity*, p. 587.
8. James Jones, *The Thin Red Line* (New York: Scribner, 1962), pp. 314, 309.
9. *Ibid.*, p. 309.
10. *Ibid.*, p. 429.
11. Frank MacShane, *Into Eternity: The Life of James Jones, American Writer* (Boston: Houghton Mifflin, 1985), p. 69.
12. Norman Mailer, *The Naked and the Dead* (New York: Holt, 1976), pp. 210–11.
13. Donald Wasson, *Library Journal* 73, 9 (May 1, 1948), 707.
14. Mailer, *The Naked and the Dead*, p. 326.
15. *Ibid.*, p. 696.
16. Richard Poirier, *Norman Mailer* (New York: Viking, 1972), p. 26.
17. Mailer, *The Naked and the Dead*, p. 682.
18. Simon Chesterman, *Civilians in War* (Boulder: Lynn Rienner, 2001), p. 2.
19. Kurt Vonnegut, *Slaughterhouse-Five* (New York: Dell, 1968), p. 27.
20. *Ibid.*, pp. 116–17.
21. Tony Tanner, *City of Words: American Fiction 1950–1970* (New York: Harper & Row, 1971), p. 199.
22. Joseph Heller, *Catch-22* (New York: Simon & Schuster, 1961), pp. 179, 373.
23. *Ibid.*, p. 76.
24. William Tecumseh Sherman, *Memoirs of General W. T. Sherman* (New York: The Library of America, 1990), p. 601.
25. Ernest Hemingway, *A Farewell to Arms* (New York: Scribner, 2003), p. 196.
26. See Samantha Power, *"A Problem from Hell": America and the Age of Genocide* (New York: Basic Books, 2002), p. 73.
27. Carl Rollyson, *Nothing Ever Happens to the Brave: The Story of Martha Gellhorn* (New York: St. Martin's, 1990), p. 225.
28. Quoted in Audrey Gillian, "Gunning for Martha," *The Guardian*, April 24, 2001.
29. Martha Gellhorn, *Point of No Return* (Lincoln: University of Nebraska Press, 1995), p. 187.
30. *Ibid.*, pp. 250–1.
31. *Ibid.*, p. 304.
32. Martha Gellhorn "Afterword," *A Stricken Field* (New York: Penguin, 1986), pp. 310, 312–13.
33. Jean Gallagher, *The World Wars through the Female Gaze* (Carbondale: Southern Illinois University Press, 1998), pp. 53, 57.
34. Thomas Pynchon, *Gravity's Rainbow* (New York: Penguin, 1987), pp. 738, 740.
35. *Ibid.*, p. 42.
36. *Ibid.*, p. 651.
37. *Ibid.*, p. 243.
38. Paul Maltby, *Dissident Postmodernists: Barthelme, Coover, Pynchon* (Philadelphia: University of Pennsylvania Press, 1991), p. 150.
39. Peter Kihss, "Pulitzer Jurors Dismayed on Pynchon," *New York Times*, May 8, 1974.
40. George Levine, "Risking the Moment," in *Thomas Pynchon*, ed. Harold Bloom (New York: Chelsea House, 1986), pp. 60, 73.

5

LEO MELLOR

War journalism in English

In the spring of 1941, the American reporter Robert St. John was not so much in the field as running through many fields. He left Belgrade, fleeing south across country and then by sea, joining British troops as they retreated through Greece to escape the rapidly advancing German army. On the way, he noted the sights produced by mechanized war: the dying soldier eviscerated but still talking, the maimed girl, and the ambulance driver who was burnt alive. On arrival in Cairo, St. John expressed disillusionment with the necessary twisting of events into a narrative suitable for transmission to London: "we were just leeches, reporters trying to suck headlines out of all this death and suffering." But then, upon seeing the military censors, it became clear that little of his material would be passed: a few sections were acceptable but the ambulance driver would have to have been "shot" – a more decorous way to die.[1]

This brief episode typifies some key practical difficulties of war journalism in the Second World War: the physical problems of reporting from a fluid battlefield; the exposure to violent death; and the pressure of censorship. Yet it also shows the level at which some correspondents were aware that they were constructing narratives – literary works – burdened by the concomitant questions of authority and authenticity. These complexities have made it harder in recent years to dismiss such journalism as valuable only for its immediate importance as reportage and its subsequent historical usefulness. A full definition of Second World War literature should include the writing that was produced in closest proximity to the action; and such writing, as I shall demonstrate in this chapter, covers a plethora of possibilities in terms of form and content. Two distinctive aspects appear in much of the English-language journalism, unifying the mass of material and marking the difference between the reporting of 1939–45 and that of other wars. Firstly there is the growth of reflexivity in journalists – the inclusion of the self as a character within the reports. Secondly is the development of a specifically laconic tone in the writing, a distancing from the propagandistic and jingoistic character of earlier war reporting.

The First World War had already offered models of how industrialized armies could accommodate correspondents and set in place mechanisms of censorship, propaganda, and the practice of "embedding" correspondents within particular units. Yet the experiences of journalists and audiences some twenty years later proved fundamentally different. The real genesis of Second World War journalism came in the reporting of the wars of the 1930s – especially those in Abyssinia (Ethiopia), China, and Spain. This was due to technical factors: the spread of radio, the invention of the newsmagazine, the expectation that correspondents would follow mobile action by car or truck. But it was also caused by the changes in literary form and in the possibilities of the journalistic mode. The war in Abyssinia (1935–36), Mussolini's attempt to reestablish a Roman Empire in Africa, gained literary immortality in Evelyn Waugh's *Scoop* (1939). While purportedly a novel, the details within it of a war reporter's scrambling chaos in leaving Britain, the disinformation to rivals, and the sheer tedium of war are drawn directly from Waugh's experience as a correspondent for the *Daily Mail*.

The Spanish Civil War (1936–39) attracted many of the journalists who later reported the Second World War. It was particularly marked by propaganda, and George Orwell's hyperbolic comment is worth recording to demonstrate the depth of his disgust: "Early in life I had noticed that no event is ever correctly reported in a newspaper, but in Spain, for the first time, I saw newspaper reports which did not bear any relation to the facts, not even the relationship which is implied in an ordinary lie."[2] Among the most systematic were the lies around the bombing of the ancient Basque town of Guernica in April 1937, and the subsequent attempts to report it. George Steer visited the next day and filed a story, printed by *The Times* in London and the *New York Times* as "The Tragedy of Guernica," detailing the fire-bombing of the town. A campaign to discredit the story and replace it with the fiction that the Basques dynamited their own town started immediately, with the support of several correspondents, and continued until the 1960s.[3] But Spain also offered other modes, with many emerging from the particularities of 1930s travel writing. This allowed modulations of tone and the intrusion of the picaresque and personal, as when the poet W. H. Auden – reporting from Valencia in Republican-held territory – recast mortal threat into incongruous campness: "There is a bullfight in aid of the hospitals; there is a variety show where an emaciated-looking tap-dancer does an extremely sinister dance of the machine-guns. The foreign correspondents come in for their dinner, conspicuous as actresses."[4] Auden also reported from China, where Japanese attacks had grown into a declared war by 1937. In his role as a correspondent in *Journey to a War* (1939), he extends and uses aspects of travel writing, producing an idiosyncratic way of reporting conflict that could include the personal. On watching the bombing of Hankow, Auden attempts reportage that moves to include the sensibility of the body: "It was as tremendous as Beethoven but wrong – a cosmic offence, an insult to the whole of nature and the entire earth. I don't know if I was frightened. Something inside me was flapping about like a fish."[5] One question that runs throughout the journalism of the Second World War is how such a contingent and fearful self could be acknowledged.

The position of the reporter

The quality of immediacy – "being there" – carries a journalistic premium. It refers to the proximity to events, the verisimilitude of observation, and the attendant problems of getting to the field of battle and sending the reports back. Yet positioning also takes place in the inclusion or omission of an authorial persona in the reports. This form of "being there" ranges from an identifiable first-person figure to that of a near-signature quality in the texture of the writing. Such presence, consciously reflexive or otherwise, changes the nature of the report – and indeed shapes the subsequent values that accrue to it. This complex self-fashioning of the journalist – and furthermore the *idea* of the war journalist – within his or her own work can be seen in three very different reporters.

The career of Martha Gellhorn (1908–98) as a war journalist spanned the twentieth century, from reports from Madrid in 1937 to Panama in 1990. She was not alone as a female journalist; over two hundred and fifty were accredited to the American forces. Yet military regulations forbade them access to any combat zone that had been deemed suitably dangerous as to be forbidden to the women actually serving in the military. Gellhorn evaded these restrictions, eventually angering the Public Relation Officers sufficiently that her accreditation was withdrawn. The role of the journalist was one that she wished to remould. Her passionate denunciation of "all that objectivity shit"[6] in postwar interviews and works makes an assessment of her Second World War writings problematic, for it cuts against her oft-stated desire to be "a walking tape recorder with eyes,"[7] a mode of apparent deep self-elision. Such a metaphor owes much to writers of the 1930s such as Christopher Isherwood and John Dos Passos, and its genuflection to the idealized photographic state of absolute objectivity. But Gellhorn's reports throughout the war show how her "camera-eye"[8] evolved to be coupled to a persona. Her reports from the Italian front in 1944 revel in the flatness of descriptive prose, laying out the constellations of troops and battle lines amid hostile landscapes and the chaos of war. While they cannot escape from adjectival scene setting – a soldier has "a good face"[9] and "the mountains of Italy are horrible"[10] – they rely upon incremental description; and most importantly a continual self-elision or self-disparagement: "it makes me ashamed to write that sentence,"[11] or "you hear a lot of rot, traveling around the world."[12]

Gellhorn crossed to France and returned on a hospital ship on D-Day itself – continuing the feud with Ernest Hemingway, then her husband and also a correspondent for *Collier's* magazine – but she only joined the land forces months later. She then followed the advance and, as the war continued, deployed more overtly cohesive tropes. This is typified in her piece from the last town captured by Allied paratroops in Operation Market Garden, the attempt to end the war in 1944: "This is a story about a little Dutch town called Nijmegen." It carries a blunt purpose expressed in the following line as "the moral of the story."[13] This lesson in narrative structure is made absolute in the staccato ending, which focuses on the abject figure of a wounded young girl. Here the lesson is explicated and the report curves back to repeat the initial formulation: "a story with a moral should be short. Even the moral should be short. What best points the moral of this story is short."[14] The repetition of "short" – carrying anger in form as well as overt content – culminates in the final paragraph in: "the moral of the story is really short: it would be a good thing if the Germans were never allowed to make war again."[15] Sparseness now becomes a laconic redundancy, a literary mode that could reach back within American Modernism to the Gertrude Stein. Nevertheless Gellhorn draws our attention to the meaningfulness of the small or the "short," but here the camera-eye has been focused to pass judgment. Minimalism becomes a morality; her own laconic sparseness becomes a mechanism for condemnation as well as reporting.

The most famous correspondent to be killed on active service in the Second World War was Ernie Pyle (1900–45). He had followed the American army in North Africa, in the Italian campaign and the invasion of Normandy, dying in April 1945 on Ie Shima, a small island near Okinawa. Writing despatches, often daily, for the Scripps-Howard *Washington Daily News*, he attempted to live a life as close to the troops as possible. His reports disdain strategic views, as he explained: "I haven't written anything about the 'Big Picture,' because I don't know anything about it."[16] Instead the reports concentrated on the corporeal experience of the soldiers as they lived cold, frightened, and arduous lives; however, Pyle's route towards this mode of detailed, anti-glamorous truth-telling required the construction of a rhetorical framework where his own role – as reporter – could be explained. His despatches from North Africa and into the Italian campaign largely follow a pattern of set-pieces, accounts which triangulate his role held between the "you" or "you folks" in the United States and the "they" of the soldiers. A focus on the human became a dynamic of "introduction" in his reports, where the actual dates and home-towns of the individual soldiers would frame encounters.

So while reporting on the American defeat at the Kasserine Pass in February 1943 he moves from an overview to focus on "Maj. Ronald Elkins, of College Station, Tex."[17] Then on the frontline, as the advance begins for Tunis, Pyle attributes the description to a specific voice "Lieut. Mickey Miller of Morganstown, Ind. says this lifeless waiting in a wheat-field is almost the worst part of the whole battle."[18] Pyle's fame grew throughout the war, with his reports syndicated in some three hundred American daily papers; while the issues he chose to expose changed policy – with the United States Congress nicknaming the $10 per day extra pay for a combat soldier the "Ernie Pyle bill." His campaigning inspired a reflexivity on the part not only of the soldiers – "Wait'll Ernie Pyle hears of this!"[19] – but also of the generals, such as Omar Bradley's quip: "My men always fight better when Pyle's around."[20] Pyle responded in his hymn of praise: "I love the infantry because they are the underdogs. They are the mud-rain-frost-and-wind boys. They have no comforts, and they even learn to live without the necessities. And in the end they are the guys that wars can't be won without."[21] Yet when he disembarked in Normandy the day after D-Day on Omaha Beach, the bloodiest landing ground, it was the debris of war that preoccupied him. In the mass of equipment and possessions – helmets, letters, guns, and clothing – he found a "long thin line of personal anguish" spread on the sand. The repeated formula on discovering more objects – "here are" – gives an incremental weariness, only momentarily broken when Pyle picks up a Bible. But this moment of significance is denied: "I don't know why I picked it up, or why I put it back down."[22] Among detritus, Pyle observes the rituals of mourning, becoming so engrossed as to assume a sleeping soldier is actually a corpse. The piece closes with an individual – but he is dead and no more than debris, with only his feet exposed and the toes "pointed toward the land he had come so far to see, and which he saw so briefly."[23]

Pyle's subsequent reports from Normandy continued with the reemergence of the trope of "introduction" and dramatizing key personae. "This Weird Hedgerow Fighting" gave a step-by-step account of what it was like to clear a field of dug-in German infantry. Here the reader also slowly moves towards the action, from being a "you" who observes "our men" when they "sneak up" to lob mortars and rifle grenades into the German dugouts, to the ambiguity, folding readers and soldiers together as Americans, in the line "so we've taken another hedgerow," at the close.[24] A similarly instructional, if more direct, approach is taken in Bill Mauldin's explanatory text accompanying the reprinting in the United States of his cartoons from the American Army newspaper *Stars and Stripes*. A civilian wishing to experience army life should:

> Dig a hole in your back yard while it is raining. Sit in the hole until the water climbs up around your ankles. Pour cold mud down your shirt collar. Sit there for forty-eight hours, and, so there is no danger of your dozing off, imagine that a guy is sneaking around waiting for a chance to club you on the head or set your house on fire.[25]

The apotheosis of the correspondent as soldier, but soldier on his own terms, is the Second World War reporting of Ernest Hemingway (1899–1961), already by the 1940s styling himself "the man who goes to wars." Indeed a line of descent of the laconic as the central tone in war reporting could be linked back to Hemingway's dispatches from the battle of Caporetto in 1917. His reports from Spain – and books and collaboration on a film – had given way in 1941 to a series of reports from China, assessing whether the Japanese advances could be resisted and what a Chinese air force would resemble. But it was the Normandy despatches from 1944 that secured his final complex reputation. Hemingway crossed the channel from Britain to France on D-Day itself, establishing both the dateline and the participatory position of the journalist in the second sentence of his report: "Nobody remembers the date of the battle of Shiloh. But the day we took Fox Green Beach was the sixth of June, and the wind was blowing hard out of the northwest."[26] The movement into the collective ("we") elides his position as specifically a reporter rather than a soldier, but it also establishes a seemingly irreproachable veracity.

Yet Hemingway did not land on the beach itself, as the report indeed concludes, but rather made runs into the shore on a landing craft, dodging between the German sea-mines and beach obstacles. Here the apparent verisimilitude is in the flatness of diction, but this had already become a stylistic tic in his reports from as long ago as Spain and the Greco-Turkish war in 1922. The fragments of dialogue within the landing craft he includes are not explained and the piece closes with an invocation of what the correspondent has left out: "[t]here is much that I have not written."[27] That authenticity is the province of the reporter who is there but does not tell all amounts to the incorporation of censorship until it becomes a stylistic effect. Such a position of the correspondent as – ironically – the non-divulger is a dominant trope in his report on the fighter aircraft combating the V1 flying bombs: "I hope the enemy never shoots down a Tempest, that the Tempest will never be released from the secret list, and that all I know and care about them can never be published until after the war."[28]

In Hemingway's 1944 reports, "How we came to Paris" and "Battle for Paris," he covers the period immediately before the city was liberated. He locates himself here in the text as part journalist, part guerrilla, and part tour-guide: "I had bicycled, walked, and driven a car through this part of France for many years."[29] His subsequent days in the fast-moving front line, despite being self-deprecatingly contextualized in the second person as something which "as a correspondent, was none of your damned business,"[30] was significant enough to earn him a formal reprimand: "war correspondents are forbidden to command troops."[31] Yet the persona in these reports is so Hemingwayesque that even his attempted moments of deflation – "my aim was to get to Paris without being shot" – only adds to the impression that style damned the greatest exponent of laconicism to self-caricature. Indeed, later he apparently recognized this, as seen in this memoir from a fellow journalist Charles Collingwood:

> After the war [Hemingway] asked me if I remembered a time in France when he had asked my opinion of a piece he had written for COLLIER'S and I said it sounded like a parody of Ernest Hemingway. "You were right of course" he said.[32]

Yet such individualism and easily recognizable authorship contrasts sharply with the experience of maneuver through anonymous communiqué and censorship that makes up the vast mass of Second World War reports. There was a weekly intake of three million words from nearly a thousand correspondents, 35,000 photographs, and 1,000,000 feet of newsreel film for the Allied public relations headquarters in Paris in late 1944.[33] Such a plethora of possible stories, however controlled and compromised by censorship, contrasted strongly with the paucity of information earlier in the war. This earlier reliance of journalists on interpreting and rewriting official briefings is behind the cynicism in this remark from 1942: "The two most important American war correspondents are the two men who sit in Washington & prepare the Army and Navy communiqués."[34]

Where is the "front"?

The "front" is a problematic concept in both the military and literary history of the Second World War. A concept of total war meant the enmeshing of the military and the industrial, the logistical and the strategic; but such all-engulfing totality also meant that all journalism became, in some form, "war journalism" for the duration of the conflict. The complexities of reporting in spheres that had hitherto been distinct from battlefields mean that the range of writing is vast. However the following examples will illustrate how the twin pressures of reflexive reporters and the laconic as an ever-present form reached out far beyond the immediate conventional battlefields.

Britain and Germany were at war from 1939, the United States and Germany from 1941. In these intervening months, American reporters in Germany and France, with their neutral status prominently displayed, were granted, through Goebbels's propaganda ministry, a villa in Berlin, a generous petrol ration, and – at first – relatively light censorship. American journalists followed the Panzer spearheads in the attacks into the Low Countries and France, reporting on the extent of success and German optimism. In some reports, typified by Louis Lochner's despatch, this was nearly uncritical: "They had covered themselves with military glory during the battle of Kutno in Poland. In the General's words: 'they have fought on fifty battlefields. They are sculpted of the best German oak. Their eyes shine'."[35] The censors did not hesitate to pass such a message, with all of its implications for anti-interventionist American politicians. But in William Shirer's broadcasts from Berlin throughout the autumn of 1940 the changing state of Germany and the limits of what could be spoken about were tested. The continual rewriting of scripts – causing him to miss his broadcast times – and the ever-growing length of forbidden subjects meant that Shirer's role became undermined by the subsequent mantra: "But we couldn't tell the story."[36] The absence of declared war did not stop the information conflict by proxy, with the prize of the United States' continuing neutrality.

In Britain, throughout the summer of 1940, one form of anti-invasion journalism flourished, predicated upon the "front" that was apparently inevitable following the surrender of France. Tom Wintringham (1898–1949) had commanded the British battalion of the International Brigade in Spain. He wrote a series of articles in the British photo-magazine *Picture Post* with titles that ranged from "Against Invasion" to "How to Fight a Panzer." But along with the advice on stopping tanks with petrol bombs and a step-by-step guide to strangling German sentries at night, an idea vividly developed by others into the motto "take him so he cannot squeak,"[37] these articles contained a revolutionary lyricism. The apotheosis of this tendency came in the piece "Arm the Citizens!" Here, he inspects volunteers at Osterly Park training school in West London, where instructors, including Yank Levy who had fought in Spain, taught British civilians to fight:

> And as I watched and listened I realised I was taking part in something so new and strange as to be almost revolutionary – the growth of an "army of the people" in Britain – and at the same time something that is older than Britain, almost as old as England – a gathering of the "men of the counties able to bear arms."[38]

This palimpsestic juxtaposition of the old and the new locates this journalism within a strain of neo-Romanticism, an aesthetic dominant within British culture at the outbreak of the war. It bears comparison with the sequence in Powell and Pressburger's film *A Canterbury Tale* (1944) where the hawk transforms into the fighter aircraft – and the pilgrims into soldiers. The guerrilla-centric practical journalistic impulse draws from similar themes as those that structure more rarefied cinema.

The problematic nature of the "Front" is perhaps best seen in the status of reporting from London in 1940–41, when the Blitz killed over 30,000 people. Until mid-1944 more British civilians than members of the armed forces died due to enemy action. Yet reports from London specifically mix tropes of normality with those of war. The photographer and writer Lee Miller (1907–77) worked for *Vogue* throughout the war. The paradox of her wartime reportage was announced in the title of her book of documentary Blitz photographs, *Grim Glory* (1941); that is to say, the coexistence of darkening mortality and ideal exaltation, like a Baroque conceit. In her juxtaposition of report and caption, extended in her later work into full articles, she played off the expectation of images with the totemic typewriter smashed into a "Remington Silent" and the "Non-Conformist Chapel" with only an avalanche of rubble through a solitary surviving door. The Blitz also offered the prospect of reports moving immediately into designations of the literary in magazines such as *Horizon* and *Penguin New Writing*. William Sansom's work as a fireman led to the four-page reportage fragment "The Wall," detailing the "timeless second" as a burning building collapses on a fire crew.[39] Here escaping, by being "framed" by a window in best Buster Keaton fashion, also meant an escape back into reality. In London some magazines allowed writing about the extent of injuries faced by rescuers, such as in this piece by Rose Macaulay: "jammed [are] those who lived there; some call out, crying for rescue. Others are dumb ... The demolition squad stumble in darkness about the ruins, sawing, hacking, drilling, heaving; stretcher bearers and ambulance drivers stand and watch."[40] Yet this journalistic naming of a landscape of pain and fracture in the bombsites was also a way of designating a space to which she would return five years later, when the ruins were cloaked in vegetation and becoming a sinisterly bucolic London jungle, in her novel *The World My Wilderness* (1950).

The American journalist Edward Murrow made live broadcasts for CBS radio from London throughout the autumn of 1940. Collected as *This is London*, the transcripts mix the residue of live journalism with the considered opinion of retrospect. Yet the deictics of the repeated formula for opening every broadcast, "This is London," immediately collapses space. His stories mixed points of resistance with the narration of the civilian move to deep-sheltering, the growth of a subterranean city: "At dawn we saw Londoners oozing up out of the ground, tired, red-eyed, and sleepy."[41] The continual signifiers of normality and domesticity fall amid those of war, with the London gunners "working in their shirt sleeves"; but this is balanced in later pieces with an undercutting of the popular slogan, and a propaganda film title, "London Can Take It," for, as Murrow notes, continual bombing engenders doubt that unsettles: "They don't know themselves how long they can stand up to it."[42]

Indeed radio waves – moving unhindered across airspaces – were the antithesis to concepts of reporters at the front, a fact used by those journalists who worked for the Axis countries during the war. The broadcasts of William Joyce (Lord Haw-Haw) to Britain were only part of an Axis strategy that attempted to use the authenticating form of journalism to cloak propaganda. Shirer's report "The American Radio Traitors" for *Harper's* magazine in October 1943 individually assesses the eight individuals who were indicted for treason, including the poet Ezra Pound, with the question "Why did they do it?"[43] Across the group Shirer does not find clear ideological answers from the contingency of biography. However Pound's broadcasts from Fascist Italy – over a hundred and ten reports or commentaries on the progress of the war – can only be understood as ideologically driven, but with the ideology being a particularly Poundian culmination of his preoccupations from the 1920s and 1930s. The identification with Fascism is typified in his gleeful first broadcast: "It's a DITCH all right. Democracy has been LICKED in France";[44] yet this sits beside a rampant inclusivity and digressive form that only connect in the continual return to the broadcaster himself. Such self-aggrandizing reflexivity is itself ironically framed by the fact that the broadcasts were largely inaudible to their target, the United States.

But absurdity in trying to locate the front line in the war was also to be found within Britain. In *Passed as Censored*, with its very title drawing attention to the pressures exerted upon it, Macdonald Hastings collected his reports from 1939–41. Central among them was a despatch from a rural cattle auction consisting of verbatim reportage of countryside banter, tailed off by the description of the cows. Here laconicism gives way to bathos: "Like Spitfires they too are helping us win the war."[45]

Endings

The official diplomatic terms for ending the Second World War were "Unconditional Surrender." But the reporting of the end of the war shows how much exceeds or is incommensurate with the neatness of the phrase. After the airborne crossing of the Rhine in March 1945, Germany was progressively occupied, and Gellhorn's despatches become progressively star-ker and angrier. Her report "Das deutsche Volk" (April 1945) opens with a focused passage of controlled rage as she ventriloquizes the self-exculpation of typical civilians:

> No one is a Nazi. No one ever was. There may have been some Nazis in the next village, and as a matter of fact, that town about twenty kilometers away was a veritable hotbed of Nazidom ... I hid a Jew for six weeks. I hid a Jew for eight weeks. (I hid a Jew, he hid a Jew, all God's chillun hid Jews.) ... It should, we feel, be set to music.[46]

But such anger is transformed in her report, and those of others, from the concentration camps. News of the Holocaust had emerged throughout the war, with evidence broadcast in late 1944 and into the spring of 1945, confirming smuggled news and documents. Yet the manufactured propa-ganda of atrocity stories in the First World War had left a lasting cynicism among the public in both Britain and the United States, when they were confronted with evidence of the Holocaust. Mollie Panter-Downes wrote in one of her "Letters" to the *New Yorker* that "atrocity stories that everyone remembers from the last war have turned up again, as good as new but with different details."[47]

Various journalistic strategies cut through this desire to look away (in some cases quite literally when films of the camps were shown in cinemas). Gellhorn's report from Dachau takes her mode of the incremental moments of focus, joined to interpolated speech, to create a narrative where the distance between what the reporter sees and what her readers can hope to see is emphasized: "Behind the barbed wire and the electric fence, the skele-tons sat in the sun and searched themselves for lice. They have no age and no faces; they all look alike and like nothing you will ever see if you are lucky."[48] The incremental fragments that make up the report – the voice of the Polish doctor, the details of the Nazi experiments on humans, the different piles of bones – refuse to exploit emotion or pass explicit judgment: "What had killed most of them was hunger; starvation was simply routine."[49] But the report ends by emphasizing the limits of what even a reporter can endure to see and therefore offering hope that war is right in that only it could "abolish Dachau ... forever."[50]

The photographs and writings of Lee Miller were central to the June 1945 issue of *Vogue*. Her pictures of the guards at Dachau – some dead, some drowned, and some beaten – forced the reader into a confrontation with perpetrators rather than victims. But the technically adroit and menacing beauty in the images of their bodies complicates this encounter. Here the violence of the liberation and the defeat of Fascism are experienced as catastrophe, of undreamt of horrors that have to pass, for the reader, from the incommensurable to recognition. Such a trajectory was urged on the public who bought the June 1945 New York edition of *Vogue* by her imperative to "'Believe It' / Lee Miller cables from Germany,"[51] which was printed above the text. Such an obligation is also found in the opening of Gellhorn's report from Dachau. After visiting the concentration camp she flew out on a transport aircraft, refusing to look out of the window: "No one ever wanted to see Germany again. They turned away from it with hatred and sickness"; but the reported words of an accompanying soldier, his desire to witness and to tell, end the opening paragraph and give the moral authority for the piece: "We got to talk about it, see? We got to talk about it, if anyone believes us or not."[52] The British broadcaster Richard Dimbleby reached the concentration camp at Bergen-Belsen on April 15, and, broadcasting the same day, repeated a variant of this: "I must tell the exact truth, every detail of it, even if people don't believe me, even if they feel they should not be told."[53]

Here, perhaps, is the ultimate position for the two qualities tracked throughout this chapter. The positioning of the self within these reports becomes predicated upon the idea of bearing witness. The war journalist's "self" constructed in the despatches is defined by this outward turn to listener or reader; beside this the formal development of "the laconic" as a mode comes to a comparable end point. These reports not only refute the historic tropes of war, courage, and descriptive excess; they also offer a starting point for a literary question that has proved central since 1945: what language might be adequate to engage with the Holocaust?

NOTES

1. Philip Knightley, *The First Casualty: The War Correspondent as Hero, Propagandist and Myth-Maker from the Crimea to Vietnam* (London: André Deutsch, 1975), p. 307.
2. George Orwell, "Looking Back on the Spanish War," *The Collected Essays, Journalism and Letters of George Orwell*, Vol. II: *My Country Right or Left*, ed. Sonia Orwell and Ian Angus (London: Secker & Warburg, 1968), p. 256.
3. See Ian Patterson, *Guernica and Total War* (London: Granta, 2007).
4. W. H. Auden, "Impressions of Valencia," *New Statesman* (January 30, 1937), 159.
5. W. H. Auden, *Journey to a War* (London: Faber, 1939), p. 61.
6. Quoted in Caroline Moorehead, *Martha Gellhorn: A Life* (London: Chatto & Windus, 2006), p. 6.
7. Quoted in Kate McLoughlin, *Martha Gellhorn: The War Writer in the Field and in the Text* (Manchester University Press, 2007), p. 59.
8. *Ibid.*
9. Martha Gellhorn, "Three Poles," *The Face of War* (London: Granta, 1998), p. 103.
10. Gellhorn, "Visit Italy," *The Face of War*, p. 115.
11. Gellhorn, "The Gothic Line," *The Face of War*, p. 143.

12. Gellhorn, "Visit Italy," p. 118.
13. Gellhorn, "A Little Dutch Town," *The Face of War*, p. 151.
14. *Ibid.*, p. 157.
15. *Ibid.*
16. Ernie Pyle, "This is Our War," in *Reporting World War Two: Part One* (New York: Library of America, 1995), p. 569.
17. Pyle, "Overrun Before They Knew What Was Happening," in *Reporting World War Two: Part One*, p. 539.
18. Pyle, "The Greatest Damage is Psychological," in *Reporting World War Two: Part One*, p. 553.
19. Quoted in Bill Mauldin "My Business is Drawing: A Cartoonist in Combat, 1943–44," in *Reporting World War Two: Part Two* (New York: Library of America, 1995), p. 379.
20. Quoted in Knightley, *The First Casualty*, p. 326.
21. Pyle, "The God-Damned Infantry," in *Reporting World War Two: Part Two*, p. 556.
22. Pyle, "This Long Thin Line of Personal Anguish," in *Reporting World War Two: Part Two*, p. 148.
23. *Ibid.*, p. 150.
24. Pyle, "This Weird Hedgerow Fighting," in *Reporting World War Two: Part Two*, p. 213.
25. Mauldin, "My Business is Drawing," p. 397.
26. Ernest Hemingway, "Voyage to Victory," *By-line Ernest Hemingway: Selected Articles and Despatches of Four Decades* (Scribner: New York, 1967), p. 340.
27. *Ibid.*, p. 355.
28. Hemingway, "London Fights the Robots," *By-line Ernest Hemingway*, p. 358.
29. Hemingway, "Battle for Paris," *By-line Ernest Hemingway*, p. 364.
30. *Ibid.*, p. 370.
31. *Ibid.*, p. 365.
32. Quoted in McLoughlin, *Martha Gellhorn*, p. 141.
33. Knightley, *The First Casualty*, p. 315.
34. Quoted in Joseph J. Matthews, *Reporting the Wars* (Minneapolis: University of Minnesota Press, 1957), p. 257.
35. Quoted in Knightley, *The First Casualty*, p. 229.
36. William Shirer, "The Hour Will Come When One of Us Will Break," in *Reporting World War Two: Part One*, p. 123.
37. Brutally illustrated with drawings in Yank Levy's *Guerrilla Warfare* (Harmondsworth: Penguin, 1940), p. 70.
38. Tom Wintringham, "Arm the Citizens!" *Picture Post* (September 21, 1940), 9.
39. William Sansom, "The Wall," *Fireman Flower and Other Stories* (London: Hogarth, 1944), p. 109.
40. Rose Macaulay, "Notes On The Way," *Time and Tide* (October 5, 1940), 981.
41. Edward R. Murrow, "Can They Take It?" in *Reporting World War Two: Part Two*, p. 99.
42. *Ibid.*, pp. 85, 87.
43. Shirer, "The American Radio Traitors," in *Reporting World War Two: Part Two*, p. 644.
44. Ezra Pound, *"Ezra Pound Speaking": Radio Speeches of World War II*, ed. Leonard W. Doob (Greenwood: Westport, CT and London, 1978), p. 3.

45. Macdonald Hastings, *Passed as Censored* (London: Harrap, 1941), p. 78.
46. Gellhorn, "Das Deutsches Volk," *Face of War*, p. 176.
47. Mollie Panter-Downes, *London War Notes*, ed. William Shawn (London: Longman, 1972), p. 62.
48. Gellhorn, "Dachau," *Face of War*, p. 195.
49. *Ibid.*, p. 200.
50. *Ibid.*, p. 202.
51. Lee Miller, "Believe It," *Vogue* (US edn) (June 1945), 104.
52. Gellhorn, "Dachau," p. 195.
53. Quoted in Jonathan Dimbleby, *Richard Dimbleby: A Biography* (London: Hodder & Stoughton, 1975), p. 193.

PART II

Global perspectives

6

DEBARATI SANYAL

The French war

In 1942, a Russian-Jewish émigré named Irène Némirovsky was deported from France under the Jewish Statutes and sent to her death in Auschwitz. Her daughters went into hiding and survived the war, all the while carrying a suitcase that contained their mother's notebook. They did not decipher its pages until half a century later, when the elder daughter resolved to confide her mother's last words to the archives of the *Institut mémoire de l'édition contemporaine*. When she opened the notebook, what emerged was a fierce portrait of France's defeat and occupation by Germany and one of the first literary works to document the country's wartime experience.

The fate of Némirovsky's unfinished book, which lay dormant in its box until it surfaced several decades later to unanimous acclaim, captures the belated quality of France's memory of the war. The period 1940–44 is known as the dark years, or *les années noires*. Its memory has been described as an ever-growing corpse that remains too warm for an autopsy and resists the closure of national burial. Historian Henry Rousso describes the Occupation and its afterlife as a "syndrome" from which the nation has yet to recover: "The Vichy syndrome consists of a diverse set of symptoms whereby the trauma of the Occupation, and particularly the traumas resulting from internal divisions within France, reveals itself in political, social, and cultural life."[1] Indeed, the French defeat provoked a veritable civil war between different sectors of the nation's population, a *guerre franco-française* pitting those who supported or accommodated the occupying forces against those who resisted. As the metaphor of the syndrome suggests, the trauma of France's wartime experience is far from over. Its after-effects continue to reverberate in the nation's collective memory and cultural imagination.

The war was swift but devastating. In a mere six weeks, some 90,000 soldiers were killed and almost two million French troops were taken prisoner in German camps. A harsh armistice was signed in June 1940 and France was divided into two zones. Paris and the northern areas were occupied by

Germany, whereas the southern "free zone" had its headquarters in the spa town of Vichy, at least until 1943 when the Germans occupied the entire country. Under the leadership of Maréchal Pétain, a military hero of the First World War, Vichy's right-wing state dissolved the democratic and parliamentary institutions of France's Third Republic and replaced the revolutionary slogan of "Liberty, Equality, and Fraternity" with the conservative motto of "Work, Family, Nation." Pétain's puppet regime collaborated extensively with German forces and passed a number of discriminatory laws of its own accord. Vichy France participated in the deportation of close to 76,000 French and foreign Jews, of whom less than 3 percent returned alive. In the aftermath of Liberation, however, the shocking memory of France's official collaboration with Nazism was erased. Instead, under the leadership of Charles de Gaulle, postwar France cultivated the vision of a "true" French Republic that had never ceased to exist thanks to the exiled Free French Forces and the clandestine Resistance movement. This mythic view of a France wholly united in its opposition to the Third Reich remained largely in place until the 1970s, when a series of books and films began to explore the era's ambiguous interplay of collaboration, resistance, accommodation, and *attentisme* (a "wait and see" stance). This ongoing inquiry into the moral and political compromises of the period makes the trauma of wartime France a "past that refuses to pass."[2]

Representations of the Occupation

Written between 1941 and 1942, the two volumes of Némirovsky's *Suite française* record France's defeat and occupation virtually as events unfolded, and before the war's outcome was known. Yet Némirovsky lays out the moral topography of the wartime experience with uncanny foresight, sketching what will become the dominant motifs of its literature: the slippery lines separating collaboration, accommodation, and resistance, the Occupation's regime of coerced hospitality, and the erotic valences of France's relationship with the enemy. The first volume, *Tempest in June*, depicts the exodus of May–June 1940, when eight million French people left their homes in a scramble for safety as the German army approached. Inspired by nineteenth-century realists such as Tolstoy and Flaubert, Némirovsky depicts the flight of several representative social types such as a wealthy bourgeois family, a bombastic writer, and an egotistical collector. Through the use of free indirect discourse, the narrative shuttles from one perspective to another and discloses the stores of avarice, corruption, bad faith, and cowardice that motivate most of its characters. In Némirovsky's darkly comic *tableaux*, the defeat merely crystallizes existing class tensions, the flight for safety becomes a savage, Darwinian struggle, and France is portrayed as a nation poised for collaboration.

The following volume, *Dolce* (*Captivity*), meditates on the ambiguities of the Occupier-Occupied relationship, one pervasively rendered in terms of hospitality, cohabitation, and eroticism in the period's literature. The women of the town of Bussy watch the arrival of strapping German soldiers with a kind of lustful hatred: "the men were absent, imprisoned or dead. The enemy took their place. It was deplorable, but no one would know tomorrow. It would be one of those things that posterity would ignore, or from which it would modestly avert its eyes."[3] Not only does Némirovsky anticipate sexualized portrayals of the Occupation in the postwar cultural imagination, she also foresees France's disavowal of collaboration. Lieutenant Bruno von Falk is billeted to the Angellier household, where Madame Angellier lives with her lonely daughter-in-law Lucille. A taboo attraction forms between the lieutenant and Lucille during this enforced intimacy. Their idyll is interrupted when a jealous villager shoots a German officer who has attempted to seduce his wife. Lucille hides the fugitive villager under her own roof without telling her own occupant, thus choosing her solidarity with France over her attraction to the enemy: "She felt herself – chained-captive-in solidarity [sic] – with this country that sighed with impatience and dreamed."[4]

Dolce captures an essential feature of much wartime literature: the domestic sphere as a site of eroticized resistance, collaboration, or accommodation with the enemy. Yet Némirovsky's ambiguous vision of complicity stands in sharp contrast to the period's most canonical representation of the domestic space as a site of occupation and resistance, *The Silence of the Sea* (1942). Written by Jean Bruller under the code name Vercors, and published by the clandestine *Éditions de minuit* (a house that produced over twenty volumes under German censorship), *The Silence of the Sea* became an instant classic and symbol of the Resistance. As in *Dolce*, a German officer is billeted to a French household. But in spite of the silent attraction between the officer and the household's niece, his coerced hosts remain implacably mute and refuse to collaborate with the occupant's attempts to engage them in dialogue about a utopian Franco-Germanic alliance. Vercors's clandestine novella suggested that to withhold action or speech could become a profound act of resistance in a captive nation silenced by the threat of Gestapo torturers and collaborationist informants.

The intrusion of foreign troops into the domestic space of French civilians was a daily literal reminder of Occupation. It was also a synecdoche for France's historical predicament as the Reich's coerced host. In his evocative essays on Paris under Occupation, philosopher Jean-Paul Sartre describes the German military presence as a faceless, tentacular infiltration that over time fostered a sense of complicity and even biological kinship with the enemy ("*une accoutumance biologique*").[5] For Sartre, one of the most painful aspects of life under occupation was the impossibility of maintaining a stance of opposition when German officers politely asked for directions on the streets, or ate at your table, or pressed up against you in the metro. Under Nazi surveillance, each utterance or gesture could betray one's intention and serve unpredictable ends. An act of resistance could potentially lead to complicity with the occupant, as when a resistance fighter broke down under torture at the Gestapo quarters and imperiled his comrades. In this climate of surveillance and forced complicity, the writing and reading of literature raised crucial questions. Was apolitical art possible? What made a work of art serve collaboration or resistance? How could a legible political message be encoded under censorship?

Theatre, allegory, and censorship

The theatre of the period provides a complex forum for investigating these questions. Since theatre companies were forced to "Aryanize" their personnel and get their plays approved by the *Propaganda-Abteilung* or Nazi censorship apparatus, the mere fact of producing a play suggested a certain compromise or accommodation with the occupying forces. If a play staged a subversive message of resistance, it was particularly important to cloak this message in allegorical form. But was it possible to ensure that an allegory's meaning would be understood by its intended audience?

Two plays in particular illustrate the ambiguities of cultural production in the Occupation's state of surveillance and censorship. *The Flies* (*Les Mouches*) was composed by Sartre in 1942, after the first anniversary of the armistice. Sartre turned the fatalism of Greek tragedy on its head by using the *Oresteia* to affirm the inexorability of human freedom in a godless world. After many years of exile, Agamemnon's son Orestes returns to his hometown of Argos, which has been under the despotic rule of Agamemnon's assassin Aegisthus. To expiate his crime, Aegisthus has imposed an order of guilt and repentance upon the people of Argos. A plague of flies sent by Jupiter maintains the inhabitants in a state of cowering penitence, thus ensuring the authority of kings and gods. Orestes is urged by his sister Electra to avenge their father and reclaim his kingdom. When he slaughters Aegisthus (along with his mother Clytemnestra), Orestes discovers that his attempt to liberate Argos from the tyranny of repentance has only led to a realization of his own individual freedom, for "Each man must invent his own path."[6] Orestes is an existentialist hero: he has assumed his freedom in a world of pure contingency through a horrific act for which he takes complete responsibility.

At the time of its performance, Argos clearly stood for the oppressive surveillance of Vichy France. The citizens' coerced penitence for a crime they did not commit also recalled Pétain's declaration that France needed to atone for the sins of the past.[7] The protagonist's rejection of religious and political authority was a call to arms against Vichy's cowed collaboration. The play also addressed the burning question of ends and means, since Orestes' murder and matricide aimed to liberate Argos. According to its author, *The Flies* justified Resistance terrorism in the face of Germany's retaliatory execution of French hostages. Yet despite Sartre's intention, his allegory fostered contradictory readings. Where some saw a call to resistance, others such as the German censorship bureau deemed it harmless enough to authorize its performance, while one German critic went so far as to interpret it as a pro-Nazi celebration of Nietzsche's superman.[8]

In a similar vein, Jean Anouilh's *Antigone*, produced in the final year of Occupation, unleashed a storm of controversy. Like Sartre, Anouilh recast classical Greek tragedy (Sophocles) in a contemporary context. The rebellious Antigone defies her uncle Creon's edict and buries her dead brother Polynices with full knowledge that she will be sentenced to death. If Anouilh's play is now primarily read as an allegory of Resistance, at the time of its first performances both the Resistance and the Collaboration claimed its message. Although many saw the anarchist Antigone as a martyr to the tyranny of Creon's Vichy, the play was also perceived as a legitimation of collaborationism. Anouilh's sympathetic portrayal of Creon as a Man of State whose rational pragmatism prevents social chaos was interpreted as an apology for the compromises of Pétain's regime. Furthermore, the defiant Antigone embodies traits that were aligned with Fascist ideals of heroism: youthful intransigence, moral grandeur, suicidal irrationality, and a belief in the innate superiority of her race. Anouilh claimed that his play was devoid of ideological content, but the climate of the Occupation gave his domestic drama a potent if contradictory political charge. Both *The Flies* and *Antigone* illustrate the referential instability of allegory and its dependence on a work's context of reception. Despite their authors' intentions, these plays harbored competing and irreconcilable meanings actualized by different communities at the same historical moment.

Literature and collaboration

The Occupation saw the rise of a generation of French fascist writers who collaborated with the German presence and formed a new cultural élite. These writers often belonged to an existing French tradition of right-wing, anti-parliamentary, and anti-Semitic nationalism. French collaborationist fascists condemned the Third Republic's parliamentary democracy and its associations with cosmopolitanism, freemasonry, corruption, and "Jewish profiteering." Common themes in the fascist literature of the period were a return to the soil and forms of rural primitivism (which echoed Pétain's national revolution), the cult of virility, virulent anti-Semitism and anti-communism, praise for the Franco-German alliance, and the celebration of violence as a means of purging social corruption. A canonical example of these Fascist themes is Drieu la Rochelle's *Gilles* (1939), a *Bildungsroman* or novel of education that records the disillusionment of the interwar generation. During the Occupation, Drieu became editor of the prestigious literary journal *La Nouvelle Revue française*. A bestseller of the time, Lucien Rebatet's *The Ruins* (*Les Décombres*) celebrated the virile, military values of fascism. Robert Brasillach, the editor of the anti-Semitic journal *Je suis partout* was a brilliant novelist, scholar, journalist, and critic of fascist convictions. He also was one of the only writers executed for treason during the *épuration* or purge of collaborators at the end of the war.

One of the most fascinating literary figures to emerge from the shadow of collaboration is Louis-Ferdinand Céline, a doctor whose prewar epic novel *Voyage au bout de la nuit* (1932) is an established classic of modern French literature. Céline wrote *Bagatelles pour un massacre* (*Trifles for a Massacre*, 1927) and *L'École des cadavres* (*School for Corpses*, 1938), pamphlets advocating the extermination of the Jews that were reedited with illustrations during the Occupation. Despite his declared anti-Semitism and anti-communism, however, Céline's enraged, ironic, and innovative prose vexes political labels to this day. Still, when the Allies landed in Normandy, his reputation as a collaborator warranted his flight to Germany in order to escape the summary executions conducted by the Resistance.

Literature and resistance

France's defeat and occupation drove several writers to choose underground action over public aesthetic expression. The poet René Char, along with his fellow poets Pierre Reverdy and André Leynaud, refused to publish any texts during the Occupation. Char joined the *Section Atterrissage Parachutage* of de Gaulle's Fighting French Forces; André Malraux, the celebrated author of *The Human Condition*, commanded a Free French Army brigade in 1944. Others risked their lives to disseminate patriotic, anti-Nazi prose and poetry in clandestine journals, while poets such as the surrealist Robert Desnos and the Catholic Jean Cayrol wrote from their captivity in the concentration camps.[9]

Simone de Beauvoir's novel *The Blood of Others* (1945) conveys the key preoccupations of the Resistance: the awakening of one's sense of historicity and solidarity with others in times of collective crisis, the limits of pacifism, the necessity of commitment, and the dilemma of whether an end justifies the means used to attain it. De Beauvoir's novel is in dialogue with Sartre (and with *The Flies* in particular) on the moral dilemma of political commitment: under what circumstances can "the blood of others" be sacrificed? And who gets to decide? Set in the interwar and wartime years, the novel traces the evolution of Jean Blomart, a passionate left-wing activist who refrains from any political or personal commitment after inadvertently causing the death of a friend. Catapulted out of his passivity by the Occupation, Jean heads a Resistance network whose terrorist actions lead to the execution of twelve hostages by the Germans and eventually cause the death of his ex-girlfriend Hélène. Although Jean is initially racked with guilt as he watches Hélène die, he realizes that just as every life is connected to the lives of others, every action exacts a certain price. He concludes that, like Hélène, each person must choose their destiny and actualize their freedom, even if it is at the cost of their life. De Beauvoir's existential novel of education also anticipates her postwar feminist masterpiece, *The Second Sex*. Hélène's initial torment arises from her individualistic petty bourgeois background, but also from her status as a woman conditioned to find happiness in the private realm of love. When she joins the Resistance and helps a Jewish friend escape a round-up, Hélène experiences a profound conversion from individual suffering to selfless solidarity. Once she has given up private forms of selfhood and acquisitive definitions of happiness, she discovers that "the entire world was a fraternal presence."[10]

This discovery of community within crisis is at the heart of Albert Camus's canonical allegory of the Resistance, *The Plague* (*La Peste*, 1947), written partly during the Occupation while Camus was chief editor of the underground journal *Combat*. Where Sartre used a swarm of flies to convey the oppression of occupied France, Camus invokes a plague that transforms a sunny Algerian city into a contagious prison. Camus's allegory of the plague was readily discernible at the time. The Fascist peril was often portrayed as a deadly virus and Nazis were commonly referred to as "the brown plague" due to their uniforms. "I write in a country devastated by the plague," declared the communist poet Louis Aragon in the opening line of a clandestine poem titled "The Grévin Museum," while the poet Robert Desnos invoked the same disease in his terse poem "The Plague" before his deportation and death.[11]

Camus's *The Plague* is the chronicle of an epidemic that suddenly sweeps over the city of Oran. A state of emergency is declared and Oran is quarantined to prevent further infection. To counter the plague's devastation, a sanitary cordon is formed by ordinary citizens and led by the narrator

Dr. Rieux. In their tireless efforts to find a cure while caring for the sick and keeping track of the rising body count, these volunteers exemplify Camus's ethos of modest and ordinary commitment. Significantly, the protagonist-narrator is a doctor committed to fight a losing battle against the inevitable disease of mortality. For Camus, this revolt against an absurd human condition forms the basis of human solidarity (as his reformulation of Descartes suggests): "I rebel therefore we are."[12]

Camus's description of an exiled city in the shadow of death captures the carceral menace of everyday life in occupied France, and more generally, of Western Europe under the threat of Fascist domination. Yet its treatment of the epidemic's unimaginable human cost is also haunted by the specter of the Nazi genocide, making *The Plague* an enduring reflection on the representation of the Holocaust. Indeed, the novel addresses the challenges of conveying catastrophic events in historical writing. In his attempt to "be an honest witness," the narrator has "deliberately taken the victims' side," refusing ideological fictions of History that try to explain away the injustice of human suffering.[13] Instead, the epidemic is portrayed from a range of perspectives that even include a fragmentary micro-history of insignificant events and marginal figures. *The Plague* and its meditation on the unthinkable horror of history anticipate the central preoccupations of Holocaust testimony and concentrationary art.

The concentrationary experience

The Holocaust is often said to provoke a crisis of representation and of witnessing. Indeed, how is it possible to recover and convey the horror of the concentrationary experience in language, especially when its traumatic conditions could unravel one's identity altogether? Survivor testimonies are haunted by the question of who – or what – survived the camps. "I died in Auschwitz, but nobody knows it," declares a fellow survivor of Charlotte Delbo's, while Elie Wiesel's *Night* concludes with the image of the survivor who stands before a mirror and sees a corpse gaze back at him.[14] This "demolition of a man," as Primo Levi called it, was the aim and organizing principle of the Nazi camps.[15] When prisoners were not exterminated upon arrival or during selections, their physical and psychological dehumanization left them at the very threshold of man and thing, as well as of life and death.

Robert Antelme's aptly titled *The Human Species* (1947) is one of the first analyses of the concentrationary experience and its structures of dehumanization. A political prisoner deported to Gandersham, Buchenwald, and Dachau, Antelme was barely alive upon his return to Paris. Years later, writer Marguerite Duras (his wife at the time) described her agonizing wait for his rescue and recovery in the sparse and haunting *La Douleur* (1985). *The Human Species* recounts the bodily torments endured by the deportees in the camps – hunger, lice, cold, fever, dysentery, and overcrowding – in excruciating sensory detail. Yet Antelme also provides a philosophical inquiry into the logic of extermination, a logic that authorizes murder by denying a victim's belonging to the human species. Despite their attempt to sunder one species into several competing species, for Antelme, Nazism's exercise of power only served to unveil the indestructible unity of humankind: "There are not several human species, there is one human species. It is because we are men like them that the SS will be powerless before us in the end ... the power of the executioner can only be that of a man: the power to kill. He can kill a man, but he cannot change him into anything else."[16]

The concentration camps left survivors such as Antelme feeling as though they were the depository of "a kind of knowledge that is infinite, incommunicable."[17] For Delbo, a Resistance fighter deported to Auschwitz and Ravensbruck, it was a "useless knowledge" in the world of the living. Delbo invokes the chasm between the camp survivor's knowledge of suffering and the epistemological certainties of "normal life" thus:

> Oh you who know
> did you know that hunger makes the eyes shine
> that thirst dulls them.
>
> . . .
>
> Did you know that suffering has no limits
> horror knows no frontier
> Did you know
> You who know.[18]

How to convey such useless and incommunicable knowledge to others, and to what ends? The transmission of Holocaust experience has provoked heated debates that often oppose historiography to literature. For some, the historical specificity of the Holocaust is betrayed by artistic or imaginative representations. Only the most scrupulous historian can serve as an authoritative witness, especially given the threat of Holocaust denial.[19] Others believe that the aim of testimony is "to give to imagine rather than give to see" and thus defend the artifice of literary form.[20] In order to represent a reality that shatters existing frames of reference, one has to strain against the boundaries of the sayable. It follows that some of the most powerful testimonies of the camps challenge the conventional limits of language, form, and genre.

Delbo's Auschwitz trilogy is a striking illustration of the complexity of testimony as a literary genre. Her memoirs convey the shock of traumatic experience by interweaving poetry, prose poetry, narrative, and dramatic elements. In *None of Us Will Return*, Delbo declares, "Today, I am not sure that what I wrote is true [*vrai*]. I am sure that it is truthful [*véridique*]," thus distinguishing factual historical record from the fluidity of memory and imagination in an individual's testimony.[21] Delbo's writings do not give a chronological account of events from the perspective of a unified autobiographical subject. Instead, her fragmented scenes of horror seem petrified in an anonymous, eternal present:

> A corpse. The left eye eaten by a rat. The other eye open with its fringe of lashes.
> Try to look. Just try and see. [*Essayez de regarder, essayez pour voir.*][22]

In French, "essayez pour voir" functions both as an injunction and a challenge to the reader: try to see (if you can). For Delbo as for Buchenwald survivor Jorge Semprun, the problem with trauma's transmission into collective memory is not language and its capacity to communicate. At stake is the responsibility of those who did not suffer the camps to see, imagine, and in turn bear witness to the survivor's testimony.

One of the most moving illustrations of the survivors' need for a witness is found in Jorge Semprun's first literary work, *The Great Journey* (*Le Grand Voyage*, 1963). A Spaniard who joined the French Resistance in 1942, Semprun survived Buchenwald and wrote fictionalized accounts of his experience in French. Significantly, *The Great Journey* was classified as fiction rather than memoir or autobiography. It recounts Semprun's boxcar journey to Buchenwald in the company of a "guy from Semur." A no-nonsense fellow Resistance fighter to whom Semprun confides his thoughts and memories, the "guy from Semur" tragically dies upon their arrival. Forty years later, Semprun disclosed that "the guy from Semur" was an invention, a "warm and pertinent fiction" that kept him company as he revisited the atrocity of his past through the act of writing. For Semprun, such literary artifices do not mask, evade, or betray reality, but rather, make this reality more tangible: "reality often needs invention to become real [*vrai*]. That is to say, realistic [*vraisemblable*]."[23] To this day, his work is an incisive defense of literature as a means of survival and remembrance, indeed of survival *in* remembrance.

Phases of memory: resistancialism and the "retro mode"

Memory is frequently described as the organization of forgetting. With de Gaulle's ascent to power in the aftermath of the war, the memory of Vichy's official collaboration with Germany was repressed. In its stead emerged a mythic vision of France victimized by Nazism yet heroically united in its resistance to the enemy. This version of history is established at Liberation in a famous speech by de Gaulle: "Paris! Paris humiliated! Paris martyrized!

But Paris liberated! Liberated by itself, by its own people ... with the support and aid of France as a whole, of fighting France, of the only France, of the true France, of eternal France."[24] The high-ranking officials who had accommodated or collaborated with the enemy were either demonized by the purges or forgotten in the amnesties of the early 1950s. Sartre himself contributed to this vision of a predominantly resistant France, despite his writings on the ambiguities of the Occupation: "Never have we been more free than under the German occupation," he provocatively declared in an essay titled "The Republic of Silence," written immediately after the Liberation.[25] The philosopher cast the Occupation in existential terms, as an extreme experience of peril (a *situation limite*) that awakened all French citizens to their freedom, responsibility, and collective solidarity. Sartre's essay conjured the vision of an austere and invisible republic within Vichy France, one composed of ordinary citizens who participated in the anti-Nazi struggle through each of their daily thoughts and acts. Such performative declarations of a nation unified under the banner of Resistance are part of what Henry Rousso has termed "the Resistancialist myth."

The memory of Vichy France's collaboration did not begin to resurface until the seventies, with the fall of Gaullism and Giscard d'Estaing's election to the presidency. A wave of books and films turned to the Occupation's murky legacy and explored different facets of collaboration, inaugurating what is called the "retro mode" (*la mode rétro*). Marcel Ophüls's devastating documentary *The Sorrow and the Pity* (1971) dealt a crushing blow to the resistancialist myth. A chronicle of daily life under Occupation in the provincial town of Clermont Ferrand, the film exposed the extent to which ordinary citizens actively or passively collaborated with the German presence.[26] This was followed by American historian Robert Paxton's groundbreaking *Vichy France: Old Guard and New Order 1940–1944* (1972), which offered documented evidence that Pétain's Vichy deliberately sought to collaborate with the Third Reich and its anti-Semitic policies.

A cinematic landmark that illustrates the ambiguities of *la mode rétro* as an aesthetic movement is Louis Malle's *Lacombe Lucien*. Based on a screenplay by Patrick Modiano, it approaches the Occupation through the experience of an uneducated peasant who is turned away by the Resistance and falls into the arms of the Gestapo. Malle's portrayal of an ordinary individual buffeted by the winds of history suggested that resistance or collaboration were a matter of accident or circumstance rather than of political conscience and commitment. The protagonist's sexual relationship with his young Jewish hostage also probed Fascism's erotic appeal, and blurred the opposition between victims and executioners. The "retro mode" and its fascination with complicity, eroticism, and the "banality of evil" were criticized for turning the period's vexed political history into a nostalgic fetish and for displacing the myth of universal resistance with a countermyth of universal complicity.[27] Nevertheless, it is a historical moment that initiated a crucial investigation into the challenges and compromises of Occupied France, one that continues to this day.

Holocaust memory

The repression of French collaboration with Nazi Germany had a considerable impact on the shape of postwar Holocaust memory. Despite publications such as Elie Wiesel's French version of the classic *Night* (1958), which addressed the deportation of Romanian Jews, it was not until the 1970s that France acknowledged the particular status of Jews as a population designated for extermination. Initial representations of deportation focused primarily on political prisoners and did not distinguish between concentration camps and extermination camps. This failure to reckon with the status of Jews as a particular target of the Nazi genocide was linked to France's amnesia about Vichy's anti-Semitic laws. But it is also explained by the nation's Jacobin legacy of universalism, which refused to treat Jews as an isolated population. Another factor was the postwar deployment of Holocaust memory towards anti-colonial ends. For instance, Alain Resnais's watershed documentary on Auschwitz, *Night and Fog* (1955), only mentioned Jews once and concluded (following Camus) with a general warning about the ongoing plague of Fascism. Resnais's omission of the Judeocide, however, sharpened his documentary's relevance for the colonial crisis. According to its director, *Night and Fog* was not meant to be a monument to memory. Rather, it was an urgent, ever-actual warning about France's own deportation, internment, and torture of Algerians during the struggle for independence. Francophone writers from the colonies such as Aimé Césaire and Frantz Fanon also mobilized the memory of the Nazi genocide in the struggle to end France's ongoing colonial occupations. These political uses of memory drew powerful analogies between French imperialism and Nazism, identifying their shared structures of racism, reification, and elimination. Yet such comparisons inevitably erased the Jewish specificity of the Final Solution.

It was not until Claude Lanzmann's monumental *Shoah* (1985) that the magnitude of the Final Solution truly surfaced in France's national consciousness. A nine-hour documentary on the extermination of Jews, *Shoah* is composed exclusively of first-hand oral accounts by victims, perpetrators, and bystanders. Lanzmann's refusal of archival footage or the traditional devices of documentary stem from his conviction that any representation of the Jewish extermination constitutes a betrayal of its horror: "There is an absolute obscenity in the very project of understanding the Holocaust."[28] Lanzmann criticized filmmakers such as Resnais for using archival footage or attempting to recreate what is – and should remain – unimaginable. He argued that images of atrocity were bound to give a sense of closure and catharsis to their viewers, thus preventing the infinite work of mourning.

Despite Lanzmann's influential prohibition on imagery and the imagination, Holocaust memory continues to be a fertile terrain for creative literary experimentation in France. Georges Perec's *W or the Memory of Childhood* (1975) is a fascinating blend of anecdote, history, and fantasy. The narrative alternates between the author's fragmentary autobiography of his wartime childhood and a fantasy Olympian island that mutates into an allegory of the camps. Patrick Modiano, a novelist who had unveiled the legacy of French anti-Semitism in his scandalous *La Place de l'Étoile* (1968), continues his haunting investigations into the Holocaust's traces in the amnesia of urban modernity. *Dora Bruder* (1997), for instance, blends archival investigation, the detective genre, and personal recollection in its poignant attempt to reconstruct the last days of an adolescent Jewish runaway who eventually died in Auschwitz.

The cultural memory of France's wartime experience is not a fixed monument to the past but a dynamic process of critical revision and creative reimagination. Recent works have sought to open up a more decentered and multidirectional perspective on the era by interweaving its history with other histories and memorial legacies. For instance, crime fiction writer Didier Daeninckx's *Murders for Memory* explores the historical continuities between the massacres of the war and the violence of decolonization. Postcolonial Francophone authors and filmmakers probe points of conjunction and collision between the trauma of the war and the wounds of colonial history. A glance at France's war from alternate places such as its colonies, for example, yields a very different picture of defeat, occupation, and liberation.[29] As the preceding examination suggests, artistic representations of the war in France are not bound to its historical occurrence. They are contested sites of memory that continually challenge and redefine the nation's center and margins.

NOTES

1. Henry Rousso, *The Vichy Syndrome: History and Memory in France since 1944*, trans. Arthur Goldhammer (Cambridge, MA and London: Harvard University Press, 1991), p. 10. Rousso refers to Pétain's collaborationist regime established in the French town of Vichy.
2. Eric Conan and Henry Rousso, *Vichy: un passé qui ne passe pas* (Paris: Fayard, 1994).

3. Irène Némirovsky, *Suite française* (Paris: Denoël, 2004), p. 384. The erotic coupling of France and Germany became a recurrent theme after the Liberation. The famous collaborator Robert Brasillach, for instance, cast France as an adulterous woman who had slept with Germany. This projection of national betrayal in feminized terms can be seen in the wave of postwar ritual scapegoating when women accused of sexual relations with the enemy had their heads shorn in public.

4. *Ibid.*, p. 494.

5. Jean-Paul Sartre, *Situations III* (Paris: Gallimard, 1949), p. 20.

6. Jean-Paul Sartre, *Les Mouches* (Paris: Gallimard, 1947), p. 237.

7. "Vous souffrez, et vous souffrirez longtemps encore, car nous n'avons pas fini de payer toutes nos fautes." Pétain's allocution of June 27, 1941.

8. See Allan Stoekl, "What the Nazis Saw: *Les Mouches* in Occupied Paris," *SubStance* 32, 3 (2003), 78–91. An even more disquieting reading of *The Flies* occurred when a German production set the play in a concentration camp in 1948, turning Sartre's critique of repentance into a rejection of German guilt for the Holocaust.

9. In the vast field of Resistance poetry key poets include Louis Aragon, René Char, Robert Desnos, Paul Eluard, Pierre Jean Jouve, Francis Ponge, Pierre Reverdy, Pierre Seghers, and Jean Tardieu. For a concise overview, see Ann Smock, "The Honor of Poets," in *A New History of French Literature*, ed. Dennis Hollier (Cambridge, MA and London: Harvard University Press, 1989), pp. 948–53. A comprehensive anthology of the genre edited by one of its notable poets is *La Résistance et ses poètes*, ed. Pierre Seghers (Paris: Seghers, 2004).

10. Simone de Beauvoir, *Le Sang des autres* (Paris: Gallimard, 1945), p. 303.

11. Aragon, "La Musée Grévin," *La Résistance et ses poètes*, p. 254; Desnos, "La Peste," *La Résistance et ses poètes*, p. 422.

12. Camus reformulates Descartes's definition of the human cogito "I think therefore I am" in *The Rebel: An Essay on Man in Revolt*, trans. Anthony Bower (New York: Knopf, 1956), p. 22 (translation modified).

13. Albert Camus, *The Plague*, trans. Stuart Gilbert (New York: Vintage, 1948), pp. 302, 301.

14. Charlotte Delbo, *Auschwitz and After*, trans. Rosette C. Lamont (New Haven: Yale University Press, 1997), p. 267.

15. Primo Levi, *Survival in Auschwitz*, trans. Stuart Woolf (New York: Collier, 1961), p. 22.

16. Robert Antelme, *L'Espèce humaine* (Paris: Gallimard, 1957), pp. 229–30.

17. *Ibid.*, p. 301.

18. Charlotte Delbo, *Aucun de nous ne reviendra* (Paris: Minuit, 1970), pp. 21–2. Also see the volume *Une connaissance inutile* (Paris: Minuit, 1970). The trilogy has been translated as *Auschwitz and After*, trans. Rosette C. Lamont (New Haven: Yale University Press, 1997).

19. On Holocaust denial in postwar France, see Pierre Vidal-Naquet, *Assassins of Memory: Essays on the Denial of the Holocaust*, trans. Jeffrey Mehlman (New York: Columbia University Press, 1992).

20. Jorge Semprun, *L'Écriture ou la vie* (Paris: Gallimard, 1991), p. 167.

21. Delbo, *Aucun de nous*, epigraph.

22. *Ibid.*, p. 137.

23. Semprun, *L'Écriture*, p. 336–7.

24. Rousso, *Vichy Syndrome*, p. 16.
25. Sartre, *Situations III*, p. 11.
26. For an important discussion of accommodation, as distinct from collaboration, see Philippe Burrin, *France under the Germans: Collaboration and Compromise*, trans. Janet Lloyd (New York: The New Press, 1997).
27. See Michel Foucault, "Anti-Retro," *Cahiers du cinéma* 251–2 (July–Aug. 1974), 5–15. A fascinating revival of the retro mode is Jonathan Littel's *The Kindly Ones*, winner of the prestigious Goncourt prize in 2006. It is a fictional yet meticulously researched first-person account of the Third Reich from the perspective of an idealistic and not unsympathetic SS officer.
28. Claude Lanzmann, "Hier ist kein Warum," *Au sujet de Shoah* (Paris: Belin, 1990), p. 279.
29. In this vein, Senegalese film director Ousmane Sembène draws an analogy between Nazism and French imperialism in *Camp de Thiaroye* (1984), the devastating account of a massacre of West African colonial troops in June 1944. After risking their lives to defend a "homeland" that did not recognize them as citizens, a force of African servicemen are interned in a transit camp that visually recalls the Nazi camps, and offered lower service pay. This return to colonial subjection provokes a mutiny. In retaliation, French tanks shell the camp, killing thirty-five servicemen and wounding many others.

7

DAGMAR BARNOUW

The German war

Speechless in the dead German cities

The most destructive war in Western historical memory, World War II was also the first to target large civilian populations strategically and explicitly erase the distinction between combatants and non-combatants. In the 1930s, partly in reaction to trench warfare in the Great War and technological developments in the interwar years, air war had become increasingly attractive to the Royal Air Force. By the spring of 1942 Churchill was offering Stalin "total air war" as a "second front," promising to burn down every house in every German city. This promise of total air war was largely kept, and it would dramatically change the Allies' views of the sustainability of hyper-technological warfare, physical, psychological, and moral. Acceptance of "total," "moral," "strategic" war in the air meant that there would be no difference between soldiers fighting the enemy at the front and women and children at home awaiting the enemy's bombs, who, paradoxically, had lost their civilian status because they had been turned into the bombs' targets. Utterly helpless in the hyper-sentient fear of being sucked up and consumed by huge storms of fire, they were passive victims of the mass killing of air war that left only the insentient matter of rubble and ashes.

In an intelligent world, this massive-scale targeting and killing of enemy civilians might never have happened again.[1] But the Allies, particularly the Americans, focused exclusively on the "good, clean, just war we won" against Germany and Japan, and their unconditional victory would spawn more wars and war-like invasions employing ever more sophisticated deadly weapons that would kill and maim ever more civilians because they could be targeted at any time, from anywhere on the earth and in the sky. No matter how horrible the lives and deaths of soldiers in World War II, there were parallels to their experiences already in Napoleon's wars, particularly on the Eastern Front. But the near-total destruction of the enemy's cities and the mass killing of their civilian inhabitants were new phenomena.

The kind and scale of Germany's losses are still not fully comprehensible, unspeakable – a fact reflected in the general scarcity and reticence of German literary representations of the war, and particularly the war in the air. Moreover, this enduring silence has been expected by both the victors and the defeated: after a war that had proved both disastrous and dishonorable for the nation, German writers could not really assess the losses, much less mourn them.[2] Six decades later, the British moral philosopher A. C. Grayling has offered the generous judgment that Allied air attacks from 1943–45 constitute a war crime. But the Allies' hands in their "just war against morally criminal enemies" were "far cleaner than those of the people who plunged the world into war . . . and the explanation – not the excuse – for why we allowed our own hands to get dirty at all is because of what we had to clean up."[3]

I

The publication in the *New Yorker* of W. G. Sebald's essay "A Natural History of Destruction" in the fall of 2002 provoked letters to the editor declaring as immoral any sympathy for German wartime experiences.[4] Readers were "shocked and offended" by a text they thought suggested that Allied fire bombing of Germany did not simply signify deserved punishment for German collective guilt: whatever the war experience of German civilians, it would "be forever trumped by Auschwitz, Sobibor, and Buchenwald, a fact that may explain why Germans have continued to show penitence in public for the horrors that they visited on others but have chosen to regret in more secluded ways the suffering that others brought on them."[5]

German memories of the war are still so much dominated by the evil of Nazism that writers are reluctant to explore the suffering endured in wartime by those who were not designated victims of Hitler's regime. Indeed, Sebald was absolutely clear on the issue of German "suffering": it did not interest him; nor did the morality or immorality of Allied bombing. He was fascinated by the *new phenomenon* of the huge firestorms – hurricanes, tidal waves, moving mountains of fire – that from July 1943 to mid-April 1945 raged through German cities. Set off by the ingenious new British combination of high-explosive and incendiary bombs, they caused unimaginable devastation – for Sebald an intriguing challenge to the literary representation of that fiery apocalypse.

Sebald's focus on the literariness of remembrance, on the ways in which eyewitness accounts are legible as creative artifacts, redirected attention away from the terrifying reality of what many ordinary Germans saw and experienced. He concentrated on the hyper-physical effects of huge masses of fires falling and rising, a sublime "natural history," as he called it, of heretofore unknown technological forces of destruction, of burning skies that fused heaven and hell. And he described in the sharply detailed, enameled style of a miniature the fantastic rock formations of ruined cities, the shrunk purple corpses, the yellow puddles of congealed fat of the bodies cured by fire. Confronted with that surreal, incomprehensible mass transformation, Sebald presented its metaphysical horror beyond any moral imagination and responsibility because "the Germans" had abdicated all morality and responsibility.

He was very clear on that abdication also in the *New Yorker* excerpt from a longer text, "Air War and Literature," where he claimed that there had been almost no literary representation of Allied bombing in postwar Germany.[6] Critics asserted that the "self-pitying" Germans had always dwelt on their suffering, though Sebald had clearly not meant German memories of air war but its literary representations.[7] Moreover, any reasonably unbiased study of German postwar political culture shows that German remembrance of their losses had been safely put to sleep for many decades in order to keep awake the guilt and shame of their bad past.[8] As the letters to the *New Yorker* confirmed, the world, including the German intellectual and political elites, has for many decades been satisfied with this arrangement.

This public deep sleep meant strong resistance to any shift in the interpretive conventions that have controlled postwar German historical memory. All public critique of this control has been rejected as heretical "revisionism," implying accusations of Holocaust denial and anti-Semitism.[9] It was precisely this control that motivated the military historian Jörg Friedrich to write his powerful, provocative documentary of Allied bombing to reacquaint ordinary Germans with their experiences of that still largely hidden part of the war. Friedrich's *Der Brand* (*The Fire*, 2006) came out in the fall of 2002, preceded by Günter Grass's *Im Krebsgang* (*Crab Walk*, 2003) in the early spring of that year, a novel that seemed to signal the possibility of a greater public openness on the subject of the troubled German past.

At the center of Grass's novel is the sinking of a German ship vastly overloaded with German refugees from the East and wounded soldiers. Torpedoed by a Soviet submarine on January 30, 1945, it was one of the greatest disasters in maritime history with 9,300 lives lost in the Baltic Sea. The novel's commercial and critical success can be attributed to Grass's realistic, virtuoso descriptions of the sinking ship, the fearful chaos of women and children screaming and flailing helplessly in the icy black waves, the terrible silence after their mass drowning. Whether it concerned the enforced mass-migrations from the East with an estimated loss of two and a half million lives, mostly women and children; or the firestorms of the air raids when Germany was already defeated and in chaos: such focus on

German wartime experiences was completely new to German audiences almost six decades after the end of the war. They responded with gratitude to Grass's narrative of that tragic marine disaster and Friedrich's documentary of the burning of German cities and their inhabitants.

An *Economist* review of Friedrich's *Der Brand* commented that "it is still rare for a German to take a public look at the second world war from a German perspective. But things are changing. Earlier this year, Günter Grass, a Nobel prize winner, caused a tidal wave of agonized German heart-searching with his novel 'Krebsgang'."[10] And the review quotes the Old Man, Grass's *alter ego*, that Germans should never "have kept silent about all that suffering simply because our own guilt was overpowering and our professions of regret paramount for all those years, for we abandoned the suppressed reality to the right-wingers."

In his rhetorically powerful role as Germany's moral-political conscience, Grass had for many years supported this silence. *Crab Walk*, too, framed the drama of mass drowning with intertwined moralizing stories, as has been his pedagogical habit for half a century. Yet where he tried to diffuse his German readers' politically incorrect feelings of personal and cultural loss, they craved the past actuality, the evidence of their pasts as they had lived them and then been told to forget what they had remembered. Sebald's complaint about the lack of effective literary representation of Germany's devastation by "total air war" was largely correct.

Only recently, and mainly in response to Grass's and Friedrich's books, have Germans begun to remember. *Der Brand* may well turn out to be the most effective representation of air war in its combined technological account and often stunning description of the extreme sensations triggered by air raids: the verbal recalling of the physical and psychological terror of being bombed. In that, *Der Brand* shares certain traits with docufiction, which some historians fear undermines its documentary reliability. Others have praised the book precisely for the epistemological power of its unconventional style. It took Friedrich's disturbing verbal explosions to shake the dead German cities – the Germans – out of their speechlessness; to make them speak of pain. Not as *their* pain but as the general human pain of such wholesale destruction, Dresden and Tokyo as well as Baghdad. In contrast, Sebald's descriptions are exercises in a verbal aestheticism whose very perfection closes rather than opens painful memories.

Controversial, both attacked and admired, *Der Brand* is objective in its relentless focus on the impact of bombs unleashing the storms of fire that sweep up and annihilate everything in their way; so, if less controversial, is Grass's focus on the wounded sinking ship, the mass of the waves' icy darkness and of mass death by drowning. Questions of morality and immorality come mostly after the calamitous events have been represented in a future present, the respective readers' or viewers' short-lived Now. Vulnerable to perspectival distortions, this Now is nevertheless the space where audiences may think and feel that Grass's and Friedrich's representations show it as it *was*: *their* past experiences, *their* memories of war.

II

The omnipresent ruins and rubble left behind by Allied bombing were not so much a "terra incognita" as a visual and semantic paradox. In the literally "bombed-out" cities with their houses broken up and broken open, what had been visible was now invisible, what had been invisible was now visible. The physical, political, and moral devastation at the chaotic end of the war seems most "naturally" expressed in the incomprehensibly altered cityscapes that, profoundly disorienting even to the cities' lifelong inhabitants, defied all familiar human meaning and seemed beyond the reach of human speech. The weight of the ruins and mountains of rubble that *were* the dead cities was too overpowering to be invoked in speech or writing. Speechless, they documented the certainties of total destruction and, beyond that, the painfully ambiguous burden of guilt, retribution, and remorse.[11] Film rather than literature best conveys their magnitude and their meanings.

Wolfgang Staudte, who conceived and directed the first German postwar film, *Die Mörder sind unter uns* (*The Murderers Are Among Us*, 1946), made the rubble and ruins of Berlin his film's main protagonist. It was a brilliant, seemingly spontaneous response that had everything to do with the fact that his medium was visual and that making this film of the end of the war was a collaborative enterprise. No matter how "authorial" the director, filming means the direct involvement of other people and of the world out there: an unimaginably changed world, melted down and reshaped by mass death and destruction.

Staudte had worked for the German film company UFA almost until the day Soviet soldiers invaded the Babelsberg studios in the spring of 1945, and he wanted to get back to making films as quickly as possible. The American Forces Film Section told him that "in the next five years no film will be made in this country except by us"[12] – echoing the sentiments of the American film industry where many German exiles had found work. Ironically, had they not rejected his exposé out of hand, they would have seen that it affirmed the official Allied attitude toward vanquished Germany as a collective of guilty perpetrators. Moreover, his "politically correct" perspective on the unredeemed, unmastered German past would not change over the decades. Unwilling to engage with the uncertainties and ambiguities of the troubled past, he intended to seize what was known as *Stunde Null* ("Zero Hour"), that important point in time when the end of the war would turn into a new beginning. *Stunde Null* was an illusion; and the chaotic end would just merge with a no less chaotic and obscure beginning. But for Staudte, all that was needed now was an immediate confrontation with the military and moral catastrophe that the Germans had brought on themselves.

The Soviet sector's DEFA, the first postwar German film company, was eager to promote democratic reconstitution by German reeducation. *Filmoffiziere* of the Soviet occupation read Staudte's script and were persuaded that it fit their concept of film as art by and for the masses, *Massenkunst*, in the service of a new correct collective consciousness.[13] The film is set in Berlin, a few months after the end of the war, when Dr. Mertens by chance meets his former commanding officer Brückner whom he had last seen at the front. Traumatized by his war experiences, the former surgeon has become a cynical, self-absorbed alcoholic drifter. In contrast, the businessman Brückner has no problems adapting to the new situation and is doing very well. Only Mertens knows that he ordered the shooting of Polish civilian hostages on Christmas Eve 1942 and he plans to revenge the victims by killing their murderer – the ending of the film. Such violence did not fit the new consciousness and Staudte had to shift the murder to a symbolic level that allowed a choice of interpretations. In the end, Brückner may or may not be judged and sentenced; Mertens may or may not be walking into a better future with Susanne, whose patient love may or may not have redeemed him, though it has prevented him from shooting Brückner.

Fortunately, Staudte's desire to confront the German past made him more interested in the visual grandeur of Berlin's horrifying transfiguration than in the film's characters. His combined documentary and artistic vision shared certain aspects of Sebald's attempts, half a century later, at representing the scarcely believable scope of destruction by invoking the surreal dimension of the sublime. He shot the film from March to July 1946 in the Babelsberg studios and, in an unusual approach, the streets of Berlin. Since they were all lined by the most gorgeous ruins and magnificent mountains of rubble, it would have made no sense to build ruins and pile up rubble in the studio, though American movies set in early postwar Germany tended to do just that.

A contemporary observer described the scene of the shooting: endless lines of ruins, bombed-out tanks, ubiquitous machine guns, and helmets shot to pieces left by the huge bloodbath of the battle for Berlin. It is a shattered world suddenly lit up by the film crew's glaring floodlights that both lure and blind the people living in the ruins. Emerging from the rubble fearfully, they seem to be drawn back into its darkness, merging again with the ruins. A shadowy, pitiful sight, they are also a disturbance to be shushed away like moths because the film calls for eerily empty streets. But an empty street is not as disquieting as a street where "people emerge who no longer exist, who have been dead for a long time, even though they do not know it."[14]

Shot under very difficult conditions – the crew's daily experience of chronic hunger, illness, lack of medical care and shelter, constant problems with obtaining enough film and electricity – this early film is remarkably successful in representing the sheer material mass of destruction as the disquieting insubstantiality and instability of the ruined city. No literary text of that time or later achieved anything close to it. What the camera sees is a surreal, hostile world in some ways reminiscent of the expressionist sets of earlier silent movies.[15] Werner Fiedler, in a review of 1946, rightly pointed out the camera's aggressive focus on the "frighteningly beautiful landscapes of ruins. It homes in on shattered lives, creating gloriously gloomy psychic landscapes."[16] The dominant elements of the film are not light and shadow but shadows darkened by the lighting technique, a play with gradations of darkness. A staircase appears as a shaft of shifting darknesses; a human face as a field of blackish rubble; and the slanting camera angle intensifies the sense of disorientation among the mountains of rubble. The effect is a feeling of dizziness, like stumbling and groping amidst a plethora of visually disturbing images that simultaneously pull the viewer in different directions.

Fiedler emphasizes the challenge for the director of "this first German anti-fascist film" to "document the new German attitude" and awaken a lethargic German population to sweep away the "rubble of the soul." Yet he also thinks Staudte's moral perspective on the immediate postwar period too harshly judgmental and selective. Every character, with the exception of Susanne just returned from a concentration camp, has to be guilty, deeply flawed, or seriously damaged; and the dark times of the rubble do not support hopes for the future. Friedrich Luft, in contrast, was disappointed that the film did not deliver the "clarification," "accounting," and "finally a new view and liberation" so much needed in 1946.

In Luft's view, Staudte's great visual sensitivity to the filmic potential of Berlin's ruins and rubble had prevented him from dealing coherently with the all-important topic of German guilt and atonement.[17] He was blind to Staudte's extraordinary cinematic treatment of the omnipresent mountains of rubble as dangerously treacherous living matter. Left behind by the planes and tanks of mid-twentieth-century hyper-technological warfare, these mountains are both unyielding and shifting: alien monsters of unearthly proportions that swallowed hundreds of thousands of human habitations and everything in them, alive or dead. The film's beginning is visually powerful: the camera pauses on a soldier's grave; a crane shot reveals a huge mountain of rubble; some small children are tracked as they clamber across those ruins in search of something they will most probably never find.

In a later scene, the camera follows two men rapidly walking across an endless mountainous wasteland of rubble. Mertens, the man in the lead, is disoriented and diminished by the war but, as if on native ground, he unerringly finds his way in even the most confusing terrain of rubble. Unable to keep up with Mertens, Brückner panics for fear that he will be left behind in this nowhere, a chaotic wasteland without any traces of human cultivation and habitation, with no signs for direction, nothing to establish meaning. The film's evil human character, he seems at the mercy of the rubble whose ominous physical presence is the film's star actor. Secretive, inscrutable, unreliable, it distorts and disorients by constantly changing underfoot as if in reaction to the person walking on it – perhaps innocent, certainly fearless like Mertens; certainly guilty and apprehensive like Brückner. Staudte gave him immoral innocence, the extreme opposite of Susanne's moral innocence. Not knowing, not caring about the distinctions between good and bad, he is, in most situations, without fear or suspicion. As long as he stays with him, Mertens will have no difficulties luring him into the terra incognita, the post-civilization wilderness of the rubble, where he intends to kill him.

In the psychologically complex reality of the postwar era, both kinds of innocence are too radical and therefore abstract, even if the victors, and then the German political and intellectual elites, held up the ideal of radical moral purification as a measure of successful denazification. For Mertens, a more credible character, the past horrors of warfare are still in the present; there do not seem to be rupture and change. The film's visual focus on rubble and ruins appears natural and, documenting the city's near total destruction itself, Staudte's cinematography is both realistic and surrealistic: it manages to represent the all-enveloping alienness and familiarity of that destruction, its shocking sublime attraction and persistent ordinary repulsion.

It seems strange that the extraordinary nature of the destruction the film documents so faithfully and artfully could not be acknowledged again for almost six decades. Until Friedrich's attempts to do so in *Der Brand*, it remained hidden in the *moral* history of destruction. The ideological restrictions and selectiveness of this history were in some ways helpful, in others harmful. For its early supporters, the West German élites who saw themselves as the heirs of Weimar's pre-Nazi and therefore Good, if unreal, Democracy, this was undoubtedly the easiest way to cope with a host of postwar difficulties. Perhaps in spontaneous reaction to the visual power of Berlin's unimaginable destruction, Staudte managed to circumvent the moral history of destruction in his filmic recordings, the "pure" images of the gloriously horrible rubble and ruins. But the moral lessons he extracted from his human characters are much too certain and predictable, as if to balance the ambiguities and ambivalences of their war memories in the images of darkness and shadows. If the film has rightly been seen as one of the most important documentations of the devastation left by air war, it is for the unmediated, unredeemed, unmatched visual power of its literally inhuman protagonist.

III

German political and psychological preoccupation with guilt and retribution proved to be tenacious, outliving German rubble and ruins by many decades and re-energized by re-unification forty-five years after the war. Yet in their emotional urgency and intellectual openness, discourses of German guilt and remorse appear most nuanced and searching in the immediate postwar years, before the return of a more organized political life that would also politicize and thereby diffuse the powerful physical and mental effects of the German war experience.[18] A good example are Erich Kästner's articles in the American-controlled *Neue Zeitung* from 1945 to 1947 where he tried to develop a more differentiating view of the *Schuldfrage*, the question of German guilt.

A well-known liberal journalist, essayist, and novelist during the interwar years whose books were burned by the Nazis, he stayed in Berlin all through the war and, like many Berliners, lost all his possessions in air raids. After the war he would be criticized for staying, as if he had not been sufficiently loyal to anti-Fascism. But it was precisely his experience of the war, his witnessing of the destruction of Berlin and other German cities, that had made him such an intelligently critical observer of the immediate postwar era, which in his, as in most Germans' experience, extended the war for several years. It was particularly the horrendous difficulties of the cruel winter of 1946–47 – hunger, cold, lack of shelter, illness, death on a catastrophic scale – that Kästner linked to the Allied power politics of separate "Zones." These politics were motivated by the victors' self-interest and ignored the desperate needs of the population, in their great majority still women, children, and old people; and they were serious problems of the "liberating" Allied occupation that, like air war, are just beginning to be discussed now, sixty years later.

Kästner's description (in the *Neue Zeitung*, November 1946) of his first visit to the destroyed city of Dresden, the serenely beautiful, beloved city of his youth, is one of the most effective texts of the immediate postwar years because it interweaves mourning and hope, emotion and reason. There are the devastating images of irrevocable transformation, radical reduction, and yet, at the moment of the visitor's speechless despair, they are already retreating into the past. It will be a past that, though painful, will not resist a future gradual normalization, because the war left the Germans with "the two fires of guilt and of pain." Inconsolable, Kästner does not search for a higher meaning of this unspeakable absence of what was once Dresden. In order to accept the openness of the future, he looks for ways of dealing realistically with the challenges of the past and the present. But he would also soon resign his post as feuilleton editor, frustrated by the rigid media control of the occupying powers. It saddened many readers who had found particularly useful his discussions of how to deal with the Nazi past, among them the advice to recall their own experiences of these years and not settle for what the Allies had told them to remember.

Many of Kästner's readers would also recently have seen *Die Mörder sind unter uns*, reviewed by Luft in the *Neue Zeitung* just two days later. Staudte's filmic creation of Berlin's transformation into a monstrously sentient rubble protagonist beyond human time and conscience differs dramatically from Kästner's verbal reflections on the political and social meanings in human time of a city's radical transformation into nothing but rubble, insentient matter. The difference of the medium is crucial here. The power of *Trümmerfilme*, of which Staudte's film is the first and most significant example, can be to make immediately visible the extreme, amoral nature of war and shock the viewer into isolating incomprehension: how could it have happened? In theory, literary reflections on the cruelties of war and the moral dilemmas of its aftermath can work to create a shared understanding of how all this could have happened and what it might mean. In practice, this proved a difficult task in the postwar era.

Heinrich Böll and Günter Grass, canonical literary figures in West Germany, both Nobel Prize winners (1972 and 1999), both prolific writers, both (sometimes ironically) admired for their high-serious self-perception as the moral-political conscience of West Germany, dealt with issues of war and guilt but not with the experience of air war. Born in 1917, Böll was drafted in 1939 and spent six years as a terrified common soldier fighting in France, Russia, Romania, and Hungary – experiences that he drew on for his early collection of stories, *Wanderer, kommst du nach Spa . . .* (1950), and a novel, *Wo warst du, Adam* (1951). Though critical of war in general and this war in particular, these early texts were too oblique, too private to be persuasive.[19] Like most young and middle-aged German men, he experienced the uncommon life of the common soldier but had little experience of air war.

Ten years younger than Böll, Grass published his first novel, *Die Blechtrommel* in 1959 (*The Tin Drum*, 1961).[20] An instant bestseller, it put "German literature back on the market" because it forcefully confronted "the Germans" with the unspeakably bad past they did not want to remember. In George Steiner's reading, the issue was not partial, provisional illumination of an extraordinarily difficult and on many levels painful past – Kästner's approach. It was the wake-up call to the collectively guilty Germans of "in your face" accusations delivered in Grass's "bawling voice."[21]

A more openly sinister version of Peter Pan, Oskar is the archetypical unreliable narrator of his picaresque story – as is his author, a few years younger and sharing part of that story. The novel is artfully meandering and deliberately ambiguous. Is Oskar a Jesus figure or the anti Christ?[22] Is he or is he not responsible for the deaths of his mother, his uncle, and his father who suffocated trying to swallow the Nazi Party badge that he thought safely hidden from the Russians but that was found by nosy Oskar? Is he or is he not the real father of his father's son by his second wife? He seems to think that he is guilty on all counts. Whose past is being represented by him and his comical-demoniacal petit-bourgeois family? Hardly those of the readers who made *The Tin Drum* such a success. Oskar is the artist son who exorcizes his Nazi father by (perhaps) killing him at the age of twenty-one and then giving up his drum, his art, promising to grow up after all and become a responsible member of society – the conclusion of all *Bildungsromane*.

Oskar's refusal to grow up exemplifies the cultural critic Theodor Adorno's simplistic Freudian-Marxian theory of fascism: all Germans were Nazis and the price they all had to pay for their regression – their Oskar-like arrested development – was acceptance of collective guilt in confrontation with their bad past. Defeated, they did as they were told and then they fell silent. But what did that silence say about *their* memories that might have been of some historical interest, even relevance?

Grass would become the most visible German literary figure and in the end he would change some of his long-held views about the bad German past: it was time to turn condemnations into questions. Time will prove him wrong or right. When *The Fire*, the American edition of Friedrich's *Der Brand*, came out in late 2006, the review in *The Economist* would not be as welcoming as it had been four years earlier. Praising the author "for both his diligence and his descriptive powers," it also asserts that "Mr. Friedrich's desire to puncture Anglo-American self-satisfaction comes perilously close to suggesting that the Germans were right to defend Nazism, and the allies were wrong to attack it."[23] This is a troubling misreading of Friedrich and of history. In the last years of the war, when Nazi Germany was already defeated, the Allied air war was waged against German civilians – at unimaginable cost to the guilty and innocent alike.

IV

On the night of July 24–25, 1943, Erich Nossack, a forty-two-year-old coffee merchant and aspiring novelist, watched the destruction of his native Hamburg from across the Elbe River, spellbound by the apocalyptic vision of countless airplanes diving down on his city in intricate, ever-changing formations. They seemed to be riding on the all-enveloping drone of their engines, a "monstrous fury of noise" that spawned an unearthly stillness just before the attack. Diving and rising with the drone's rhythm, the airplanes obliterated and cleared the sky, lighting a myriad fires that would transform the city into mountains of rubble. Nossack experienced the attack as a "spectator," grateful that he "was spared playing a role in it" and fascinated by the fantastic audio-visual performance of the so-far worst attack on a German – or any – city. He was also shaken to the core because he realized that it changed everything: "For me the city went to ruin as a whole, and my danger consisted in being overpowered by seeing and knowing the entirety of its fate."[24]

Nossack's account of the destruction of Hamburg in "Der Untergang" (*The End*), from November 1943 describes in sober detail the overwhelming sensory phenomenon of the firestorms and reflects on the calamity's entangled private and public meanings. It is a carefully worked literary and documentary essay, expansive and terse, passionate and reticent, on the topic of irreversible personal and cultural loss: the sudden explosive absence of familiar people, animals, sacral and secular buildings, artworks, books, manuscripts, musical instruments, furniture, crockery, clothing that had defined his human identity. One of the most compelling testimonies to the inhumanly destructive power of air war, not unlike Staudte's filmic representation of Berlin's rubble, Nossack's verbal exploration of its human meanings presents the evidence that what had happened was "something completely new ... It was the end" – of the world as he – we – had known it.

NOTES

1. See Vera Brittain, *One Voice: Pacifist Writings from the Second World War* (London, New York: Continuum, 2005).
2. Volker Hage, *Zeugen der Zerstörung: Die Literaten und der Luftkrieg* (Frankfurt/M.: S. Fischer, 2003), p. 69.
3. A. C. Grayling, *Among the Dead Cities The History and Moral Legacy of the WWII Bombing of Civilians in Germany and Japan* (New York: Walker, 2006), pp. 276–80.
4. W. G. Sebald, "A Natural History of Destruction," *New Yorker*, (November 4, 2002), 66–77.
5. Letters to the *New Yorker* (December 2, 2002), 10.
6. The text was excerpted from W. G. Sebald, "Air War and Literature," *On the Natural History of Destruction* (New York: Random House, 2003), pp. 1–104.
7. See Bill Niven, ed., *Germans as Victims: Remembering the Past in Contemporary Germany* (New York: Palgrave Macmillan, 2006).
8. See Dagmar Barnouw, *The War in the Empty Air: Victims, Perpetrators, and Postwar Germans* (Bloomington: Indiana University Press, 2005), pp. 1–29, 165–207.
9. *Ibid.*, pp. 1–29, 102–64.

10. Unsigned review, "A German Review of History: Another Taboo Broken," *The Economist* (November 23, 2002), 47.

11. See Dagmar Barnouw, *Germany 1945: Views of War and Violence* (Bloomington: Indiana University Press, 1997), pp. 1–87, 136–98.

12. Malte Ludin, *Wolfgang Staudte* (Rowohlt: Reinbek bei Hamburg, 1996), pp. 123n., 56.

13. *Ibid.*, p. 32.

14. *Ibid.*, p. 34.

15. *Ibid.*, p. 36.

16. Werner Fiedler, "Der Weg durch die Trümmer" (*Neue Zeitung*, October 17, 1946), now in *Edition Filme 6, Staudte* (Berlin: Wissenschaftsverlag Volker Spiess, 1991), pp. 176–7. See the large number of contemporary reviews listed, *ibid.*, pp. 300–1.

17. Friedrich Luft, "Der erste deutsche Film nach dem Kriege" (*Der Tagesspiegel*, October 16, 1946), now in *Edition Filme 6, Staudte*, pp. 173–6.

18. Jürgen Steinle, *Nationales Selbstverständnis nach dem Nationalsozialismus. Die Kriegsschuld-Debatte in West-Deutschland* (Bochum: Universitätsverlag Dr. N. Brochmeyer, 1995).

19. For documentation of Böll's war experiences see *Heinrich Böll: Briefe aus dem Krieg 1939–1945*, 2 vols., ed. Jochen Schubert (Köln: Kiepenheuer & Witsch, 2001).

20. *The Tin Drum* is now the first part of the *Danzig Trilogy* that includes *Katz und Maus* (1961) and *Hundejahre* (1963). For secondary literature on the trilogy see Volker Neuhaus, *Günter Grass* (Stuttgart: Reclam, 1999), pp. 219–32.

21. George Steiner, "The Nerve of Günter Grass," in *Critical Essays on Günter Grass*, ed. Patrick O'Neill (Boston: GK Hall, 1987), pp. 30–1.

22. Neuhaus, *Günter Grass*, pp. 54–61.

23. Unsigned review, "Bombing Germany: Bad, but Was it Wicked too?" *The Economist* (December 2, 2006), 85–6.

24. Hans Erich Nossack, *The End: Hamburg 1943*, trans. Joel Agee (Chicago and London: The University of Chicago Press, 2004), pp. 1, 8.

8

KATHARINE HODGSON

The Soviet war

The Soviet context

World War II proved to be an enduring theme in literature by Soviet writers, particularly in work written by the generation who had experienced the war directly themselves. Yet in the years that followed the end of the war, many young writers returning from the front were silent. Much of what they wrote about the war only began to emerge over ten years after the victory had been won. While the war had been in progress there had been an immediate, lively, and prolific response to it, mostly in the form of poetry, journalism, or short stories. At the end of the war, however, war literature, with a few exceptions, became ponderous and formulaic. The reason for this change can be found in the way the Soviet state understood the role of writers and of literature. Writers were expected to serve the state by producing works on themes approved by the authorities, written in a plain, accessible style, which educated their readers "in the spirit of socialism." The censors and the critics enforced strict controls over what could be published, and failure to conform could bring about serious consequences.

While censorship continued to operate during the war, it had been relaxed to some extent, allowing writers more freedom in their work. As the war came to an end, the state began to tighten its control over literature once more. It was made clear to writers that the war was to be represented and interpreted in certain ways only. This period of repressive cultural control only came to an end after Stalin's death in 1953; significant changes came about after his successor, Nikita Khrushchev, made a speech in 1956 condemning Stalin and the "cult of personality" that had built up around him. Numerous controversial novels about the war appeared through the 1960s, although the state still operated a system of censorship, removing material felt to be undesirable. In the case of one novel, to be discussed further below, the authorities seized the manuscript, stating that publication would only be thinkable in a couple of hundred years. This chapter will provide an overview of how representations and interpretations of the war developed, and will then explore in more detail three aspects of Soviet war literature. First it will consider wartime journalism, then the poetry of wartime, as immediate responses to the conflict in progress, before moving on to look at the novel and the broader perspectives that this genre introduced.

During most of the 1930s, Soviet writers were urged to prepare themselves for the expected war with fascist Germany, to familiarize themselves with military subject-matter, and to celebrate the heroism of the Red Army. Following the Nazi–Soviet Pact of August 1939, Germany was no longer mentioned as a potential enemy, but the war theme continued to be promoted. The vision of war put forward in 1930s Soviet literature conformed to the state-prescribed norms of socialist realism, being far from realistic and extremely optimistic. It portrayed heroes who were wholly dedicated and fearless, and declared that victory depended on the wise guidance of the Party and Stalin. When the war came, however, it brought bitter experience of retreat, encirclement, and masses of fleeing civilians, rather than the rapid, near-bloodless victory that the authorities had been expecting. The idealized norms of pre-war literature were, to say the least, inappropriate for the circumstances. Many writers adapted quickly, pushing at the boundaries of censorship to reflect to their readers something of the reality of the suffering war had brought, and to depict the people's endurance of this suffering. The authorities had little choice but to allow writers some leeway. It was clear, in the face of the disastrous retreats of summer 1941, that the war effort would demand real popular commitment which could not be won by mouthing empty slogans about the might of the Party, or by making groundless claims that the war was going well, when large numbers of people had direct evidence to the contrary.

Although censorship did continue to operate, writers were able to give a soberly realistic picture of war and the suffering it brought, as well as of the bravery and self-sacrifice of the people. Readers recognized that something in Soviet literature had changed. As Don Piper puts it: "the measure of literature became its approximation to the realities of the front and its distance from the cant of the past decade."[1] The heroism portrayed by many wartime writers had little to do with the kind of heroism that was inspired by devotion to the Communist Party and more to do with a heroism rooted in a largely apolitical patriotism and the desire to protect home and family. Poets were able to write lyric poetry about the emotional experiences and undeniable hardships of the individual at war, whereas previously, war poetry of this kind had been viewed with suspicion, particularly if those emotions were anything other than happily optimistic. War reporters, including Vasily Grossman, whose work will be discussed below, set aside routine invocations of Stalin's inspirational role and tales of easy victories in favor of representing the harshness of conflict and the soldier's stubborn endurance.

Gradually writers began to hope, together with many other Soviet citizens, that the end of the war would bring further liberalization. Yet even before victory had been achieved, the authorities were beginning to instruct writers that they needed to convey the message that victory was owed to the Party, to Stalin, and to the Soviet system. Victory, Stalin declared in February 1946, had been won because of the socialist system.[2] His words implied that people should forget their wartime hopes of change to a more humane regime, without the kind of terror that had been inflicted by the state on society in the late 1930s, or the savage censorship that had shackled writers and artists. People who had fought in the hope that their committed efforts to help win the war would be rewarded by greater freedom were rewarded instead by renewed repression. The victory was stolen from the people who had brought it about, and attributed instead to the wisdom of Stalin and the Party. Writers were expected to collaborate in this theft by providing large-scale, epic works which emphasized the historic significance of the war as a victory for the socialist system, and downplayed the cost in terms of individual lives, suffering, and sacrifice. Although some isolated works which did not conform slavishly to postwar norms were allowed through by the censors, a good deal of the war literature published in the Soviet Union in the first decade or so after the war was intent on portraying a version of the war which served Stalinist propaganda aims and had little in common with the war as it had been experienced by most Soviet citizens.

The Stalinist propaganda machine suffered a near-fatal blow in 1956, when Khrushchev addressed the Twentieth Party Congress with a fierce condemnation of Stalin, who had died three years earlier. Stalin's prowess as a military strategist was roundly mocked, and Khrushchev paid tribute to the people whose collective efforts had in fact won the war. In the period of cultural liberalization that followed, literature about the war returned to its wartime roots, sloughing off much of the Stalinist baggage in favor of a realistic portrayal of events. The "truth of the trenches" which many authors described was based on their own experiences at the front. They produced grim accounts of war experienced by the ordinary soldier, with little interest in its "historic" significance, but a consuming interest in exploring individual responses to the pressures of war. The subversive potential of the war theme, which had lain dormant for years, now reemerged. Literature written during the war emphasized the immediate: the struggle for victory and the need to overcome hardship and suffering. The literature that followed after 1956, as Piper points out, looked to the problems caused not by the enemy, but by the Soviet system itself.[3] It asked questions about the disastrous retreats of summer 1941 and Stalin's failure to respond to the threat of invasion. It examined the ways in which the Soviet ability to fight the war had been undermined by the terror inflicted on the peasantry as they were forced into collective farms in the early 1930s. It showed how the arrests of large numbers of army officers in 1937 took away experienced commanders, leaving others unwilling to show initiative. The question of the German persecution and murder of Soviet Jews, often with the willing assistance of Soviet citizens, was one of the most controversial issues raised.

Journalism: Grossman as war reporter

Many writers volunteered or were called up to serve as war correspondents, including Ilya Ehrenburg. His predominant concern was with telling Soviet troops about their enemy, sometimes through mockery, but sometimes through condemnation of their vicious and criminal behavior, as in an article of May 1942:

> To us the Hitlerites are not merely enemies: we do not regard them as human beings, but as murderers, executioners, moral degenerates, and cruel fanatics, and that is why we hate them. At the beginning of this unusual war, many of us did not realize the true nature of the people who were invading our country. People . . . naively presumed that we were being attacked by human beings. But they turned out to be monsters who had chosen a death's head for their emblem, young brazen-faced robbers and vandals, who yearned to destroy everything in their path.[4]

Ehrenburg received many letters from soldiers at the front, thanking him for putting their thoughts into words.

Also popular with front-line readers were articles by Vasily Grossman, which concentrated on the actions and experiences of Soviet soldiers. Ehrenburg admired Grossman's work: "In the defense of Stalingrad he found his theme, his heroes, war without any glamour, without the conscious or subconscious romanticism of Kipling, a war which was gloomy, harsh, and honest."[5] Both men were correspondents for the army newspaper *Red Star*. Not all war correspondents took the risks Grossman did, some preferring to remain in the relative safety of headquarters rather than at the front line. This helped him to gain the respect of the soldiers he interviewed. Grossman experienced the disastrous retreat of summer and autumn 1941, escaping on one occasion just before enemy forces arrived, and later spent many months in Stalingrad as the battle for the city raged. Before the German surrender he was sent to territory south of Stalingrad which had just been regained from enemy occupation, where he heard from witnesses evidence of the brutal treatment they had suffered, and unsettling details of collaboration with the enemy. Early in 1944 he joined the Red Army in its advance westward, arriving at his hometown, Berdichev, where most of the town's Jewish inhabitants, including his mother, had been murdered in 1941. Grossman pursued information about the Holocaust, and learned of Ukrainian collaborators who helped occupying German forces to eradicate their Jewish neighbors. His report on the systematic mass murder of Jews at Treblinka in Poland, based on interviews with survivors and local people, was one of the first detailed accounts of the Nazis' "Final Solution." It was widely translated and reprinted, and later used as testimony of the Nazis' crimes against humanity at the Nuremberg Trials.

Grossman's reports for *Red Star* were frequently reprinted in *Pravda*; his Stalingrad articles appeared in book form in 1943. His work was often based on long interviews with soldiers and officers, and drew on their individual perspective to give an impression of the war as experienced by one particular individual. He accompanied the famous Stalingrad sniper Anatoly Chekhov to his post and observed him at work, before writing a lengthy article using Chekhov's own words to describe the minute detail of his daily campaign, and his hesitation over making his first kill:

> "When I first got the rifle, I couldn't bring myself to kill a living being: one German was standing there for about four minutes, talking, and I let him go. When I killed my first one, he fell at once. Another one ran out and stooped over the killed one, and I knocked him down, too ... When I first killed, I was shaking all over: the man was only walking to get some water! ... I felt scared: I'd killed a person! Then I remembered our people and started killing them without mercy."[6]

The picture that emerges of Chekhov is of an individual who is committed to his duty, but who retains human feelings. Grossman focused on the personal rather than on the collective, and rooted his accounts in sober detail. He rejected tales of improbable (and probably untrue) heroics, of the kind that appeared frequently in the early weeks of the war, describing them as: "complete rubbish, with stories such as 'Ivan Pupkin has killed five Germans with a spoon'."[7] The heroism Grossman celebrated was the heroism of Soviet forces at Stalingrad withstanding days of enemy bombardment but continuing to hold their positions and go about their routine business. He describes an army typist from Siberia, Klava Kopylova, who is twice buried by explosions while typing a battle order in a bunker at headquarters, and who nevertheless completes her work and presents the order for the commander's signature.[8] Grossman's attempts to bring readers an accurate account of war often resulted in his articles being altered and distorted by the *Red Star* editorial team, to his intense frustration.[9] His notebooks contain the raw material for his articles, but also details which could not have been published at the time: information about cases of cowardice and desertion, insubordination, and evidence of religious belief among soldiers (in a militantly atheist state). Keeping a record of such details was risky behavior; if discovered, his notebooks would most probably have been seen as criminally "anti-Soviet," but they help to give a more rounded picture of the war, and became a valuable resource for Grossman's novels.

Grossman ran into particular problems when it came to writing about the Nazis' systematic extermination of the Jews in occupied territory. The official Soviet line was that Jews were not to be singled out; all victims of enemy massacres were to be described as Soviet citizens first and foremost. At the same time, the Jewish Antifascist Committee, which included Ilya Ehrenburg among its leaders, was engaged in collecting evidence of Nazi crimes against Jews. Ehrenburg invited Grossman to contribute to the work of the Committee, and Grossman provided a large amount of material to the Committee's planned *Black Book*, which was to present interviews with survivors and other witnesses as evidence of the Holocaust. Grossman had serious difficulties with the censors over his articles "Ukraine without Jews" and "The Killing of Jews in Berdichev," although he was eventually allowed to publish them. The Soviet authorities were uncomfortable with the *Black Book* project, as it raised awkward questions about collaboration and Soviet anti-Semitism. They granted it official approval in summer 1943, probably to a large extent because the project had been suggested by prominent American Jews, including Albert Einstein, but eventually banned it in October 1947 when the USA and the USSR were no longer allies. This was a very clear signal of the anti-Semitic campaign which would follow over the next few years; thirteen members of the Jewish Antifascist Committee were executed in 1952.[10] It was not until 1991 that a Russian-language edition of *The Black Book* was published in Kiev.

Poetry during the war

From the beginning of the war Soviet newspapers printed poetry alongside articles by war correspondents. While many of these poems were of little lasting significance, some of the work that first appeared in wartime newspapers went on to become established classics. By the end of 1941 it was clear that poets were abandoning themes of devotion to the Party and Stalin, as well as exaggerated accounts of heroic exploits. Instead, they began to give their readers a more realistic impression of the experience of war, with the emphasis on the perceptions and emotions of the individual.

Lyric poetry, suppressed for years because it was thought to encourage unhealthy introspection, enjoyed a wartime revival which was welcomed by readers, if not always by critics. In December 1941, Aleksey Surkov published a poem addressed by a soldier in a dugout to his wife far away. Critics took exception to a couple of lines:

> It is not easy for me to reach you.
> But death is only four paces away.[11]

Mention of the possibility of death and of separation from loved ones, it was feared, would undermine soldiers' morale. The popularity of Surkov's poem suggests that his readers did not agree; they responded readily to poetry which reflected their own experiences and feelings. One of the most popular wartime poets was Konstantin Simonov, author of "Wait for Me," a poem many soldiers carried with them or copied in letters to their wives. It is an appeal from a soldier at the front to the woman he loves, asking her to wait for him and to believe that he will one day return home – her faith will guarantee his survival.

Poets also began to write in a far more realistic way about the experience of war at the front, the younger generation often drawing on first-hand experience of conflict. Censors would not allow too graphic a representation of battlefield realities, but poets were able to convey the brutality of the war quite adequately through sparse but telling details. Semyon Gudzenko, who served as a soldier, then a war correspondent, concluded his poem "Before the Attack," written in 1942, as follows:

> Afterwards,
> we swilled down icy vodka,
> and I used a knife to scrape
> from under my fingernails
> another man's blood.[12]

In poems like this, authentic detail acts as a guarantee of emotional authenticity.

There was no shortage of authentic detail in poetry written about the experience of civilians in cities such as Leningrad, where enemy encirclement brought the front line into ordinary people's lives. The Leningrad siege lasted almost three years; its first winter brought severe cold and starvation as well as the constant danger of enemy bombing raids and artillery fire. Olga Berggolts became famous through the poems that she read on Leningrad radio to her audience in the besieged city. Her voice was far better known to them than her face; in late 1938 she had been arrested on political charges and spent several months in prison before her release the following summer. Still considered ideologically suspect, Berggolts had great difficulty publishing her work, until the outbreak of war meant that her skills were needed as part of the war effort.

Her long poem "February Diary" was written in the winter of 1941–42, at a time when her husband was dying of starvation. It took considerable effort to have this work passed by the censors for broadcast and publication because of its bleak descriptions of the Leningraders' predicament. For those in Leningrad, the poem was, if anything, understated, but for the audience in Moscow, unaware of the extent of the city's hardships, it was a shock to learn of the inhuman conditions in which the Leningraders resisted the enemy, cold, and hunger. Yet while Berggolts described the physical hardships she faced with other Leningraders, she also evoked a paradoxical feeling of freedom:

> In dirt, in darkness, in hunger, in sadness,
> where death dragged at our heels like a shadow,
> we were sometimes so happy,
> we breathed such stormy freedom,
> that our grandchildren would have envied us.[13]

It is probably fair to say that the most popular poetic work of the entire war was a narrative poem, published episodically between 1942 and 1945, with an ordinary soldier as its central hero. *Vasily Tyorkin: A Book about a Soldier*, by Aleksandr Tvardovsky, followed its hero as he took part in battles, was wounded, spent time recovering, and returned to join the advance on Berlin. Tyorkin's cheerful resourcefulness makes him an appealing character. He is also strikingly apolitical, making no reference to Stalin or the Party, apart from a single passing mention of the Central Committee and President Kalinin. It is hard to identify him as a figure from the Soviet era at all, something which attracted increasing criticism as the war neared its end.

Vasily Tyorkin is, however, far more than a light-hearted tale of a likable hero. The voice of the narrator features prominently, adding depth through his reflections and comments. A large part of the poem's appeal to readers is in its commitment to bringing them the truth about the war. In the poem's introduction the narrator asks what is most needed in wartime. After a list of several essential items: fresh water, good food, tobacco, humor, he arrives at the answer:

> But what do you need most of all,
> What can you not live without –
> What's that? The essential truth,
> Truth that strikes you to the core,
> Just as long as it's substantial,
> No matter how bitter it might be.[14]

Tvardovsky's poem does not overlook the loss of life that war brought, or the tragedy of soldiers who return to their villages after the enemy had been driven out, to find that their whole family has been killed. Tyorkin's latent subversiveness emerged more fully in a later work, *Tyorkin in the Next World*, published in 1963. This is an account of his journey to the under-world, due to an administrative error rather than his actual death. The next life resembles in its bureaucratic repressiveness the world of the living in the Soviet Union.

The novel: changing perspectives

Tvardovsky was not alone in his use of the war theme to reveal shortcomings in the Soviet system. Deming Brown notes that many war novels of the 1960s "used the conflict to evaluate the recent past and, by implication, the present."[15] But as the end of the war came in sight, Soviet literary critics were on the lookout for the epic novel that would do justice to the heroic scale of the war against Hitler's Germany, and give due recognition to the role of the Communist Party, led by Stalin, in bringing this victory about. They called for a twentieth-century version of Tolstoy's *War and Peace*. Such vast and wide-ranging novels took a long time to emerge. Literature in wartime was pre-occupied with giving an immediate response to events while they were still in progress; the broader perspective had to wait. Most prose fiction written during the war was short and focused on a single limited aspect of the war. While some novels did emerge while the war was still in progress, including Grossman's *For a Just Cause*, serialized in *Red Star*, most of them appeared well after the war was over.

One of the best early pieces of war fiction was Viktor Nekrasov's *In the Trenches of Stalingrad*, published in 1945. The author was rewarded with a Stalin Prize in 1947, although what he wrote was rather different from most of the works published about the war in the early postwar years. It is a soberly realistic, semi-autobiographical account, from the point of view of the first-person narrator Lieutenant Kerzhentsev, of the near-disaster at Stalingrad; the narrative ends before the final victory, and is focused on the fate of a small group of soldiers. Like Tvardovsky's *Vasily Tyorkin*, Nekrasov's work makes few gestures in the direction of conventional Soviet pieties. It even implies that one of the characters, the resourceful Valega, is the son of dispossessed kulaks who has served a term in a labor camp. The emphasis is on the war as a people's war, with ordinary people bearing the burden of sacrifice and hard-ship to bring about victory. Stalin features only as a portrait kept in a dead soldier's dugout next to a portrait of the author Jack London; Kerzhentsev takes the latter with him, but leaves the former behind.

In the early postwar years there was a concerted effort to make writers fall into line with the Party's view of the victory and of postwar priorities.

Emphasis was shifted from war heroes to portraying the achievements of the civilian population instead, echoing Stalin's actions to neutralize any potential threat to his leadership from leading military figures. His postwar treatment of several celebrated wartime generals ranged from demotion to execution. As the Cold War began, narratives of the war were devised which made the Western allies look as though they were already engaged in the Cold War; they were portrayed as little better than Nazis, capitalist plotters scheming to destroy the Soviet Union. Nekrasov's book about Stalingrad was already at odds with the official line that the victory was owed to the tactical genius of Stalin and the Party's wise leadership. Grossman's *For a Just Cause* was published in book form in 1952 and attracted criticism because it said little about the Party's contribution to the victory, and made no mention at all of Stalin. Other authors, including Aleksandr Fadeyev, a loyal member of the official literary establishment, found that the authorities were prepared to interfere so as to ensure writers took the correct approach. Fadeyev's novel *The Young Guard*, based on the true story of an underground resistance group organized by young people in an occupied city, had to be rewritten because it gave insufficient attention to the role of the Party. The initial version of 1945 suggests that the Party proved ineffective in the face of enemy occupation; the revised version of 1951 builds up the role of the Party as mentor to the young members of the Resistance.

Most of the war fiction published in the first postwar decade was made to serve the ends of Stalinist propaganda. It was only after public criticism of Stalin in 1956 that a new wave of war novels began to appear which were concerned far less with the struggle against the enemy than with internal conflicts and the individual psychology of the soldier. Authors like Grigory Baklanov, Iury Bondarenko, Konstantin Simonov, and Vasil Bykau took the tendencies already evident in wartime literature towards greater realism and a focus on the individual, and developed them further. In their novels they highlight the problems caused at the start of the war by military unpreparedness, a result of Stalin's unwillingness to act on warnings of an imminent invasion, and show how the rigid and suspicious thinking of military commanders led to the squandering of lives and resources. Their work often focuses on a single hero or small group of characters placed in a situation of extreme crisis, and portrays war as a nightmarish physical, psychological, and moral ordeal. Critics attacked them for showing a partial and distorted version of the war, and admired instead the formulaic productions by novelists such as Ivan Stadnyuk, who produced panoramic accounts of wartime heroism, and did not raise awkward questions about the Party or the system.

Vasily Grossman's *Life and Fate*, completed in 1960, is written on an epic scale, with a large cast of characters. This is the novel most deserving of being seen as the twentieth-century *War and Peace*. It shows both the heroism and the tragedy of the war. As well as depicting the battle at Stalingrad, it shows the life of a physicist's family in Moscow, Soviet prisoners in a German concentration camp, and the last days in the life of a Jewish boy as he is transported from the ghetto to the extermination camp. Grossman raises unsettling questions, including the idea that the Stalinist and Nazi systems are fundamentally the same. It was emphatically not the kind of novel that the Soviet critics of 1945 had been expecting. When it was submitted for publication to a Moscow literary journal, the authorities moved to confiscate all the manuscript copies of the book they could find, and all the typewriter ribbons used to produce it, telling its author that his work would not see the light of day for at least two hundred years. Their prediction was far from accurate: *Life and Fate* was published in Switzerland in 1980, and eight years later it appeared in the Soviet Union, thanks to the liberal policies of Mikhail Gorbachev.

The novel is centered on the battle for Stalingrad, where victory marked a turning point of the war, and the Soviet state began to feel secure enough to assert itself once more. The novel shows the hopes for change that people felt, and particularly the freedom discovered by a small group of military personnel fighting in an isolated outpost behind enemy lines in Stalingrad. At the same time, it shows that these hopes were illusory. There are plenty of incidents that show the dehumanizing and humiliating effects of the totalitarian system on the novel's many characters. The tank commander Novikov delays an attack by eight minutes to avoid incurring unnecessary casualties; his action saves lives, but he is denounced by a commissar for disobeying orders. The physicist Viktor Shtrum is confronted by the need to make humiliating compromises. He also encounters the state's anti-Semitism (rather in advance of the actual anti-Semitic campaigns). Grossman's guilt at not having invited his mother to come and live at his small Moscow flat, when escape from the advancing enemy had still been an option, is mirrored in Shtrum, whose mother dies in precisely the same circumstances.

Life and Fate can be distinguished from the majority of Soviet war literature by the way it sets the war in a broad historical context, looking backwards to the terror of the 1930s, as well as forward to the repressive chauvinism of the late Stalin era. Piper sums up the narrative trajectory of *Life and Fate* as follows: "The novel plots the erosion of patriotism and liberty, as a chauvinistic, anti-Semitic nationalism is deliberately grafted onto the cynical predatoriness of the 1930s."[16] Grossman, of course, was writing with the benefit of hindsight, something that was not available to him when he was chronicling events at the front line as they unfolded, or to the poets whose work can be read rather like a seismograph, charting the emotions of a nation at war.

Whether it takes in a broad panorama or focuses on a single moment, Soviet war literature reveals the complex ways in which the war was represented and interpreted. While the state exerted pressure on writers to show a heroic conflict which demonstrated the virtues of Soviet man and the system, writers continued to draw on the legacy of wartime literature in order to represent the war with integrity and honesty, and to question received opinions and values. Ultimately, instead of confirming the version of reality promoted by Stalinist propaganda, the most enduring works of Soviet war literature offered an alternative view. The war theme, which the authorities intended to promote in officially acceptable literature, proved to be a powerful weapon in the service of artistic, psychological, and moral change.

NOTES

1. Don Piper, "Soviet Union," in *The Second World War in Fiction*, ed. Holger Klein (London: Macmillan, 1984), p. 144.
2. Adam Ulam, *Stalin: the Man and his Era* (New York: Viking Press, 1973), p. 630.
3. Piper, "Soviet Union," p. 163.
4. Ilya Ehrenburg, "Hatred," *Russia at War* (London: Hamish Hamilton, 1943), pp. 130–1.
5. Quoted in Frank Ellis, *Vasiliy Grossman: The Genesis and Evolution of a Soviet Heretic* (Oxford and Providence: Berg, 1994), p. 62.
6. Vasily Grossman, *A Writer at War: Vasily Grossman with the Red Army 1941–1945*, ed. and trans. Antony Beevor and Luba Vinogradova (London: Pimlico, 2006), p. 157.
7. *Ibid.*, p. 9.
8. *Ibid.*, pp. 181–2.
9. *Ibid.*, p. 198.
10. *Ibid.*, p. 349.
11. Aleksey Surkov, "In the Small Stove," my translation. See also Aleksey Surkov, "In the Small Stove," in *Russian Poetry 1917–1955*, ed. and trans. Jack Lindsay (London: Bodley Head, 1957), p. 117.
12. Semyon Gudzenko, "Before the Attack," my translation. See also Semyon Gudzenko, "Before the Attack," trans. Gordon McVay, in *Twentieth-Century Russian Poetry*, ed. Albert C. Todd and Max Hayward (London: Fourth Estate, 1993), pp. 711–12.
13. Olga Berggolts, "February Diary," my translation. See also Olga Berggolts, "February Diary," trans. Walter May, in *Soviet War Poetry*, ed. L. Lazarev (Moscow: Progress, 1976), p. 55.
14. Aleksandr Tvardovsky, *Vasily Tyorkin: A Book about a Soldier*, my translation. See also Aleksandr Tvardovsky, *Vasily Tyorkin: A Book about a Soldier*, trans. Jill Higgs (Spalding: Hub Editions, 2003), p. 2.
15. Deming Brown, *Soviet Russian Literature Since Stalin* (Cambridge University Press, 1978), p. 271.
16. Piper, "Soviet Union," p. 169.

9

ROBERT S. C. GORDON

The Italian war

Italy's war

In standard histories, the Second World War is dated from 1939 to 1945, from Germany's invasion of Poland to surrender in Berlin and atom bombs over Hiroshima and Nagasaki. But global chronologies can obscure local histories, and often a simple adjustment of dates is useful as a first step towards understanding the particularities of a single nation's experience of the war and the literary representations that came out of it. The chronology of Italy's Second World War was complex and fragmented, producing distinct layers of memory and representation (and, indeed, silence and oblivion) within its war literature. So, if we were to start with a bald chronological adjustment to reflect this complexity, we should first replace 1939–45 with something like: 1940–43/45.

Mussolini's regime – in power since 1922 (and in full dictatorial control since 1926) – had been the founding model of modern, Fascist totalitarianism and a key inspiration for Hitler's Nazi movement and rise to power. By 1939, Fascist Italy had long been talking of war, militarizing its youth, and fighting colonial or proxy wars (Ethiopia, Spain). It had formally allied itself to Nazi Germany in the Axis Pact of Steel in May 1939. However, when war was declared in September, Italy's armed forces were, in reality, drastically under-prepared and ill equipped and could not hope to respect the Axis pact. Only when the astonishing Nazi sweep across Europe seemed to herald victory did Mussolini hastily join battle, in June 1940, invading southern France. In the following three years, Italy fought in several European and African theatres (Greece, Ethiopia, Egypt, Libya) and in the doomed Axis advance into Russia of 1941–43, and administered various occupied territories (parts of the Balkans, France); but in almost every arena, they were dogged by failure, leading to rescue or retreat. By mid-1943, the pressures of these failures – and the increasing likelihood of Axis defeat – were accentuated by food shortages, workers' protests, and, worse still, by the Allied landings in Sicily in July. This was the last straw and, after nearly twenty-one years of rule, Mussolini was deposed by his own Fascist Grand Council on July 25, 1943. A great deal of public euphoria[1] and institutional delay, weakness, and uncertainty followed, until, on September 8, Mussolini's successor Marshal Badoglio declared an armistice with the Allies. Formally at least, Italy's war (1940–43) was over.

In reality, the fighting was far from over. Over the ensuing eighteen months (1943–45), Italy became a theatre of war, split between *de facto* occupying Nazis in the north and center, and Allied forces advancing slowly from the south. Almost the entire Italian army was left stranded without orders, close to now hostile German forces, who promptly imprisoned 800,000 of them. Mussolini was rescued by the Germans and reinstalled in the north as a puppet leader of a "new" Fascist republic (the "Republic of Salò"). A mass partisan resistance campaign emerged, with the active involvement of tens of thousands of Italians and networks of support of hundreds of thousands and more. The best organized and most numerous sector of the Resistance was communist-led, but there were also monarchist, Catholic, liberal-socialist, and other formations. As the Allies fought hard battles all the way up the Italian peninsula, the partisans made telling contributions to the liberation campaign. Rome – nominally an "open city" from 1943, but for all intents and purposes German-occupied – was liberated on June 4, 1944; Florence on August 11. Italy's liberation was complete on April 25, 1945. Days later, Mussolini was captured in flight by partisans and was summarily executed, his body hanged upside-down in Piazzale Loreto in Milan.

The home nation – twice invaded – had been turned once again into a territory over which other powers fought, as it had been for centuries before unification in 1861. But, all the while, Italy was still fighting its own wars. In an influential formulation, historian Claudio Pavone argued that three over-lapping wars were being fought in Italy between 1943 and 1945: a patriotic war of liberation against the Germans; a class war fought by an oppressed people dreaming of revolution; and a *de facto* civil war between partisan Italians and Italians who stayed loyal to Fascism and the Salò Republic.[2] In amongst these wars, the Resistance offered a kernel of possible national redemption – of Italy taking control of its destiny – that would be of extra-ordinary importance in the memories, histories, and literature of the war to come (and in the politics of postwar Italy also).

War literature: three fields

The literature of the Second World War in Italian[3] inevitably reflects the wide range of experiences and sites of action and struggle set out above. It shares many general aspects of the literature of twentieth-century "total" warfare, in which violence encroached so directly on the everyday lives of mass populations, including women, children, and the elderly, and in which mass conscript armies were sent to fight across thousands of miles, to sites of empires and colonies. It followed other literatures in producing a flow of non-fictional, non-literary autobiographical writing by "ordinary" men and women, each with extraordinary experiences to relate, alongside works of war *literature* as such. National war literatures inevitably acquire distinct characteristics and emphases also, however; in particular in the way they are necessarily selective and incomplete in their scope, clustering, in symptomatic fashion, around key localized events or fields (and ignoring certain others), as they build shared narratives of the war. In the case of Italy, we can identify three fields of this kind, three dominant experiences and narrative paradigms within its war literature: the fighting war (in particular, the Russian campaign); imprisonment (of soldiers, partisans, and, particularly, Jewish survivors of genocide); and – casting its shadow over the other two – the Resistance (and other wars) of 1943–45.[4]

I. The fighting war: Russia, Europe, and the home front

One writer and one book in particular was responsible for giving voice to the appalling stories of 200,000 Italian troops involved in the advance on and retreat from Russia between mid-1941 and early 1943, and for rooting that campaign in collective memory as an emblem of the devastating experience of ordinary soldiers on the ground, in a war incompetently run and lost from above.[5] The book was Mario Rigoni Stern's 1953 memoir, *The Sergeant in the Snow*.

Rigoni Stern, a native of the northeastern Italian mountains, had fought in France, Greece, and Albania and would later write about all of these, but it was his account of Russia that struck the most resonant chord. The book is loosely shaped and decidedly oral and diaristic in its language and story-telling, focusing on details of equipment, food, communication, rotas, or makeshift Christmas and New Year celebrations, as much as on occasional flashes of action, gunfire, and death. The narrative slowly builds towards the long, appalling sequence of the retreat of December 1942–January 1943. It is, crucially, choral: naming and gathering around the author-protagonist a grouping of young soldiers from different parts of Italy, with different accents and dialects, sketched in vignettes and stock phrases that are caricatural, but also intensely and memorably human. There's the Venetian, Giuanin, for example, who (echoing stock Venetian comedy characters) looks up to the rather patrician young officer Rigoni, asking "Sergeant-Major, shall we ever get home?" (in broad Venetian, "Sergentmagiú, ghe rivarem a baita?").[6] Meanwhile, Rigoni's physical and moral exhaustion builds to extremes, in the minus-30-degree cold and the sleepless, foot-slogging confusion of the retreat. The book starkly captures elements of landscape around the river Don – the open skies and huddled Ukrainian villages, with their wooden huts or *isbas* – through which what is left of the Italian force flees and fragments, with Germans, Russians, and Hungarians often commingled with them.

Rigoni Stern – like other soldier-writers such as Nuto Revelli (and indeed their friend the survivor-writer Primo Levi) – was a respected but relatively marginalized figure in postwar literary circles in Italy; in part because literary intellectuals are naturally suspicious of the non-literary narratives of "real" lives; but in part also because the fighting war of 1940–43, the Fascist war fought alongside the Germans, was hard to assimilate into a new vision of Italy founded on the collapse of that war and the redemption of the Resistance against the Germans. There are precious few narratives of recruitment or training or the journey to war in Italian, for example. But, somehow, the Russian campaign managed to slip through the censoring mechanism, especially narratives of human dignity and loss of life in the face of defeat and retreat, such as Rigoni Stern's, which established the Russian front as part of that narrative of the collapse of Fascism.

One work, however, stands as an extraordinary exception to the pattern of censorship in the collective memory of the wider European war and Italy's role in it; a semi-journalistic, semi-literary text which is one of the most vibrant, jarring, and mannered of all accounts of the Second World War: Curzio Malaparte's *Kaputt* (1944).[7]

Kaputt flits around the vast expanse of Axis Europe, following the military progress, the grotesque violence, and the sometimes absurd socialite grandeur of the occupying powers and their military élite. Malaparte was a war correspondent and former Fascist (and later Communist). His mercurial character and his travels across Europe at war – including witnessing the genocide of the Jews at first hand – are reflected in the dark, expressionistic style of *Kaputt*. In the following extract, set in the Ukraine – the same part of Europe as Rigoni Stern's chronicle – the narrator sees for the first time the signs of defeat in the faces of German soldiers:

> It had been raining for days and days and the sea of Ukrainian mud slowly spread beyond the horizon . . .
>
> The Germans soldiers returning from the front line, when they reached the village squares, dropped their rifles down in silence. They were coated from head to foot in black mud, their beards were long, their hollow eyes looked like the eyes of the sunflowers, blank and dull. The officers gazed at the soldiers and

at the rifles lying on the ground, and kept silent. By then, the lightning war, the *Blitzkrieg*, was over, the *Dreissigjährigerblitzkrieg*, the thirty-year lightning war had begun. The winning war was over, the losing war had begun. I saw the white stain of fear growing in [their] dull eyes.[8]

Malaparte's merciless dissection of the transition in the Germans, visible in their very physiognomy, from a "winning war" to a "losing war" in part slyly redeems Italy and Italianness in the face of both German and Russian barbarity. But it is inevitably also, at one and the same time, a coded description of Italy's very own "losing war."[9]

The same predicate of defeat and desolation governs narratives of war violence as it intruded into civilian rather than military lives. In Cesare Pavese's 1948 novel, *The House on the Hill*, there is an account of the morning after an Allied bombing raid on Turin. The protagonist, Corrado, enters the city from the surrounding hills, and surveys the damage:

> I returned to the city next morning with a crowd of people, to the distant accompaniment of roars and explosions. People were running everywhere and carrying bundles with them. The asphalt of the avenues was pitted with holes, scattered with layers of leaves, and here and there were pools of water. It looked as if there had been a violent hailstorm. The last conflagrations were crackling raw and red in the clear light of day.
>
> The School was, as usual, still intact ...
>
> A cyclist came by, put his feet down and told us that Turin had been completely destroyed. "Thousands dead," he told us. "They have smashed up the station, gutted the markets. It's been given out on the wireless that they will be returning tonight." And he pedalled off without looking back.[10]

The images of everyday life – commuting into the city, the morning damage looking like a hailstorm, school carrying on as normal, chatting in the street – mingle with explosions in the distance, fires burning on, and warnings of thousands dead, neatly capturing the mix of ordinary and extraordinary thrown up by this war. Shortly afterwards, Corrado neutrally admits that "the war was lost."[11] As winter sets in a few weeks later, he spots a rat, sitting atop a heap of rubble, insouciant: the world of humans has now, thanks to the war, become his habitat, all putrid rubble.

Rigoni Stern, Malaparte, and Pavese are all, in very different ways, interested in the violence of war and its effect on individuals: a final element worth noting in the literature is the return of an ancient, misogynist facet of war violence and a mythical topos in its representation: rape. Rape is, in history and in representation, all too central to women's experience of war, and is shown as a defining trauma in an important cluster of literary narratives from Alberto Moravia's *Two Women* (1957) to Elsa Morante's *History* (1974).[12]

II. Imprisonment and return

Rigoni Stern was imprisoned by the Germans after the Armistice from 1943 until 1945, one of approximately 1,300,000 Italians who were prisoners of either the Germans or the Allies by the end of the war.[13] Slowly over the postwar era, stories of imprisonment – for the most part stories of the vast system of Nazi camps[14] – emerged as a further key thread of writing about the war. As with the literature of military combat, these stories at first struggled to find space beside Resistance narratives. Where the latter were home-centered, proactive, and future-oriented, the literature of imprisonment was predicated on defeat, inaction, loss of homeland. It is telling how many accounts from the approximately 4,000 political deportees who survived (out of 40,000) – the earliest category of prisoner to gain a foothold within Italian war literature – were at anxious pains to assert that their Resistance fight, their ideals for a new Italy, continued unaltered at Mauthausen or similar.[15]

Within the panorama of prisoner literature, a role of special importance must be reserved for the testimonies from the approximately 1,000 Italian Jews who survived Auschwitz or other concentration camps where the Nazi genocide was enacted. If, in the immediate postwar years, relatively little separate attention was paid to the "Final Solution to the Jewish Question" within literary accounts, the latter has loomed ever larger in the literature and cultural consciousness of the war, in Italy as elsewhere, in the late twentieth century and beyond.

One of the central, emblematic figures in any canon of Holocaust writing is Primo Levi. Having fought briefly in the Resistance, Levi was captured and deported to Auschwitz in February 1944. The Russians liberated the camp in January 1945 and on his return to Turin nine months later, Levi began writing down the stories that would become his first work, *If This Is a Man* (1947).[16] The book was famously turned down by the major publisher of war and Resistance literature in Italy, Einaudi (note its prevalence in the endnotes to this chapter), reinforcing the sense of misconception of the significance of the genocide at this time.

Although Levi suggested that the book had been put together in a cathartic rush, it now appears as one of the most lucid analyses and one of the most terrible evocations of the physical and psychological experience of the Holocaust victim. The very title of the book, and the prefatory poem from which it is taken, establish Levi's interest in the systematic destruction of human identity wrought by the Nazis:

> Consider if this is a man
> Who works in the mud
> Who does not know peace

Who fights for a scrap of bread
Who dies because of a yes or a no.
Consider if this is a woman
Without hair and without name
With no more strength to remember
Her eyes empty and her womb cold
Like a frog in winter.[17]

The book takes us on a journey – in place, body, and mind – from selfhood and normality (a world of choice, doubt, and action, as Levi briefly describes his partisan days) to abjection. Each stage he passes through strips away some core element of identity. The train journey, the arrival, the initial selections for work or for death, the showers, the shaving, the tattooing, the assignment to work, the deceptions and cruelties of other prisoners: each brings loss of dignity, privacy, autonomy, individuality, solidarity, and humanity. Levi is especially alert to systems and patterns of behavior in the camp – its languages, its economies, its structures of power, its morality, the balance between competition and (rare) cooperation – and also to a residual sense of "ordinary" humanity and its habits:

consider what value, what meaning is enclosed even in the smallest of our daily habits, in the hundred possessions which even the poorest beggar owns: a handkerchief, an old letter, the photo of a cherished person ... Imagine now a man who is deprived of everyone he loves, and at the same time of his house, his habits, his clothes, in short, of everything he possesses: he will be a hollow man.[18]

The Eliotic "hollow man" (*uomo vuoto*) reaches an extreme in the figure of the so-called *Muselmann*, the ghost-like prisoner who has lost all will to resist. And here the abjection of identity is explicitly linked by Levi to his time, to twentieth-century modernity, and therefore to the global significance of this "Event" within the events of the Second World War:

[The *Muselmänner*] crowd my memory with their faceless presences, and if I could enclose all the evil of our time in one image, I would choose this image, which is familiar to me: an emaciated man, with head dropped and shoulders curved, on whose face and in whose eyes not a trace of thought is to be seen.[19]

If Levi became by far the most powerful and best-known writer on the genocide to come out of Italy, there were, nevertheless, others also bearing witness in important ways. A literary critic, Giacomo Debenedetti, wrote a pellucid short account of the roundup and deportation of over a thousand Jews in Rome in 1943. It was published in 1945 with the simple title *16 October 1943* and marks the start of a long process of integrating the persecution of the Jews in Italy into a national narrative and a national literature.[20] There is also a fascinating grouping of works by Italian Jewish women survivors, such as Liana Millu's *Smoke Over Birkenau* and Giuliana Tedeschi's *There is a Place on this Earth*.[21]

Levi's second book, *The Truce* (1963),[22] told the story of his long, meandering journey of return to Italy across a devastated Europe. The literature of return was a fundamental corollary to the literature of imprisonment. Within this category, even the several hundred thousand interned Italian soldiers found an early voice in an extraordinary 1945 play by the Neapolitan dramatist Edoardo de Filippo, *Napoli milionaria!*,[23] which centers on the return from a German camp of Gennaro, his mind close to collapse, who finds his family mired in the corruptions and temptations of the black market and prostitution. The family's story is also the story of the nation as it recovers from the moral, psychological, and material devastations of war.

III. The Resistance

The Resistance dominated Italian war literature for at least three reasons. First, it marked a dramatic break in Italians' relation to the state, the nation, and the war. Many moved from passive acquiescence to active resistance or even, as in the case of Nuto Revelli, from active fighting for Fascism to active fighting against it (Revelli became a key Resistance leader and later a key Resistance writer). It was the single most significant source of the rebirth of a positive idea of Italian national identity: its anti-Fascist ideals (despite deep ideological differences between its constituent elements) shaped the political culture of the postwar Italian Republic. Secondly, the collective experience and stories of the Resistance were crucial catalysts in forming the most influential cultural movement in postwar Italy, neo-realism, a moment of creativity, public commitment, and heartfelt, shared sentiment amongst writers and the reading public. Thirdly, the *literature* (as opposed to the public rhetoric) of the Resistance was particularly important in complicating the understanding of the role of violence in war. A myth or civic religion grew up around the Resistance (especially on the left),[24] and at times Resistance literature followed this, proposing narratives of "good" partisan violence – a heroic struggle for liberation against overwhelming odds, for the good of the nation (or group or class) – as opposed to the "bad" violence – the violence of pure power and oppression – of the Nazis and Fascists. In more interesting cases, however, writers showed an acute awareness, well before historians opened up this issue, of the moral difficulty of narratives of good violence.

One novel which contributed to the myth of the Resistance, as well as fitting in with certain aspects of neo-realist modes of writing, was Elio Vittorini's *Men and Not Men* (1945),[25] a story of Milanese partisans. *Men and Not Men* is characterized by a restless formal experimentalism and complexity. Nevertheless, it has a clear-cut sense of the rights and wrongs of the struggle depicted: the partisans are, as Vittorini would have it, "men," whereas the enemy are monstrous, non-human in some way. This issue – the humanity or otherwise of the enemy and/or the victim – and indeed its very vocabulary ("*uomo*," man or human being) were crucial focal points in political and moral inquiry about the meanings and consequences of the war. For example, Vittorini's title was self-consciously echoed in the title and content of Levi's *If This Is a Man. Men and Not Men* culminates in the death of its protagonist, a sacrifice made in the cause of the Resistance and a better future, not uncommon in positive, redemptive narratives of the Resistance.

The focus on men flags up also, if only by contrast, an emphasis in some Resistance literature on the active role women played in the struggle. Film rather than literature provided the most resonant icon for this role: Anna Magnani's Pina in Rossellini's film *Rome, Open City* (1945); but there are equivalent figures in literature also. Cate, in Pavese's *House on the Hill*, and the eponymous hero of Renata Viganò's *L'Agnese va a morire*[26] both stand at the center of local networks and communities which feed into the Resistance and both pay the price, in capture or death.

The rhetoric of "good violence" seen in many novels and memoirs from the early postwar years contrasts with a gently mocking or ironic treatment of the partisans, many of whom were presented in some other accounts as inexpert, immature, and improvised. These texts began the process of constructing a more complicated and human picture of the partisan war, which then gathered pace in work from the 1960s onwards. Italo Calvino's first novel, *The Path to the Nest of Spiders* (1947),[27] centers on a boy, Pin, his prostitute sister, and a shambolic partisan group made up of former crooks. Luigi Meneghello's autobiographical *The Outlaws* (1964)[28] is decidedly effective in deflating heroic rhetoric surrounding the Resistance, as is the work of perhaps the most significant of all Resistance writers, Beppe Fenoglio. His major work (compiled posthumously from a complicated array of manuscripts) was *Johnny the Partisan* (1968),[29] an epic portrayal of the Piedmontese landscape and its partisans, which uses an elaborate language much influenced by English and local dialect. Fenoglio had first published a collection of Resistance stories in 1952, where his ironic lightness of touch was already evident. Here is the opening of the title story:

Alba was taken by 2000 men on 10 October and lost by 200 men on 2 November 1944.
  In the first days of October, the Republican [i.e. Fascist] garrison, feeling drained by the stranglehold of the partisans in the hills around ... got the priests

to tell the partisans that they would leave, as long as they could be guaranteed safe passage out. The partisans accepted and on the morning of 10 October, the garrison cleared out.

The Republicans crossed the river Tanaro with arms and packs, watching their backs to make sure the partisans weren't following them a little too closely ... Then, once they had reached the opposite riverbank and nothing of theirs remained on this side except the settling dust, they stopped, turned towards the free city of Alba and shouted in unison: "Traitors, bastards, renegades, we'll come back and hang every one of you!"[30]

The comic vein of Calvino, Meneghello, and Fenoglio (all of whom fought as partisans) was rich and subtle, but it had its limits as a means of profound inquiry into the Resistance and its nature as war. For the latter, we can turn again to Pavese and especially his last two novels, *The House on the Hill* (1948) and *The Moon and the Bonfire* (1950).[31] In the former, Corrado is gradually drawn away from Turin and into the hills in his attempt to escape the war and the Resistance (and responsibility).[32] But in the hills, Corrado finds ever more confusion and violence. Confronted with the dead bodies of enemy soldiers, he is forced to reflect on the leveling nature of death, since a body is no longer either a partisan or a Fascist, but a demand for a moral defense: "every war is a civil war: every man who falls resembles the one who survives and calls him to account."[33] *The Moon and the Bonfire* takes this universalizing sense of the violence of the Resistance a step further, culminating in the revelation of the strange, ritual death of a (woman) collaborator, who is burned by the partisans in a horrific reprise of a seasonal ritual of sacrifice. Pavese's anthropology of violence offers an alternative to the model of ideological, symbolic sacrifice "for the cause" suggested by many Resistance narratives.

The choice

The Moon and the Bonfire is a story of return, but not of a return from war: the protagonist, nicknamed Anguilla ("Eel"), has returned to his native Piedmont hills after twenty years in America (one of Italy's many millions of modern emigrants). He and the novel's readers have to excavate the obscure, buried recent history of war, Resistance and civil war, of betrayal and violence, through the tight-lipped memories of those who stayed in his village and lived through it. Pavese committed suicide shortly after completing the novel, but the scene that it set – of the war and especially the Resistance as a site for competing and fraught memory and history, individual and collective – offers a powerful figure for Italy's postwar era and its representations of war.

As already noted, the dominant mode of war literature for the immediate postwar era was, broadly, realist and Resistance-centered. There was relatively little (or relatively little notice was taken of) literature engaged with returning prisoners or with the military campaigns; just as within the democratic, anti-Fascist cultural consensus of the postwar period, there was a relatively weak sense of a break or thorough confrontation with the Fascist period as a whole. Social and cultural changes throughout the postwar era, however, were inevitably reflected in the shifting ground of war representations, prompting new interest in, for example, the recovery of individual or marginal histories – histories of women, of racial victims, of military internees and other prisoners, and so on. Perhaps the most dramatic shift of all came as the ideological schemas of the Cold War broke down after 1989, and as the fiftieth anniversary of the Liberation approached (and, indeed, as former neo-Fascists entered the government). Forms of revisionism took hold in Italy and changed, for good and ill, the terms of representation of Fascism and anti-Fascism, stretching the foci of both histories and memories of them, and also forms of narrative about them. Thus, one of the most powerful war narratives of the end of the century was a work not of fictional narrative but of oral history; Alessandro Portelli's *The Order Has Been Carried Out* (1999), on the Nazi massacre of 335 Romans in the Fosse Ardeatine in early 1944, in reprisal for a Resistance attack which killed 33 German soldiers.[34] Most charged of all, though, has been the attempt to reclaim and rehumanize the young soldiers who ended up – by an accident of history, according to the revisionists – fighting for the Salò Republic. For many, this blurring between the so-called "Red" (Resistance) and "Black" (Fascist) sides has been anathema, a blind moral relativism. For others, though, this has been a way of rereading war narratives as a profound inquiry into national identity and national history, seen especially from the perspective of one moment, in autumn 1943, when the institutions of the nation and the state abandoned its people – one historian has called this moment "the Death of the Nation"[35] – and millions of Italians were faced with a terrible moral, political, and historical choice: to fight or not to fight, and for which Italy?

One of the greatest of all Second World War poems in Italian, Eugenio Montale's "The Dream of the Prisoner" had already dramatized, in the emblematic setting of a German prison camp in 1943, this same choice, which has come to seem to encapsulate in a single moral decision the historical problematic of Italy's war:

> They say that if we recant and sign up
> we can avoid the goose cull;
> that if we declare our guilt, but betray

and sell the flesh of others, the ladle will be ours
and we'll not end in the soup
served up to the pestilential Gods . . .

and the blows still come and the footsteps,
and I still don't know if I will come to the feast
to eat my fill or be eaten. The wait is long,
my dream of you is not over.[36]

NOTES

1. Several works of war literature spend pages evoking this illusory moment of freedom and euphoria: see, for example, Cesare Pavese, *La casa in collina*, first published as part of *Prima che il gallo canti* ["Before the Cock Crows"] (Turin: Einaudi, 1948); *The House on the Hill* (London: Peter Owen, 1956), pp. 57ff.; or Alberto Moravia, *Il conformista* (Milan: Bompiani, 1951); *The Conformist* (London: Secker & Warburg, 1952), pp. 291ff.

2. Claudio Pavone, *Una guerra civile. Saggio storico sulla moralità della Resistenza* (Turin: Bollati Boringhieri, 1991). For a general survey, see Philip Cooke, ed., *The Italian Resistance: An Anthology* (Manchester University Press, 1997).

3. This chapter is about literature in Italian. It is worth noting, however, a seam of war literature in English about Italy, often written by participants in the Allied Italian campaign. See, for example, autobiographical work such as Norman Lewis, *Naples '44* (London: Collins, 1978) and Eric Newby, *Love and War in the Apennines* (London: Hodder & Stoughton, 1971) (both had important subsequent careers as travel writers and novelists). See also the (often stereotypical) use of Italy or Italians in English-language war fiction (with a Great-War precursor in Hemingway's *Farewell to Arms* [1929]), from Joseph Heller, *Catch-22* (New York: Simon & Schuster, 1961) to Louis De Bernières, *Captain Corelli's Mandolin* (London: Secker & Warburg, 1994) and Michael Ondaatje, *The English Patient* (London: Bloomsbury, 1992).

4. On Italian war literature in general, see chapters in Helmut Peitsch, Charles Burdett, and Clare Gorrara, eds., *European Memories of The Second World War* (Oxford: Berghahn Books, 1999).

5. In this respect, Russian-front literature resembled the literature of the Great War: see, for instance, Emilio Lussu, *Un anno sull'altipiano* (Paris: Edizioni italiane di cultura, 1938); *Sardinian Brigade* (New York: Knopf, 1939).

6. Mario Rigoni Stern, *Il sergente nella neve. Ricordi della ritirata di Russia* (Turin: Einaudi, 1953); *The Sergeant in the Snow* (London: MacGibbon & Kee, 1954), p. 20.

7. Curzio Malaparte, *Kaputt* (Naples: Casella, 1944); (London: Alvin Redman, 1948). See William Hope, *Curzio Malaparte* (Market Harborough: Troubador, 2000).

8. Malaparte, *Kaputt*, p. 204.

9. Cf. Wolfgang Schivelbusch, *The Culture of Defeat: On National Trauma, Mourning and Recovery* (London: Granta, 2003).

10. Pavese, *House*, pp. 22–3. On Pavese, see Doug Thompson, *Cesare Pavese* (Cambridge University Press, 1982).

11. Pavese, *House*, p. 25.

12. Alberto Moravia, *La Ciociara* (Milan: Bompiani, 1957); *Two Women* (London: Secker & Warburg, 1958); Elsa Morante, *La storia* (Turin: Einaudi, 1974); *History* (London: Allen Lane, 1978).

13. Agostino Bistarelli, *La storia del ritorno* (Turin: Bollati Boringhieri, 2007), pp. 38–41.

14. For a rare literary product from Allied POWs, see Vittorio Sereni's 1947 collection *Algerian Diary, The Selected Poetry and Prose of Vittorio Sereni* (University of Chicago Press, 2007), pp. 75–115.

15. See Robert S. C. Gordon, "Holocaust Writing in Context: Italy 1945–47," in *The Holocaust and The Text: Speaking the Unspeakable,* ed. Andrew Leak and George Paizis (London: Macmillan, 1999), pp. 34–6.

16. Primo Levi, *Se questo è un uomo* (Turin: De Silva, 1947; 2nd edn, Turin: Einaudi, 1958); *If This Is a Man* (London: Penguin, 1979; 1st edn 1959; also known in the US as *Survival in Auschwitz*). For the best introduction to Levi, see Mirna Cicioni, *Primo Levi: Bridges of Knowledge* (Oxford: Berg, 1995).

17. Levi, *If This Is a Man*, p. 17.

18. *Ibid.*, p. 33.

19. *Ibid.*, p. 96.

20. Giacomo Debenedetti, *16 ottobre 1943* (Rome: OET, 1945); *16 October 1943* (Market Harborough: University Texts, 1996). Debenedetti's work is also part of a cluster of works – including Morante's *History* – which use Rome as a symbol of the nation and its war, with partisans, Jews, the Church, and the state in complex interrelation.

21. Liana Millu, *Il fumo di Birkenau* (Milan: La Prora, 1947); *Smoke over Birkenau* (Philadelphia: Jewish Publication Society, 1991); Giuliana Tedeschi, *C'è un punto della terra …* (Florence: Giuntina, 1988); *There is a Place on Earth* (London: Minerva, 1992).

22. Primo Levi, *La tregua* (Turin: Einaudi, 1963); *The Truce* (London: Bodley Head, 1965; also known in the US as *The Reawakening*).

23. Included in Edoardo de Filippo, *Four Plays* (London: Methuen, 1992).

24. Stephen Gundle, "The 'Civic Religion' of the Resistance in Post-war Italy," *Modern Italy* 5, 2 (Nov. 2000), 113–32.

25. Elio Vittorini, *Uomini e no* (Milan: Bompiani, 1945); *Men and Not Men* (Marlboro, VT: Marlboro Press, 1985).

26. Renata Viganò, *L'Agnese va a morire* (Turin: Einaudi, 1950); "Agnese Goes to Die" (untranslated).

27. Italo Calvino, *Il sentiero dei nidi di ragno* (Turin: Einaudi, 1947); *The Path to the Nest of Spiders* (London: Collins, 1956).

28. Luigi Meneghello, *I piccoli maestri* (Milan: Feltrinelli, 1964); *The Outlaws* (Michael Joseph: London, 1967).

29. Beppe Fenoglio, *Il partigiano Johnny* (Turin: Einaudi, 1968); *Johnny the Partisan* (London: Quartet, 1995). See Philip Cooke, *Fenoglio's Binoculars, Johnny's Eyes* (New York: Peter Lang, 2000).

30. Beppe Fenoglio, *I ventitré giorni della città di Alba* (Turin: Einaudi, 1952), now in *Opere*, 3 vols., ed. Maria Corti (Turin: Einaudi, 1978), vol. I, p. 5; my translation. (There is a small-press version of the book in English: *The Twenty-Three Days of the City of Alba* [South Royalton, VT: Steerforth Italia, 2002].)

31. Cesare Pavese, *La luna e i falò* (Turin: Einaudi, 1950); *The Moon and the Bonfire* [sic] (London: John Lehmann, 1952).

32. One literary historian has used the image of the "house on the hill" as an emblem of the betrayal, a sort of *trahison des clercs*, by a swathe of Italian writers and intellectuals, who evaded the call-to-arms of the Resistance in late 1943: Raffaele Liucci, *La tentazione della "casa in collina": il disimpegno degli intellettuali nella guerra civile italiana, 1943–1945* (Milan: Unicopli, 1999).

33. Pavese, *House*, p. 191.

34. Alessandro Portelli, *L'ordine è già stato eseguito: Roma, le fosse Ardeatine, la memoria* (Rome: Donzelli, 1999); *The Order Has Been Carried Out: History, Memory and Meaning of a Nazi Massacre in Rome* (New York: Palgrave, 2003).

35. Ernesto Galli della Loggia, *La morte della patria* (Bari: Laterza, 1996).

36. Eugenio Montale, "Il sogno del prigioniero," in *La bufera e altro* (Venice: Neri Pozza, 1956), now in *Tutte le poesie*, ed. Giorgio Zampa (Milan: Mondadori, 1990), pp. 276–7; my translation.

10

REIKO TACHIBANA

The Japanese war

The Japanese history of World War II is still incomplete and controversial, especially in relation to other Asian countries with which Japan was at war, such as China and Korea. The war ended with the "divine" Emperor Hirohito's radio announcement of surrender on August 15, 1945, followed by his declaration of his newly human status on January 1, 1946. Exempted from responsibility for the war by the Allied forces (led by the USA), he became the "symbol" of the new nation – its transition from an autocratic totalitarian regime to an American-style "democratic" one – and died in January 1989 without ever admitting his responsibility. Neither did the majority of the Japanese population. The end of World War II also meant the dawn of the Cold War nuclear age: two Japanese cities, Hiroshima and Nagasaki (on August 6 and August 9, 1945, respectively), became the first victims of the atomic bombs that displayed the feasibility of annihilating humankind. Postwar Japanese literature was produced literally from the ruins of Hiroshima and Nagasaki, as well as other cities such as air-raided Tokyo and Kobe, and from a distrust of this overnight metamorphosis of Japanese society. Then, instead of Japanese military censorship during the war, writers experienced another kind of censorship by the Allied forces during the occupation period (1945–52): anything related to the atomic bomb and its victims, nationalism, the Imperial household, and communist ideologies was vulnerable.

Japanese literature dealing directly or indirectly with the war revived by the end of the 1950s and has continued to flourish. It demonstrates diversified pictures, realistic or figurative, of the war itself and ranges from straightforward to more intricate and distanced perspectives. Focusing on how the war and people's experiences are reconstructed in narratives, section I of this chapter discusses A-bomb literature (*genbaku bungaku*), section II examines the literature of wartime; and section III will explore the indirect literature of the war, a defamiliarized and multifarious world.

I. A-bomb literature (*genbaku bungaku*)

So-called A-bomb literature was initially produced by *hibakusha* (survivors of the bombs) immediately after the blast, when writers felt it their mission to record such overwhelming experiences, and later by non-*hibakusha*, many of them basing their work on survivors' notes, interviews, records, and so on. It took more than two decades to acknowledge the genre of A-bomb literature, in part because of censorship and partly because of survivors' unwillingness or inability to express their feelings and thoughts in words (as in the case of Holocaust survivors) and their compatriots' reluctance to listen to those survivors' stories.[1] Only in 1985, forty years after the war, were the collected works of A-bomb literature finally published in Japan. A-bomb literature includes not only stories by *hibakusha* authors, but also preserves embedded excerpts from non-fiction documents, such as notes, diaries, or doctors' records of the medical treatments they provided; that is to say, the distinction between fiction and non-fiction is often obscure.

As a result of Allied censorship, A-bomb literature was not officially published until the beginning of the 1950s, although some of it was written right after the bombing. For instance, "Summer Flowers" ("Natsu no hana"), a semi-autobiographical story by Tamiki Hara (1905–51), was born, based on his notes, as early as August 7, the day after the atomic blast. This work was finally published in June 1947, in a minor journal (*Mita bungaku*, or "Mita Literature") in order to evade censorship. Despite such immediacy, the tone of the story was distanced and amazingly restrained, and its structure underlines the world before and after the bomb. The story starts with the first-person narrator's visit to the family grave where his wife's bones are buried on an early August morning a few days before the blast. We are told that his wife died of an illness the previous year in Tokyo, and that the heartbroken narrator was evacuated from the air-raided city to his hometown of Hiroshima in the early spring of 1945. Splashing water on the grave, sticking the flowers in their holders, and lighting the incense, the narrator quietly mourns his wife's (individual) death. Such a "peaceful" scene is followed in the rest of the story by hellish pictures of mass destruction and countless (impersonal) deaths. The image of the tiny yellow summer flowers, an allusion to fragile humankind, is contrasted with a city blackened and burned by the monstrous power of the atomic bomb.

However, A-bomb literature also includes writings by younger *hibakusha* authors who were children or high school students at the time of the bombings; their autobiographical stories are often requiems for family members, friends, and other people in their communities who died of radiation sickness. Representative of this category are Kyoko Hayashi (b. 1930) and Hiroko

Takenishi (b. 1929). Hayashi's "The Empty Can" ("Akikan," 1978) presents five women – Hara, Oki, Nishida, Noda, and the narrator "I" – in their mid-forties who visit their old high school in Nagasaki in the mid-1970s, after thirty years' absence. Walking around the school, entering the auditorium, they (all except Nishida are *hibakusha*) immediately return to their unforgettable memories of the day the A-bomb fell, August 9, 1945, when the seriously wounded Hara and Oki lay on the floor, along with many other injured students (three hundred students and teachers have been killed). They realize that the woman named Kinuko who could not come to their reunion due to being hospitalized in order to have glass (from the A-bomb blast) taken from her back, was the same girl who carried an empty can to school right after the war, and her classmates gradually learn that her parents were killed instantly in the blast, and that she put their remains in the can.

The legacy of the A-bomb is reflected in each woman's private life. Besides the recently widowed non-*hibakusha* Nishida, only Noda is married, while Oki and Hara are single "for no special reason" and the narrator, like her author, is divorced (Kinuko is also single).[2] While in twenty-first century Japan, social restrictions are looser, and single women and childless married couples no longer surprising, marriage and childbirth were the social norm for women in the mid-1970s, divorce was rare, and "career women" uncommon. Some of the women, like Hara and Oki, are unable to leave Nagasaki because of their fear of the recurrence of radiation sickness and their wish to be near the hospital for atomic bomb victims, even though this inhibits their chance to look for better jobs. Employing many symbolic contrasts and images, such as the distinctions between light and dark, *hibakusha* and non-*hibakusha*, the window glass and the glass from Kinuko's back, and the present and the past, the text gradually opens up those women's experiences from thirty years ago and since. The ending of the story lets in the light of hope: "How many fragments of glass from thirty years ago would come out of Kinuko's back? What kind of a glow would those smooth white pearls of fat cast when they were brought out into the light?"[3] Scars from the A-bomb never leave those women (like the remains in Kinuko's can and the glass in her back), but the narrative suggests that talking openly, bringing all out into the light, frees their suppressed memories to help them overcome the past.

Importantly, Hiroshima has also been reconstructed through visual media, as in Masaki Mori's 1983 anime *Barefoot Gen (Hadashi no Gen)*, an adaptation of the manga series of the same title by Keiji Nakazawa (a *hibakusha* born in 1939), which appeared in 1973 and 1974. Born in Hiroshima, the six-year-old Nakazawa was in the city (but miles away from ground zero) when the A-bomb was dropped. He survived, while half of his family was killed in the blast. Focusing on the boy named Gen, the anime begins with the life of his family towards the end of World War II. The scarcity of food and his mother's pregnancy have meant a difficult time for Gen's family, and especially for his pacifist father who is called a traitor to the country, and who does not attempt to get food from the black market, yet they live comparatively happily as a family. The blast overturns Gen's world. Inserting the scene in which the Enola Gay drops the bomb, the anime graphically presents people like zombies (hanging skins, popping out eyeballs, and so on), walking around a wasteland. The even more shocking scene, though, is when Gen, who miraculously survives without apparent injuries, discovers that his entire family except for his mother (i.e. his father, his older sister Eiko, and his kid brother, Eiji) are trapped under the beams of the collapsed house and that a fire has broken out in the entire area. No one is able to rescue them from the trap. In accordance with his dying father's urging him to take care of the mother and her unborn baby, Gen finally leaves the sight, dragging his frantic mother to a safe place.

Despite such horrible scenes, through the birth of his sister (named Tomoko, who dies of malnutrition weeks later) and the adoption of an orphan boy who is exactly like his dead brother, Eiji, the anime underlines the willpower and idealism of humankind, with no one truly bad and everyone helping one another, as is suggested by the hopeful ending showing the regrowth of wheat (along with the father's masculine face appearing on the screen, calling to Gen, "be strong like a stalk of wheat, which grows even after being repeatedly trodden on"). To feminist eyes, this anime raises questions in its portrayal of women such as Gen's mother and sister as submissive and powerless, while the patriarchal family is left to the child Gen (we don't know exactly how old he is, but we assume that he is around ten years old), as the eldest son of the family, who takes care of his mother in accordance with his father's last words. Yet, the anime depicts a "realistic" picture of what happened at Hiroshima and demonstrates the insanity of war through the child's eyes; and, through the experience of Gen's father, it criticizes the government and predicts Japan's defeat.

Non-*hibakusha* writers such as Masuji Ibuse (1898–1993), Yoshie Hotta (1918–98), Makoto Oda (1932–2007), and Kenzaburo Oe (b. 1935), among many others, have produced texts based on their interviews with *hibakusha* and documentary materials, displaying their own, often politicized, perspectives on Hiroshima and Nagasaki. For instance, the 1994 Nobel Prize laureate Oe's *Hiroshima Notes* (1965) is a collection of essays in which Oe underscores that Hiroshima is not over, since many of the survivors still continue to struggle with both radiation sickness and social discrimination. Nonetheless, by portraying the *hibakusha* doctors' tireless efforts to aid the sick and injured, and the survivors' indomitable resilience, Oe's book reflects a positive view of humankind. Another representative work by a non-*hibakusha* writer is Masuji Ibuse's so-called documentary novel, *Black Rain* (*Kuroi ame*, 1966). Drawing from his interviews with survivors and a review of their diaries and records, Ibuse's novel is written largely in the form of a diary. The narrator Shizuma Shigematsu and his wartime journal really exist (as do other characters such as Shizuma's wife and the doctor Iwatake). Set in 1950, five years after the war, the novel has characters such as Shizuma, his niece, Yasuko, and his wife, Shigeko, who recall their experiences at the time of the blast of the A-bomb in Hiroshima in order to function within and comprehend their current situation. The present and the past thus intermingle, or, rather, we might say that the past is part of the present for those struggling survivors.

In this context, it is worth mentioning Shohei Imamura's film of the same title, based on Ibuse's novel, from 1988, which was probably influenced by the 1986 Chernobyl nuclear power plant accident in what was then the USSR. Imamura added extra characters such as Yoichi, who, having served in the Japanese army during the war, suffers psychological trauma even five years after the war ended. He becomes "insane" whenever he hears engine noise because it brings back memories of enemy tanks. The movie focuses on the once well-to-do landowning Shigematsu family, and especially on Yasuko in her mid-twenties, whose marriage proposals fail because of the rumor that she was at the hypocenter at the moment of the blast (in reality, she was on the outskirts of the city, but returned to the center that day to look for her uncle and aunt), and thus suffers from radiation sickness (or is incapable of repro-duction, and thus of providing an heir to the household – the main purpose of marriage at that time). Towards the end of the movie, Yasuko reveals a symptom of radiation sickness, and Yoichi, who has fallen in love with her, encourages her to overcome the sickness, forgetting his own postwar trauma. Symbolizing their love as the union of two wounded hearts in the context of the war's aftermath, the movie articulates not only non-*hibakusha*'s discri-mination against *hibakusha*, but also America's (and humankind's) failure to "learn a lesson from history" by briefly inserting the news that America might use A-bombs again in the Korean War (1950–53).

II. Wartime literature: a world of ambiguity

Some writers recreate their (own or fictional) experiences of the war. The representative author of this category is Shohei Ooka (1909–88). Based on his experience in the Philippines, Ooka produced a number of stories with a wartime setting, including *Fires on the Plain* (*Nobi*, 1951), and *Taken Captive; A Japanese POW's Story* (*Furyoki*, 1952). Drafted in 1944 at the age of thirty-five, Ooka was sent in July of that year to fight on Mindoro

Island in the Philippines, where he fell ill with malaria. After being abandoned by his squad, he was captured by the Americans and became a POW in January 1945. Following his release and repatriation from the Philippines in December 1945, Ooka began writing an autobiographical account of his experiences as a soldier and as a captive of the Americans. Written in May and June of 1946, his first story, "Until Being Captured" ("Tukamaru made") was not published until February 1948, due to the Allied authorities censoring descriptions of American soldiers. Ironically, Ooka's portrayal of former enemies as humans, rather than monstrous existences without any emotions and feelings (a caricaturing of enemies typical of both sides during the war) was not yet welcomed by the Allied forces. A collection of twelve of Ooka's captivity narratives, including "Until Being Captured," was then published in book form with the title *Taken Captive* in 1952, a year after the publication of his *Fires on the Plain*, a more popular and fictionalized wartime narrative made into a film of the same name by Kon Ichikawa in 1959.

In the same year as Ooka's publication of *Taken Captive*, Nobuo Kojima (1915–2006) published his short story, "The Rifle" (1952), which focuses on a young soldier's experience in China. The protagonist's obsession with the old "Meiji model" rifle associated with his memory of a love affair with an older married woman in Japan (whose husband had gone off to war), and his bizarre experiences during the war display an abnormal and dehumanized world in which the distinction between reality and delusion is blurred.[4] Such ambiguity in the story provokes the reader to read the narrative more attentively and between the lines than Ooka's, for example, more detailed descriptions in his story.

Women's experiences of the war have also produced a valuable body of writings. Based on her childhood experience in China, the above-mentioned Nagasaki survivor Kyoko Hayashi wrote a novella, "Yellow Sand" ("Kosa," 1977), focusing on the first-person narrator's recollection of a Japanese prostitute, named Okiyo-san, in Shanghai in 1937 when the (second) Sino-Japan war was about to break out. The six-year-old protagonist's encounter with Okiyo-san, who is a "black hole," a disgrace to the nation, in the Japanese community because she, unlike other Japanese prostitutes who were superficially called "entertainers" for the Japanese, openly engaged in prostitution for Chinese and other foreigners.[5] The brief friendship between the protagonist and Okiyo-san abruptly ends with Okiyo-san's hanging herself when the Japanese (including the protagonist's family) prepare for repatriation to Japan when news comes of the outbreak of war. Throughout the story, the color yellow – dust and rape flowers in spring – permeates, and through it the "sky, the river, and the earth merge" and there is no distinction between "heaven and earth."[6] This natural abundance of springtime is contrasted with the prostitute's lonely suicide, which nobody except the protagonist remembers, in the footsteps of the (man-made) war.

Another woman author, Taiko Hirabayashi (1905–72), wrote a short story, "Blind Chinese Soldiers" (1946), set in a crowded train station near Tokyo on March 9, 1945, the day of the American air raids in the Tokyo area. Her story demonstrates people's apathy and passive acceptance of the grim wartime situation, with its delayed trains and its arrogant uniformed officials (like policemen and railway station employees). The first-person narrator, "a certain intellectual-turned-farmer,"[7] witnesses not only the handsome Prince from the Imperial family sitting alone comfortably on a blue seat in the clean first-class compartment, but also hundreds of filthy blind Chinese solders coming out of the last and shabbiest compartment of the same train. These diametrically opposed sights surprise the narrator (the rare sight of the Imperial person) and disgust her (the unbelievable sight of these smelly soldiers) at the same time, but, like many around her, she minds her own business and soon forgets the encounter. The train then departs, cutting off that last compartment from which the soldiers emerged. After the war, the narrator finds out that no one has seen those Chinese soldiers again. The disappearance of the soldiers alludes to Japan's desire to erase the dark history of the war, as if nothing happened. This short text articulates "ordinary" people's passive support of the war and their indifference to others.

III. Indirect war: a defamiliarized and multifarious world

The 1994 Nobel Prize laureate, Kenzaburo Oe wrote a few novellas about the indirect experience of war from the point of view of children, such as "Prize Stock" ("Shiiku," 1958; also translated as "The Catch") and *Nip the Buds Shoot the Kids* (*Memushiri kouchi*, 1958). Both based on his experiences during the war, the stories take place in a remote village much like Oe's hometown on the island of Shikoku, where children are exposed to violence and betrayal. In "Prize Stock," Oe's uses of the layered power structure – the village, the town, and the prefecture/central government – allude to Imperial Japan where the divine emperor is supported by military officers, townspeople, and village adults. Power is exercised and resisted in a multiplicity of force relations through the capture of the enemy. Oe's insertion of an African–American soldier as a prisoner of war also defamiliarizes Japan's propaganda about the war – protecting Asia from White supremacy.

In a primitive, confined village cut off from the outside world by flooding, the boy protagonist nicknamed Frog as well as the other children are fascinated by the idea of "rearing" the soldier until the authorities decide the prisoner's fate. Just as the soldier is treated like an animal, the villagers are treated like filthy animals by the townspeople and the higher authority; the village itself is permeated with smells and the air of animals and animalistic conduct. Towards the end of the story, the powerless soldier at the bottom of the power structure challenges the village, holding Frog as a hostage. The death of the soldier, along with the father's crushing of the boy's hand, emphasizes a world of violence and meaningless death – the battlefield per se. This story can be also read as a parody of the *Bildungsroman* genre, in which wartime cruelty forces the boy protagonist to realize the loss of his innocence and distrust of adults and authority.

Yukio Mishima (1925–70) created a more indirect presentation of the effects of the war in his novel, *The Temple of the Golden Pavilion* (*Kinkakuji*, 1960). It is based on a real incident, the 1950 act of arson on the Zen temple, the Golden Pavilion in Kyoto (declared a national treasure in 1897 due to its beauty and longevity); in Mishima's novel, the act is committed by the acolyte Mizoguchi, who is obsessed by the temple's absolute beauty. The novel is Mizoguchi's confessional account of his "killing" of this beauty. Alienated from his peers since childhood due to his stuttering and physical ugliness, he wishes for death with the Golden Pavilion during the American air raids. Yet, because the Golden Pavilion survived (historically, the ancient capital Kyoto was saved from air raids and A-bombs because of its aesthetic value), the chance for Mizoguchi to die with beauty disappeared, and the distance between him and beauty was again restored in the postwar world. His everlasting dream of dying alongside beauty leads him to destroy the beauty (the Pavilion), yet he decides to live (like the real acolyte) at the end. Wishing for his own young and beautiful death during the war, the author Mishima also lived a so-called "left over" life for a quarter century in postwar society, where, according to Mishima, Japan lost her soul through the divine emperor's human declaration and, under pressure from the USA, became a mere symbolic power in the postwar constitution. The vanity and irrationality of his protagonist Mizoguchi's burning of beauty echoes Mishima's own final act, when he committed seppuku in public decades later in 1970, leaving behind his "futile" speech to the Self Defense Force (*jieitai*) soldiers to restore the old Japan with him.

It could be said that the novel *Urashimaso* (1977), by Minako Oba (1930–2007), culminates the aftermath of the war in Japanese literature. The novel also belongs to the genre of A-bomb literature since Oba herself was an "indirect" *hibakusha* (she was not in Hiroshima at the moment of the blast, but she was taken to the city with her classmates to help survivors a few weeks later). As with her contemporary Kyoko Hayashi, Oba's witnessing of hellish sights at the age of fifteen became the source of her creative power, and the theme of the self-destructiveness of humankind permeates her writing. In *Urashimaso*, and through its transnational protagonist, twenty-three-year-old Yukie, who has just returned to Japan from the US after eleven years away, the contemporary Japan of the mid-1970s (similar to the setting of Hayashi's "The Empty Can") is defamiliarized for readers, who are required to re-view their own societies as well as the world. Yukie, half-alien in her native land, becomes an attentive and ideal listener to her quasi family, including her half-brother Morito and his mistress Ryoko (indirect and direct *hibakusha*, respectively), their son Rei (whose autism is probably due to radiation effects), their adopted daughter Natsuo (whose Japanese mother died in childbirth and whose American father died in the Korean War), and Ryoko's former husband, Ryu, who is going to marry his pregnant girlfriend, breaking off his thirty-year triangular relationship with Ryoko and Morito. (Ryu served as a soldier in the Imperial army in China, where, according to him, he raped a Chinese woman.)

Observing their alienated lives outside the norm of society and hampered by the past, Yukie's visit to Hiroshima and her "home" town becomes her journey of self-discovery as she seeks to fill in blank memories of the nation and her family, and to assure herself of an "in-between" existence in both countries and cultures. Multi-layered perspectives are employed, including the popular Japanese folk story "Urashima Taro": the title *Urashimaso* was taken from the Urashima plant whose long stem resembles the fishing line of a young fisherman called Urashima Taro in the fairytale, and the ominous black Urashima plant grows near the enigmatic old house in which Yukie's quasi family lives. Oba believes that the A-bomb is the end result of the excessive human desire and curiosity manifested throughout the traditional story of Urashima Taro, who ages and dies after opening a box he has been told to keep sealed. That is, the self-destructiveness of humankind – destroying others to survive themselves, leading them to destroy themselves – is underlined through her characters in *Urashimaso*.

The political activist and writer, Makoto Oda (1932–2007), who was the founder of the Vietnam Peace Group during the Vietnam War, published the novel *Gyokusai* in 1988, translated into English as *The Breaking Jewel* by the prominent Japanologist Donald Keene. After a long conversation with Oda, and incorporating his own experience (including witnessing the Japanese "gyokusai," or suicide attackers) as a military translator during the Pacific War, Keene completed his English translation in 2003. Taking place on a tiny South Pacific island during the last days of World War II, and focusing on the military men, the Japanese Nakamura and the Korean Kon (who became "Japanese" during Japan's colonization of Korea in 1910–45),[8] the novel portrays the madness of a war that causes people to justify such acts as suicidal attacks in the face of defeat (as in kamikaze, or suicide pilots). Towards the end of the story, the injured Nakamura reveals his prejudice against Kon, who tries to persuade him to become a prisoner of war (rather than dying in vain), angrily stating that unlike the (coward) Koreans, Japanese men fight to the very last breath. This book is particularly relevant to our post-9/11 world, born as it was from Oda's realization that he could have been one of the soldiers who killed themselves during World War II through suicidal attacks under the pretext of an honorable and heroic death for the divine emperor.[9]

One of the most popular Japanese writers in the West as well as in Asian countries, Haruki Murakami (b. 1949) has been criticized by many (including Oe) for writing books that are apolitical or unconcerned with the history of his own nation. More recent works, though, such as *The Wind-Up Bird Chronicle* (*Nejimaki dori kuronikuru*, 1998) and *Kafka on the Shore* (*Umibe no Kafka*, 2002) have begun to present the legacy of World War II.[10] While portraying the Japanese soldiers' nightmarish experiences (for instance, the skin peeling off live soldiers) on the Mongolian front in the *Wind-Up Bird Chronicle*, Murakami sets *Kafka on the Shore* entirely in Japan. Like his many other novels, the story presents two worlds alternately – one is based around the fifteen-year-old protagonist, named Kafka ("crow" in Czech), and the other is based on an eccentric man in his sixties named Nakata. The story begins with Kafka's running away from home in Tokyo, followed by an enigmatic incident in the war of more than half a century ago in a remote village where a handful of elementary school students, local ones and evacuees from Tokyo (including young Nakata), suddenly lose consciousness on a school excursion on a low mountain. All the children except Nakata regain consciousness after hours, but sent to a Tokyo hospital, Nakata finally wakes up having lost all memories and intellectual abilities. Stigmatized as mentally retarded and illiterate, he lives on a small disability stipend from the government as well as money inherited from his deceased parents (his father used to physically abuse him, and he became the "black sheep" of his élite family). Nakata, however, has a special ability: he is able to talk with cats, and his wartime experience is reported to the US officials by his teacher as well as by the doctor who treats him in the hospital. Young Kafka and the elderly Nakata, who do not know each other at all and who never meet throughout the story, are directed to the same library in Kochi in the southern part of Japan, a small private library owned by a wealthy family where Miss Saeki, its manager, works with a male-female individual named Oshima. Young Nakata's mysterious incident during the war (his lost consciousness), recounted at the beginning of the story, is, we realize, his entering and returning from the "other" world. This wartime incident is allusively connected to Kafka's experience towards the end of the story, in which two military deserters serve as guards and guides for the "other" world. Inserting various literary texts, concepts, and thoughts from outside Japan (the Oedipus complex, *The Arabian Nights*, Kafka, Goethe, Nietzsche, among others, as well as icons of capitalism like Colonel Sanders and Johnnie Walker), and from Japan (the living spirit from the *Tale of Genji* and Soseki's novels, and so on), the story presents, both metaphorically and realistically, violence, and bloody forces like the battlefield, yet the ending is positive – in returning from the other world, Kafka decides to go back to Tokyo to finish junior high school.

In conclusion, more than six decades after World War II, Japanese writers continue to produce literary texts about the legacy of the war, figurative or realistic or both. A-bomb literature began with writers' sense of mission – the need to record their overwhelming experiences – right after Hiroshima and Nagasaki, and their memories of hellish pictures become the source of their creative power. More distanced and indirect perspectives of the war appeared decades later and continue to be created in contemporary Japan. Postwar writers underline the incomplete past and what the cultural theorist Homi Bhabha has called "the "past-present', which becomes part of the necessity ... of living."[11] Opening Pandora's box in Hiroshima and Nagasaki meant the feasibility of human annihilation – or the self-destructiveness of humankind, as Oba puts it – yet the majority of the literary texts discussed here express positive hopes for the future. In using a multifaceted perspective, ambiguity, a wide range of settings and characters, images and symbols, these authors attempt to recreate an enigmatic world in which the readers are active participants in completing the meanings of the story.

NOTES

1. Pursuing reconstruction of the nation, rather than dealing with the recent past – for instance, the atrocities committed by Imperial Japan in other Asian countries – people tended to discriminate against *hibakusha*, whose illness (due to radiation sickness) prevented them from working hard and who were thus often stigmatized as lazy.
2. Kyoko Hayashi, "The Empty Can," *The Crazy Iris and Other Stories of the Atomic Aftermath*, trans. Margaret Mitsutani (New York: Grove, 1985), p. 134.
3. *Ibid.*, p. 143.
4. Nobuo Kojima, "The Rifle," in *The Oxford Book of Japanese Short Stories*, trans. Lawrence Rogers, ed. Theodore W. Goossen (Oxford University Press, 2002), p. 241.
5. Kyoko Hayashi, "Yellow Sand," in *Japanese Women Writers*, trans. Kyoko Iriye Selden, ed. Noriko Mizuta Lippit and Kyoko Iriye Selden (New York: M. E. Sharpe), p. 214.

6. *Ibid.*, p. 208.

7. Taiko Hirabayashi, "Blind Chinese Soldiers," trans. Noriko Mizuta Lippit, in *The Oxford Book of Japanese Short Stories*, p. 182. Like the author, many intellectuals and writers evacuated from big cities to the countryside during the war. Due to the lack of food everywhere, they, like farmers, had to grow vegetables and crops for themselves and their family members.

8. During Japan's colonization and annexation of Korea between 1910 and 1945, Koreans became citizens of Imperial Japan (so-called "adopted" children of the emperor). Brought to Japan as cheap laborers and, like Kon in the story, serving (voluntarily or by force) in the Imperial army, Japan's Korean subjects had to acquire a new identity expressed through Japanese names and to learn the Japanese language. At the moment of Japan's defeat (or liberation for Koreans), the majority of the two million Koreans in Japan hurriedly returned to their home country, while more than 600,000 Koreans remained in Japan. The Japanese citizenship they had held during the war was unexpectedly abrogated in 1952, right after the signing of the San Francisco Peace treaty between Japan and the Allies, and by law the Koreans became "aliens" in an unfriendly society.

9. Tina Pepler made a radio drama entitled *Gyokusai* and based on Oda's story, which was broadcast on the BBC to the world on August 6 (so-called "Hiroshima Day" in Britain), 2005. Pepler had also broadcast Oda's earlier novel, an A-bomb narrative entitled *H: A Hiroshima Novel* (1995; *HIROSHIMA*, 1982) on the BBC in 1995.

10. Murakami's involvement in social matters in Japan started around 2005, when the Kobe earthquake killed more than six thousand and destroyed cities (including his hometown) in the Kobe/Kansai area on January 17, followed by the religious sect Aum Shinrikyo's Sarin attacks (which killed twelve and injured more than five thousand) in the crowded Tokyo subways on March 20. Witnessing the aftermath of these overwhelming acts of violence in his native town and nation, he published his first non-fictional work, *Underground*, a collection of interviews with Sarin gas victims, and then another collection of interviews, this time with former members of the sect.

11. Homi Bhabha, *The Location of Culture* (New York: Routledge, 1994), p. 7.

11

DONNA COATES

War writing in Australia, Canada, and New Zealand

(Not) For God, King, and Country

Even though the 1931 Statute of Westminster had made Australia, Canada, and New Zealand independent nations with autonomous foreign policies, New Zealand and Australia nevertheless responded to the outbreak of the Second World War as if they were still colonies, automatically at war as they had been in 1914. Both relied upon Britain for strategic imperatives such as security and defence, as well as for economic reasons. Further, sentimental links between Britain and its former colonies meant many continued to call Britain "home" and to regard the British as their "kith and kin." Within hours of Britain's declaration of war on Germany, both New Zealand's Prime Minister, Michael Joseph Savage, and Australia's Prime Minister, Robert Menzies, rushed to offer the British government their support because they believed it inconceivable to do otherwise. In Canada, although the Anglophile, imperialist, and monarchist Prime Minister, Mackenzie King, was in favor of supporting Britain once war was declared, he knew he had to satisfy Francophone Quebec's concerns about the conscription issue that had proved so divisive in the First World War; thus he informed the nation he would "let Parliament decide." After very little debate, Canada, too, was at war by September 10. As news of the defeats suffered by Britain and France continued to be reported in the press, the conscription issue was once again raised, but King's ambiguous proclamation, "Conscription if necessary, but not necessarily conscription,"[1] served only to anger French Canadians. In 1944, over 16,000 conscripts were ordered overseas, provoking a political crisis that almost destroyed the government, as French Canadians felt they were being forced to serve and die for their oppressors' cause. Although not many French-Canadian writers expressed concern over "the war within the war," in *La Guerre, Yes Sir!* (1968), Roch Carrier depicts a series of bloody events that occur in the 1940s when English soldiers bring the body of a French Canadian back to his rural home, and in *The Tin Flute* (1945), Gabrielle Roy demonstrates that some French Canadians in Montreal viewed the war, tragically, as a means of escaping grinding poverty.

I

In general, though, Canadians have a profound distaste for militarism. Although they have produced numbers of heroic figures worthy of mythologizing, names of the most famous, military or otherwise, languish in obscurity because, as a nation, Canadians have been notoriously reluctant to elevate ordinary individuals to the realm of myth and heroism. Unlike other nations that proudly celebrate the victories of their political and military heroes for their fierce individualism and dogged determination, Canadians tend to reward virtues such as humility and modesty, or in a more contemporary sense, collective merits such as those embodied by the bravery of peacekeepers. For these reasons, fiction by men that emerged either during or shortly after the war is subdued. It does not perceive war as a crusade for the restoration of the Right, nor does it unquestionably assert the justness of the Allied cause, find nobility in self-sacrifice, or cling to illusions about life after the war. Perhaps because many of the writers had served overseas, their war is not about heroes. Their soldier figures are not gallant young men laying down their lives for the good of their country, but ordinary men who carry their weaknesses or limitations with them. Writers focus on the inner consciousness of the individual fighting man who is increasingly alienated in mechanized battles, yet feels a responsibility to fight to the finish.

The bravery of the "little man," who carries no deceptions about his physical or emotional strength nor sees himself as a fearless or invincible warrior, is a recurring theme, as in G. Herbert Sallan's *Little Man* (1942), which tells the story of a man who, like Sallan himself, survives the First World War, but loses (in fiction) his son to the Second. Platoon Commander Edward Meade's *Remember Me* (1946), written overseas and sent home to his wife to type, provides documentary-like descriptions of London (and Londoners) under attack, aerial dogfights, and the Normandy invasion. Although Meade conveys respect for the firm resolve of Englishmen under duress, he reserves his highest praise for Canadians on the battlefront and the home front. In *Storm Below* (1949), Hugh Garner, who served in both the Spanish Civil War and the Second World War, explores the private thoughts of a group of ordinary soldiers who spend six days in 1943 on convoy escort duty in the North Atlantic. Earle Birney, best known as a poet, also produced the military picaresque *Turvey* (1949). In part a satire on the Intelligence Corps, the work features a hapless recruit who is motivated to fight by simple patriotism, but the war ends before he gets his chance. Considered the best fiction to emerge from the war, Colin McDougall's *Execution* (1958) traces Canadian soldiers through major offensives in Italy, culminating in a bloody battle at Monte Cassino, but the "execution(s)" of the title depict the senseless killing of innocent victims in wartime and the characters' struggles to come to terms with these injustices. McDougall, who earned the DSO for bravery, served with the Canadian army in Italy. Douglas LePan, an artilleryman with the Canadian army was, like Birney, best known as a poet. In his novel *The Deserter* (1964), LePan recounts a soldier's difficulty finding a balance between apathy and commitment to the future in the demobilization period following the war in London. James Jackson's *To the Edge of Morning* (1964), a psychological case study in part based on the author's experience as a pilot, is unusual in that it deals with jungle warfare and the air war in the Indian Ocean. William Allister's *A Handful of Rice* (1961) chronicles cruelties suffered by a prisoner of war in a Japanese camp after the fall of Hong Kong in 1941. Not all fictions deal directly with soldiers' lives, however: Philip Child's *Day of Wrath* (1945) explores Nazi Germany and the impact of the Holocaust on survivors, and several of the poet A. M. Klein's stories, published in the 1930s and 1940s (collected in *Short Stories* [1983]), consider the Nazi menace, the threat of the atomic bomb, and the nascent Cold War.

Although McDougall's and LePan's works won Governor-General's Awards, few (of the few) Second World War novels by Canadian men were ever widely read or studied. Similarly, New Zealand men did not produce much fiction, but novels by writers such as M. K. Joseph, Guthrie Wilson, and Gordon Slater claim that, in spite of the setbacks and disasters of the Greece and Crete campaigns, the nation produced the best fighting formations on any battlefield, but especially the Mediterranean. According to novelist and historian Dan Davin, New Zealanders placed great stock in Churchill's description of the Second New Zealand Expeditionary Force as "the Salamander of the British Empire," and their commander, General Freyberg, as "a ball of fire." Davin, who was demobilized in 1945 with the rank of major, produced some of the country's best-known war fiction. His lengthy *For the Rest of Our Lives* (1947) examines the Western Desert campaign from the perspective of three junior officers. Intellectuals and political rebels with a love of debate, especially on subjects such as the nature and origin of war, they nevertheless recognize how limited their powers are against the forces of history. While at the front between 1941 and 1945, Davin produced a number of stories (*The Salamander and the Fire: Collected War Stories* [1986]). In the frequently anthologized "The General and the Nightingale," Davin offers his own salute to Freyberg.

Australian men, by contrast, generated a substantial number of novels, almost all about military conflict, almost all by men who had served in combat, and almost all about "big men." Jon Cleary, Lawrence Glassop, and T. A. G. Hungerford fought on the battlefields in the Middle East and New Guinea, whereas Eric Lambert worked as a journalist in the Middle East, New Guinea, and Singapore. Lambert's *The Twenty Thousand Thieves* (1952) and the sequel, *The Veterans* (1954), Cleary's *The Climate of Courage* (1954), Glassop's *We Were the Rats* (1944), and Hungerford's *The Ridge and the River* (1952) were runaway best sellers, several selling more than half a million copies. While only a few are still in print today, they remain valuable indicators of the sustaining power of the Anzac legend, initially created by novelists and poets in the 1890s and then termed the myth of the noble bushman. Essentially a form of "writing back" to the Empire, the myth decreed that (male) Australians had, despite their inauspicious beginnings, acquired a cultural and physical superiority. The social climate also dictated that the bushman was an irreverent anti-authoritarian who believed strongly in the principles of egalitarianism and mateship. During the Great War, the legend, reinforced by historian and war correspondent C. E. W. Bean, zoomed from bush to battlefield, and depicted larger-than-life warriors who liked to fight and were good at it. Their fighting prowess and capacity for combat (especially at Gallipoli) was said to have achieved nationhood, history for a new nation, and international acclaim.

The literature that emerged from the legend (which women novelists also supported unequivocally) was, even at the time, anachronistic and out of step with the anti-heroic sentiments expressed in the literature of the English war poets and in the fiction by European, American, and Canadian writers. Remarkably, it continued to hold sway throughout the Second World War, for writers were under intense pressure to prove that the Australian legend had not been a mere fluke of history, or that the "Sons of Anzacs" were neither second-rate nor second-best, but as worthy of hero worship as their forefathers. Few writers dared to challenge the legend, although George Johnston's *My Brother Jack* (1964) explores the tension between two brothers – a prototypical Anzac who appears to have stepped straight off the rocky cliffs of Gallipoli, and an introverted intellectual who has no stomach for soldiering and feels increasingly alienated from the mainstream culture that applauds men like his brother. Alan Seymour also questions the myth in his controversial play *The One Day of the Year* (1960), which consists of a series of arguments between a working-class ex-Anzac of the 1939–45 War who celebrates (and is celebrated by) his glorious military heritage on Anzac Day (April 25), and his university-educated son, who sees the legend as outmoded and irrelevant.

In the main, however, Anzacs Two demanded attention and got it, as Second World War writers, like their predecessors, hopped on the Anzac adulation bandwagon and lauded their participation in war. And, by 1939, writers were at liberty to endorse larrikin behaviour, reference to which had been carefully suppressed in the First World War. Now, Antipodean Achilles drink to excess, use foul language, and gratify their sexual urges at will. (Critics have speculated that these novelists may have realized that it was pointless to depict updated Anzacs as militarily superior to the First, so they turned them into sexual conquerors, too.) Censors did not always approve of these heroes-turned-hooligan; Sumner Locke Elliott's 1948 play *Rusty Bugles* was taken off the stage because his non-combatants at a Northern Territory ordnance station employed blasphemous and indecent language to express their boredom, and Glassop's *We Were the Rats* (1944) was banned as obscene because his Anzacs were likewise such foul-mouthed philanderers. Although few male writers questioned Anzacs' lusty encounters with alluring local women, both Xavier Herbert, in *Soldiers' Women* (1963) and Lambert in *The Veterans* invoke familiar double standards to condemn women who engage in casual sexual relationships as morally degenerate, and those who pander to the better-paid Americans as traitors to the war effort.

Perhaps because an emphasis on bravura military performance privileged foot soldiers engaged in hand-to-hand combat, only a few Australian novels – Don Charlewood's *No Moon Tonight* (1965) and John Beede's *They Hosed Them Out* (1965) – depicted hazardous night bombings over Europe. Correspondingly, fiction that situated Diggers in defeat, such as soldier Richard Beilby's *Gunner* (1977), which deals with the ruinous Crete campaign, is in short supply. More popular are novels set in North Africa, where Australians contributed to several important victories. Lambert's *The Twenty Thousand Thieves* documents the Anzacs' struggle to force the Italian Army from the Egyptian border to Benghazi in 1941, and Glassop's *We Were the Rats* chronicles the Anzacs' defence of the Libyan port of Tobruk in the same year. Glassop re-visited "the rats" in *The Rats in New Guinea* (1963), but his sequel, like Cleary's *The Climate of Courage*, which features Anzacs who serve in both North Africa and the South-West Pacific, emphasizes that the latter was a tougher testing ground than the Mediterranean. Novels like David Forrest's *The Last Blue Sea* (1959), which are set exclusively in the South-West Pacific, underscore the extent to which Anzacs find the humid climate and oppressive conditions of the jungle an even more daunting enemy than the fearless Japanese. Nevertheless, not all Anzacs were demoralized by their experiences in the jungle – those in Hungerford's *The Ridge and the River*, Lambert's *The Veterans*, and Cleary's *The Climate of Courage* resurrect the never-say-die spirit and values of the father force and become revitalized by their valiant struggles against tremendous odds.

Anzacs incarcerated as Japanese prisoners of war and thus unable to exercise their inalienable right to defend the national cause on the battlefield become morally disillusioned when they are subjected to abuse by those they considered their racial inferiors, but now realize they have underestimated. Playwright John Romeril, who draws his inspiration from POW memoirists Russell Braddon and Ray Parkin, dramatizes the atrocities men endured while they worked as slave laborers on the Burma–Siam railway in his experimental play, *The Floating World* (1974). Lambert, too, who derives *McDougal's Farm* (1965) from prison veterans' notes and conversations, writes frankly about the Japanese inhumanity towards and barbaric treatment of their prisoners as does Nevil Shute in *A Town Like Alice* (1950). (Approximately 33 per cent of all Australian POWs died in Japanese camps, whereas only 3 per cent of those held captive in German and Italian camps did not survive.) In an unusual turn of the tables, Kenneth Seaforth Mackenzie's novel, *Dead Men Rising* (1951), based on his own experiences as a prison guard, recounts the 1944 suicidal mass-escape of Japanese prisoners from the camp in Cowra, New South Wales; 234 POWs and 4 Australian guards died in the breakout.

While the interest in combat novels has now largely faded, prisoner-of-war literature, with its emphasis on the anti-warrior, the man forced out of the action, has had sustaining power. Randolph Stow's *The Merry-Go-Round in the Sea* (1965) features a soldier who returns to West Australia from a Japanese POW camp tormented by recurring nightmares, a feeling of shame, and resentful that his friends and relatives regard him as an object of pity (though these emotions are misguided). (Stow's novel, in part a *Bildungsroman*, also offers a child's perception of war, as do contemporary writer David Malouf's Brisbane novels *Johnno* [1990] and *12 Edmonstone Street* [1993]). Malouf's "At Schindler's" (*Dream Stuff* [2000]) also depicts a confused adolescent who witnesses his mother's affair with an American soldier while her husband is confined to a POW camp. In *The Great World* (1990), Malouf tells the story of two "mates" whose lives are determined by the bonds they forge as they undergo the fall of Singapore, degradation at the infamous Changi prison, and the soggy jungles of Thailand. In *The Widow and Her Hero* (2007), Thomas Keneally explores the nature of heroism from the point of view of a widow whose husband disappeared in 1945; the novel, based in part on the "true" story of soldier Ivan Lyon, pays testament to the comradeship, bravery, and sacrifices of soldier-heroes as they carry out an ill-fated commando mission which lands them in a POW camp in Japanese-occupied Singapore. Several contemporary writers have also examined the postwar experiences of POW survivors. Patricia Cornelius's *My Sister Jill* (2003) features a man whose detention at Changi has turned him into an abusive man, and his family suffers the consequences. Expatriate writer Shirley Hazzard's *The Great Fire* (2004) depicts an English survivor of a POW camp who falls in love with a young Australian in part because her purity and innocence are in such stark contrast to the death and destruction he has witnessed both during and after the war.

Often overlooked are the accounts of several intrepid Australian women nurses who were also captured and interned. Elizabeth ("Jessie") Simons's novel *While History Passed* (1954), later published as *In Japanese Hands: Australian Nurses as POWs* (1985), documents Simons's experiences immediately before, during, and after her lengthy internment in a Japanese POW camp in Sumatra. Upon reflection, Simons wrote that she did not regret having been confined, for she learned the meaning of comradeship and gained other invaluable knowledge. Betty Jeffreys's *White Coolies* (1954), drawn from diaries she hid from the Japanese, also documents her detention at a POW camp in Sumatra. Most memorable is her account of the formation of a choir that helped bolster women's spirits, especially during the initial months of captivity. In 1996, Jeffreys became an advisor to Bruce Beresford, director of the film *Paradise Road* (1997), largely because of the material in *White Coolies*.

II

Great Britain's inability to come to the aid of either Australia or New Zealand gave rise to the "friendly invasion" of one million American GIs in the South Pacific, where they rapidly became the dominant power and a powerful force in women's fiction. Florence James's and Dymphna Cusack's popular *Come In Spinner* (1951), set in 1944 Sydney, provides detailed accounts of the tensions over military might, money, and women that heated up shortly after the Americans arrived. But in spite of the GIs' lavish spending, dazzling good looks, and romantic ways, Australian women say "no thanks to the Yanks" because they have rapidly dwindled into slick and unscrupulous scoundrels. Although the novel documents the kinds of social injustices that prevailed in a wartime climate and was at the time considered politically adventurous in its representation of both class and gender, it nevertheless fails to discard or revise national values, particularly those pertaining to the impoverished relationships between women and men. (Australian men traditionally favored racehorses, beer, and their mates over dates.) In Henrietta Drake-Brockman's Ballarat novel *The Fatal Days* (1947), which also documents the American presence, one woman forms a lasting relationship with an American soldier, but only because he appreciates all aspects of Australian life. Two other novels – Eleanor Dark's *The Little Company* (1945) and Cusack's *Southern Steel* (1947) – depict the vulnerability of Australians when Japanese submarines attack Sydney and Newcastle in 1942, but neither novel, narrated from a male point of view, questions national stereotypes. The only fiction to do so is Zora Cross's clumsily written *This Hectic Age* (1944).

In Canada, Gwethalyn Graham's experimental and prophetic *Swiss Sonata* (1938), set in 1935, features a brilliant Canadian student who attends a boarding school in Lausanne, where she learns of the grim political situation in Germany through her conversations with students and teachers. Graham was reputedly delighted when the Nazis blacklisted her novel. *Earth and High Heaven* (1944), which sold over one and a half million copies in Canada and America and dominated the American bestseller lists in 1945, offers a candid exposure of the kind of xenophobia and anti-Semitism that prevailed in 1942 Quebec, but the issues Graham raises seem almost unthinkable in a nation that has since become known for its racial, ethnic, and religious tolerance. Graham was again ahead of her time, for it was some years before Irving Abella and Harold Troper's *None Is Too Many: Canada and the Jews of Europe, 1933–1948* (1982) offered an examination of a related and shameful (now almost forgotten) incident in Canada's past – the systematic exclusion of Jews as immigrants or refugees before, during, and after Hitler's genocide. (The writers derived their memorable title from the words of an anonymous immigration agent who, when asked how many Jews would be allowed into Canada, replied, "None is too many.") In the 1990s, playwright Jason Sherman was commissioned to adopt the historical work for the stage. Both historical and dramatic versions (*None Is too Many* [1997]) underscore that Canada did less than any other Western country to help Jewish refugees, a subject to which Sherman returns in *Remnants* (2003).

Because the bulk of the literature about the Second World War was at the time produced by the dominant "white" stream of Australian, Canadian, and New Zealand writers, it is now vital to include contemporary works by indigenous and multicultural writers who have been, until recently, systematically excluded by poverty and discrimination from making public their (mostly losing) side of the war story. These new works, which often revise or reshape traditional war narratives, may uncover secrets or unearth scandals hidden in the past, or reveal the kinds of power relations that have formed the complex histories of colonization in each country. For example, First Nations playwright Marie Clements's *Burning Vision* (2004) sheds light on the little-known historical fact that the uranium in the bomb dropped on Hiroshima was mined on land in the Northwest Territories belonging to the Dene group of indigenous (First Nations) people. The Canadian government, which informed the Dene in the 1930s that they were digging for a substance to cure cancer, knew then it was deadly; as a result of their work either in the mines or as transporters of the ore, many of the Dene began to die of cancer. Clements's challenging play further connects the exploitation of the Dene with the Japanese who were bombed and with the Americans who dropped the bombs. And Joy Kogawa's *Obasan* (1981), which chronicles the forced removal of 22,000 West-Coast Japanese Canadians from their homes and businesses after the bombing of Pearl Harbor, also places government policy in a poor light. Kogawa, who was interned herself as a child, describes in fiction how those designated "enemy aliens" were transported to internment camps in interior British Columbia, and then, at the end of the war, were offered either repatriation to Japan or a second dispersal to designated areas east of the Rocky Mountains. These extreme measures were put in place even though no Japanese Canadian was ever charged with disloyalty to Canada. Kogawa's novel, which depicts the child Naomi's observance of the tension between her two "obasans" (aunts) – one who vociferously seeks justice and redress, the other who remains silent and attempts to forget the past – is believed to have been instrumental in influencing the Canadian government's 1988 financial settlement with Japanese Canadians for their loss of property, liberty, and citizenship during the war. Kogawa's novel also affected writers such as Kerri Sakamoto. Unaware that her relatives had been interned until she was twenty, and after reading *Obasan*, Sakamoto wrote *The Electrical Field* (1998). Set in the 1970s before the Redress movement had attained momentum, the novel takes as its subject the residual legacy of collective silence, emotional scarring, and internalized racism on internees and their descendants. In 1992, Kogawa's *Itsuku* (*Some Day*), which tells of Naomi, now a middle-aged woman, and her outspoken aunt's gradual reconciliation with the racist policies of the Canadian government, appeared. (Stung by the harsh criticism of *Itsuku*, Kogawa rewrote the novel and re-published it as *Emily Kato* in 2005.)

Recently, Dennis Bock in *The Ash Garden* (2001), and Sakamoto in *One Hundred Million Hearts* (2003), revisited the conflict in the Pacific. Bock's novel examines the dropping of the atomic bomb on Hiroshima from the perspectives of three traumatized victims – a German scientist who defected to work on the Manhattan Project and was then sent to Hiroshima immediately after the bombing to assess its effects; his wife, an Austrian Jew who found refuge at a Quebec resettlement camp after her voyage on the doomed SS St. Louis; and one of the twenty-five "Hiroshima Maidens" brought to the United States for reconstructive surgery – whose lives intersect. (Shaena Lambert's *Radiance* [2007] offers a more sustained examination of one of the "maidens," but it is set wholly in the United States.) Sakamoto's *One Hundred Million*

Hearts recounts the story of a woman who discovers that her Canadian-born father, a kamikaze pilot who shames his family and his country by surviving the war, has a second daughter in Tokyo who bitterly resents the ideology which attempted to sacrifice the lives of so many men like her father.

Several contemporary but overlooked Australian writers have also brought to light shocking events on the home front. In *Blood Stained Wattle* (1992), Maria Gardner attempts to unveil the "truth" behind the suppression of facts pertaining to the bombing of Darwin in the Northern Territory (Japanese forces mounted two air raids, the first of sixty-four, on February 19, 1942, that killed 243 people and wounded three to four hundred), and to ascertain why it has since become known as "a day of national shame." In *Smile, the War Is Over* (1983), Robin Sheiner draws attention to the Federal War Cabinet's classified plan which determined that if Australia were invaded, it would only be defended south of the Brisbane Line, an imaginary boundary extending roughly from Brisbane to Adelaide, thereby protecting the south east of Australia, but excluding all of West Australia. Not surprisingly, when the Americans come to rescue them, the people of Perth greet the GIs as heroes. Like James and Cusack, Sheiner details the Americans' ability, thanks to their bulging wallets, to monopolize taxis, booze, and women, which then gave rise to Australian men's irate response that Americans were "overpaid, oversexed, and over here." Like *Come In Spinner*, Sheiner's text critiques the manpower legislation that forced women into poorly paid jobs in factories or munitions industries. It also chronicles the plight of Australian women who immigrated to the United States as war brides and exposes the kinds of prejudice aboriginal people, African–American soldiers, and immigrants encountered before and during the war. In *An Angel in Australia* (2003), Keneally also draws attention to racial hostility against African–American soldiers in Australia and a priest's attempt to counteract it. The novel also features a defenseless and lonely woman who succumbs to the charms of an American service man while her husband is incarcerated in a German POW camp. Although the representation of Americans in Australian texts is often negative, New Zealand writer Fiona Kidman's *Paddy's Puzzle* (1983) depicts a positive and loving relationship between an African American and a young woman suffering from tuberculosis in Auckland.

III

In the 1990s, a number of established Canadian writers turned to Second World War events as sources for their fiction. Katherine Govier's *Angel Walk* (1996) features an unconventional young Canadian woman who holds down a dangerous job in an Ontario TNT plant and then travels overseas to work as a war photographer for the newspapers of the Canadian-born press baron Lord Beaverbrook (Max Aitken) in London. Anne Michaels's *Fugitive Pieces* (1996), a poetic novel narrated from two points of view, traces time, memory, and history across several continents. The first narrator, a Polish child whose family is destroyed by the Nazis, eventually becomes a successful translator and poet in Canada, but never overcomes the sense of cultural and linguistic dislocation he suffered in his youth or comes to terms with how to honor the dead without becoming obsessed by them. The second narrator, the son of Polish Holocaust survivors, is also tormented, but by events he did not live through. Michael Ondaatje's *The English Patient* (1992) examines the socio-political implications of colonialism, history, literature, and gender; it brings together four characters in a bombed-out Italian villa at the end of the war and tells an enigmatic story of love and espionage.

Although Edward McCourt presented an unhappy Irish war bride in *Home is the Stranger* (1950), none of his contemporaries – male or female – followed his lead for some decades. Why there should have been such a paucity of stories about these war brides is curious, given that nearly 48,000 women, mostly from Britain, emigrated to Canada after the war, bringing with them some 22,000 children. That so many marriages occurred may be due to the fact that Canadian soldiers were the first to leave and the last to come home; except for the catastrophic raid on Dieppe in 1942, they did not "see action" until 1943. In the meantime, service clubs and dance halls became places to pass the time and find companionship. Not surprisingly, romance, intensified by the uncertainties of the wartime climate, began to bloom. These amorous relationships often led to much non-violent "action," for as one of playwright Margaret Hollingsworth's soldiers remarks in *Ever Loving* (1985), "We're the only outfit in military history with a birth rate higher than the death toll."[2]

Recently, war brides have appeared in novels and stories such as Margaret Atwood's *The Robber Bride* (1993), Aritha van Herk's *No Fixed Address* (1986), Suzette Mayr's *The Widows* (1998), Mavis Gallant's "Up North" (*The End of the World and Other Stories* [1974]), Joyce Marshall's "The Old Woman" (*A Private Place* [1976]), Rachel Wyatt's "Her Voice, "Stanley," and "Time Travel" (*The Day Marlene Dietrich Died* [1996]), and in plays such as Norah Harding's *This Year, Next Year* (1995) and *Sometime, Never* (2001), and Margaret Hollingsworth's *Ever Loving*. These texts demonstrate that women experience war over a different period than masculinist history usually recognizes, for the aftermath of war proved as destructive to war brides as the war years had been to men, and the pain of deracination comparable to a serious war wound. Many are miserable because their Canadian husbands have overstated their potential: dashing and gallant in uniform, full of promise and get-up-and-go in Europe, they lack initiative and resourcefulness back in the True North. These "war husbands" also appear to be stuck in the old ways of thinking. They demand that their wives – many of whom held down responsible positions under dangerous wartime circumstances – be submissive nurturers and caregivers who place their husbands' needs ahead of their own. Literary brides are also crushed by what they identify as Canada's appalling lack of culture, its hostile people, and its chilly climate.

In fairness, women writers also emphasize that war brides should shoulder some of the responsibility for their unhappiness, since their reasons for marrying Canadian men were often questionable. Few married for love alone. Many emigrated for the same reasons as the men who marched away to war – a yen for adventure, a longing to travel, and to escape low-paying, boring jobs and repressive milieus. Moreover, few had done their "home" work before leaving England and hence were, as Atwood puts it, "raw" brides, unaware of how truly strange and different Canada would prove to be.[3] Although few emerge triumphant on the home front, signs of victory arise, as they tend to in postcolonial texts, in the next generation, as several daughters resolve not to repeat their mothers' lives as subalterns, but take up unconventional careers and eschew traditional forms of marriage and motherhood.

Timothy Findley, one of Canada's most politically engaged writers, has long been preoccupied by war, but especially by the Second World War, which began when he was a child of nine. His recurring subjects are fascism, the Holocaust, and nuclear annihilation, and in "War," "Stones," *You Went Away* (1996), and *Famous Last Words* (1981), he examines the misuse of authority by patriarchal figures and the suffering they cause their sons. His *The Butterfly Plague* (1969; revised 1986) makes an unusual comparison between Nazi Germany and Hollywood, and *Not Wanted on the Voyage* (1984), a contemporary revision of the Biblical Noah's Ark myth, also retells the European Holocaust story. In *Famous Last Words*, Findley questions how writers such as Ezra Pound and public figures like the Duke and Duchess of Windsor could have succumbed to fascist intrigue. (Because of strict libel laws in Britain, Findley's publishers delayed publication of the novel until 1987, a year after the Duchess's death.)

Findley also has much in common with Keneally, for both position their readers as active and critical agents implicated in the tragedies of history. Like Findley, Keneally was a child during the Second World War, but the crucial event for him was the anticipated Japanese invasion of Australia. (Unlike Findley, though, Keneally has employed a pseudonym, William Coyle, for *Act of Grace* [1988], which features a tail gunner in the RAF who flies numerous missions over Europe, including Dresden, and *Chief of Staff* [1991], which examines the politics of the American High Command in Australia.) Like Findley, Keneally prefers home front tragedies to combat novels: *The Fear* (1965), revised and reissued as *By the Line* (1989), examines the stresses of family life during wartime; *A Family Madness* (1985) underscores the problems Belarusian emigrants encounter in postwar Australia; and *The Cut-Rate Kingdom* (1980) asserts that Australian leaders (thinly disguised Prime Ministers John Curtin and Robert Menzies, and the American General MacArthur) were insufficiently competent to handle the complexities of a nation threatened by Asian invasion. Keneally also demonstrates the extent to which events from the First World War impinge upon the Second in *Gossip From the Forest* (1975), as does Findley in *You Went Away*, and, like Findley, Keneally has also written about the Holocaust. His best-selling novel, *Schindler's Ark* (1982), based on the story of the entrepreneurial factory-owner Oskar Schindler, a complex and not wholly admirable man who nevertheless endangered his own life and future to save over one thousand Polish Jews from extermination, was retitled *Schindler's List* for the American edition and, subsequently, Spielberg's 1994 film. It won the Booker Prize, although controversy erupted over whether it was fiction or "faction," and hence ineligible for the prize. In *Searching for Schindler* (2007), Keneally reveals how he came to be fascinated by the story and how Spielberg turned it into a highly successful film.

In New Zealand, Pat Booth's *Sons of the Sword: A Novel of the Pacific War* (1993) retraces many historical events of the Pacific War that endangered citizens in Australia and New Zealand, as well as the devastation that resulted from the dropping of bombs on Hiroshima and Nagasaki. Narrated from the point of view of an adult looking back on his wartime childhood, the novel also tells of "other losses" his family suffered as a result of their brief encounter with an American soldier. Contemporary writer C. K. Stead's *Talking About O'Dwyer* (1999), narrated by a New Zealand-born Oxford professor, illustrates how his life and the lives of others are affected by the death of a Maori warrior killed on Crete by a Pakeha commanding officer. In *Tu* (2004), Maori writer Patricia Grace draws upon her father's war diaries that briefly describe his service with one of the most celebrated and decorated units of the New Zealand Army, the 28th Maori Battalion, to tell the story of three brothers who enlist separately in the Maori battalion and eventually serve in Italy together. Although Grace stresses that many Maori felt they were participating in the war as the price of citizenship – their famous marching song includes the words "For God, King, and Country" – she questions whether their tremendous sacrifices (they were often used as shock troops and hence had the highest casualty rates of any battalion) brought them any reward, or whether it was ever possible to find meaning in so much violence, devastation, and death. The answer to Grace's question, whether posed by writers from Australia, Canada, or New Zealand, is a resounding "No."

NOTES

1. Quoted in Desmond Morton, *A Short History of Canada* (Toronto: McClelland, 1994), p. 222.
2. Margaret Hollingsworth, *Ever Loving*, in *Willful Acts* (Toronto: Coach House Press, 1985), p. 56.
3. Margaret Atwood, *The Robber Bride* (Toronto: McClelland, 1993), p. 163.

PART III

Approaches and revisions

12

GILL PLAIN

Women writers and the war

"Women writers and the war" is a misleadingly straightforward title for a subject of enormous proportions, a subject that potentially embraces not only the geographical extent of a world war, but also a series of theoretical questions about writing and subjectivity, conflict and creativity. Although, as earlier chapters show, women of all nationalities responded powerfully to the events in Europe and beyond, this chapter will focus on British women's responses to the conflict.[1] The selection is not intended to suggest that British women writers can somehow stand for all women writers and their responses to war; rather it is an attempt, through selection, to indicate the complexity of the topic. Even within the confines of a small island (albeit one with a large empire attached), women responded to the war with breathtaking diversity, their writing articulating everything from anger to grief, from resentment to support. Some even avoided the conflict, relocating their fiction in imaginative spaces beyond the reach of the war machine. Yet these spaces nonetheless bore the imprint of the conditions of their construction, and can be seen as one strategy among many for imaginatively surviving war. This chapter will examine the diverse strategies of British women writers to ask a series of larger questions about war and gender, and to consider whether it is possible to identify a coherent body of writing that represents a female response to the Second World War.

Territorial claims: women's place in the Second World War

A substantial body of critical work now bears witness to women writers' production of a "distinguished and multiform literary tradition" – but this recognition has taken years to achieve.[2] As both Phyllis Lassner and Jenny Hartley have noted, the literary establishment of the 1940s was largely dismissive of women's wartime writing, and this indifference is symptomatic of the conceptual problems that surround not only women and war, but "war writing" itself. Historically, the very idea has been a gendered one, founded on the emphatic cultural distinction between male activity and female passivity, combatant and non-combatant, soldier and mother. But it was evident from long before the outbreak of the Second World War that such a clear-cut dichotomy could not be maintained in a new age of mechanized armies and airborne warfare. This was to be a "war against civilian populations" with the potential to invert traditional paradigms of suffering and sacrifice.[3] Bombing would reshape the experience of war for British women, as would the steady advance of the "war machine" in the form of conscription, evacuation, rationing, and unprecedented governmental intervention into the private spaces of everyday life.[4] The Blitz's emphatic displacement of the boundary between homefront and battlefront is a particularly visceral demonstration of the inadequacy of understanding war writing only in terms of combat experience, but it is not this alone that can be seen to give cohesion to a concept of women's war writing. Indeed, many women writers had no direct experience of war's violence and their writing cannot straightforwardly be categorized through shared trauma. They did, however, share what Elizabeth Bowen described as a "climate" – the atmosphere of Britain in the period 1935–50.[5] The attempt to articulate this climate gave rise to a complex body of writing that grapples in particular with issues of belonging and exclusion surrounding the perceived cultural disjuncture between "woman" and "war."

The historian Sonya Rose has observed that the public discourses surrounding women during the war were riddled with contradictions. Women were told to "be truly feminine" while at the same time their sexuality was understood as a potential threat to the security of the nation.[6] Women were the symbolic representatives of the home front, but they were needed in the public sphere, and magazines, posters, and advertisements struggled to reconcile women's agency with their traditional roles, usually by offering the reassuring message that "love and marriage would follow wartime service and sacrifice."[7] As Rose observes, the very articulation of this narrative invokes the specter of its feared alternatives: the career woman and the undomesticated female. Women writers also raised these specters, depicting in their non-compliant, doubtful, and questioning women the breakdown of patriarchal authority within the home and the displacement of heterosexual norms. In Mollie Panter-Downes's *New Yorker* short stories, for example, a light comic touch softens but does not disguise the seismic shift in gender relations brought about by the war. In "Fin de Siècle" (July 12, 1941) Panter-Downes depicts a bohemian couple whose comfortable, companionate 1930s existence is remorselessly overwritten by the new narrative of the 1940s. In an uncanny regression, the heterosexual dyad is usurped by the return of the homosocial community as – much to the horror of his wife, Ernestine – Don Merrill discovers he relishes the return to school that is army life:

> When he was singled out for a commission, it became apparent that the keenness was real, not ironic. The first few times she heard him talking about "we" it took her a moment or two to realise that he didn't mean the calm domestic "we," Don and Ernestine, but the regiment to which he was going to be attached. Already he had identified himself with it.[8]

As the weeks progress, Don is gradually absorbed by his new wartime identity, and Ernestine is left uncertain as to how to read his "unsmiling" face.[9] All around she finds people talking about "their version of Don's new 'we'," but for her this transition means the denial of their past life, and the translation of her status from artistic equal to subordinate wife.[10]

In Panter-Downes's story, war intensifies hierarchical gender relationships, as men, by becoming soldiers, assume a higher purpose and an identity that definitively distinguishes them from women. It is a depressing vision in which a relative pre-war equality is displaced by a wartime doctrine of separate spheres; but amongst women writers more widely, this perception of renewed difference coexisted with a sense that the war nonetheless offered considerable opportunities to women. In her study of "middlebrow" fiction, Hartley has argued that "even when it is critical," British women's writing constitutes "a literature of commitment and citizenship."[11] Hartley is relatively optimistic about the impact of the war on gender relations, believing that it offered women unprecedented access to the public sphere, to "value, status and pay."[12] These are not insignificant considerations, but are they actually synonymous with citizenship? Susan Gubar's work suggests not. In her influential examination of war writing and gender, Gubar argues that irrespective of her wartime utility, woman remains a foreign body within patriarchal concepts of nationhood. While not actually the absolute other of the enemy, she remains a potential other, a suspect figure within a structure of national homogeneity that distrusts and fears the feminine.[13] This tension between pragmatic inclusion and fundamental distrust characterized almost all dimensions of women's entry into the public sphere, and in women's writing it resulted not so much in a "literature of citizenship," as an interrogation of such a concept. A wide range of women's wartime fiction encodes a debate about and a questioning of women's relationship to what Virginia Woolf described in *Three Guineas* as the "unreal loyalties" of "old schools, old colleges, old churches, old ceremonies, [and] old countries."[14]

Citizens or traitors? Women and nation

From the work of Rose, Hartley, and Gubar, and from the contemporary interventions of Woolf, it would seem that women were not granted citizenship in the Second World War; rather, they were forced to negotiate for it. And when attained it was provisional, subject to an ongoing program of proof emerging from a basic cultural assumption of women's unreliability. Women occupied a compromised position in relation to state structures, as Elizabeth Bowen makes clear in her novel *The Heat of the Day* (1948). When the heroine Stella threatens to expose the blackmailing spy Harrison, he tells her in no uncertain terms that her version of events will not be believed: "a woman's always a woman, and so on."[15] Irrespective of the role she is performing, woman's preeminent subjectivity is sexual, and she remains categorized by her sex in a way that displaces her from the wartime construct of citizenship. Indeed, in an ironic foreshadowing of poststructuralist thought, wartime women were assumed to be performing rather than inhabiting the identity of public citizen, and the assumed instability of this reiterated act of being was reinforced by media images that endlessly reminded women not of their singular subjectivity, but of their multiple roles (feminine lover, masculine worker, ideal homemaker). Margaret Higonnet puts it most succinctly: "Propaganda reminded female defense workers that they were not themselves – that is, not 'natural' – but behaving temporarily *like men*."[16] What emerges most clearly from this message is an underlying fear of a loss of definition – a fear of losing the clear-cut boundaries distinguishing the male subject from his female other. Women consequently become even more disturbing in wartime, as through employment in the public sphere they come closer to the possibility of citizenship – and thus it is that films, advertising, and fiction often encode a sting in the tale. Wartime gender representation ultimately falls back upon the exposure and reiteration of difference, through love or some other form of bodily collapse that emphatically reminds women that they are *not* citizens, but rather essential servants to the male citizen class.

Given the anxieties surrounding the female body in time of war, it is perhaps not surprising that the relationship of women to the body politic was more emphatically the subject of women's writing before the outbreak of hostilities. The events of the 1930s, in particular Hitler's rise to power in Germany and the Spanish Civil War, prompted writers such as Woolf, Storm Jameson, and Naomi Mitchison to produce novels and essays urging political and spiritual resistance to fascism. In *Three Guineas* (1938), probably the most famous of these early polemical interventions, Woolf is faced with the question of why women's enfranchisement has not put an end to war. She responds to this impossible question with an extended parody of scientific inquiry that links fascism and patriarchy in its argument that the seeds of dictatorship are rooted in domestic tyranny. The public and the private, argues Woolf, cannot be divided, "the tyrannies and servilities of the one are the tyrannies and servilities of the other."[17] Patriarchal society has, for centuries, oppressed women and denied them the fundamental rights of citizenship. The rise of fascism, however, has exposed "the private brother, whom many of us have reason to respect" to the alienating experience of otherness and oppression:

> You are feeling in your own persons what your mothers felt when they were shut out, when they were shut up, because they were women. Now you are being shut out, you are being shut up, because you are Jews, because you are democrats, because of race, because of religion.[18]

For Woolf this shared experience is "inspiring" and she imagines a future in which men and women work together in the common cause of peace.[19] But in spite of this unity of purpose, she refuses to join her correspondent's society for the prevention of war, and proposes instead an alternative: the Outsiders Society.[20] With exemplary logic, Woolf questions how women can be part of a culture that has so long excluded them, and asks what possible investment they might hold in the emotive concepts of patriotism and nation. The Outsiders Society, she maintains, must "maintain an attitude of complete indifference" to the claims of country, for the country does not and has never recognized them: "As a woman," writes Woolf, "I have no country. As a woman I want no country. As a woman my country is the whole world."[21] In a radical inversion of the binary oppositions so often used to condemn women, Woolf compares their rational, adult indifference to the arrested development of men and nations who are "fighting to gratify a sex instinct" which she "cannot share."[22] Women, so long associated with the body, are here linked to the mind, and they represent the best hope of thinking a future beyond the irrationality of war.

Woolf was not alone in expressing anxiety about the triumph of instinct over rationality. As the war progressed, the pacifist Frances Partridge struggled in her diary to make sense of a conflict that violated her deepest beliefs and filled her with "thoughts of death and suicide":

> I put on records, Monteverdi and Haydn, hoping that music would have its usual magical effect in restoring belief in the existence of logic and sanity, but tonight it seemed impossible to correlate the two disparate worlds, the musical one of reason and the mad one of events.[23]

Partridge's pacifism makes it doubly hard for her to reconcile the violence of war with reason and progress, but women across the political spectrum also articulated a sense of war as regression. In Betty Miller's *On the Side of the Angels* (1945), Andrew, sidelined from the services through ill health, becomes a detached observer of the conflict. His Freudian conclusions stress the vulnerability of civilization and the power of atavistic, repressed desires: "it's war itself which is the biggest piece of escapism of all – escapism *par excellence* – a flight from reason, from everyday duties and responsibilities."[24] Andrew's critique is non-gender specific, but the context of the novel, in which a small-town doctor is seduced from his wife and family by the homosocial lure of the military, firmly genders the "flight from reason" as male. In thus identifying war as a failure of civilization, writers such as Woolf, Partridge, and Miller challenge assumptions of masculine rationality and female irrationality to suggest, in the words of the poet Wrenne Jarman, "Men are but dreamers: only we are real."[25]

Woolf's *Three Guineas* was not, however, an isolated response to the threat of war. As early as 1936, Storm Jameson's *In the Second Year* depicted the consolidation of a fascist dictatorship in Britain, and an even more disturbingly dystopian future was imagined by Katharine Burdekin's *Swastika Night* (1937). For Stevie Smith, however, the impending crisis had its roots not in public policy but in the corruption of the individual psyche. *Over the Frontier* (1938) was Smith's second novel and readers would have been familiar with the intimate confiding voice of her narrator, Pompey Casmilus, from the earlier *Novel on Yellow Paper* (1936). But while the opening of the book reacquaints us with Pompey the skeptical observer, as the novel progresses the reader is increasingly discomforted by a surreal transition in which Pompey the outsider becomes Pompey the disciple – a believer in some unnamed creed, fighting for an unspecified cause, she is seduced into uniform by the rhetoric of a "righteous pure intolerance."[26] The parallels with fascism are obvious, and in allowing her own familiar narrative voice to succumb to its promises, Smith demonstrates that the capacity for fascism lies within us all.

Smith's depiction of a traitorous and barbaric inner self suggests a bleaker vision even than that of Woolf, who had at least imagined in women a saving quality of indifference to the rhetoric of power. But whatever the differences in their understanding of the danger, both writers were acutely aware of the attraction posed by concepts of belonging and the difficulty of maintaining a critical distance from the emotive discourse of patriotism. This desire for distance is not synonymous with opposition to the war. Indeed, of the writers discussed in this section only Frances Partridge maintained an unwavering belief in pacifism throughout the conflict. It is, however, indicative of a widespread recognition across the political and literary spectrum that there was a disjuncture framing women's relationship to nation. A brief examination of this "gap" in the middlebrow world of popular fiction serves to indicate just how difficult it was for writers to produce Hartley's literature of "commitment and citizenship."

Agatha Christie and Margery Allingham were two of the most successful writers of the interwar years, their detective fiction winning both critical and popular acclaim.[27] When the war began, they deployed familiar characters in this unfamiliar territory, seeking – like most popular writing in wartime – both to excite and reassure their audience. These were fantasies of agency designed to suggest that in time of peril, the individual, however insignificant, could make a difference. But although the fiction of both Christie and Allingham features a range of strong women characters, the conception of female wartime agency that emerges from their writing seems fundamentally limited. For Allingham, the fantasy of agency is primarily addressed to the middle-class man in the street, who will, her novel *Traitor's Purse* (1941) suggests, be ably assisted by both women and the working classes. Her detective Albert Campion has a plucky girl assistant in the shape of Lady Amanda Fitton, but in spite of her evident capabilities and public role as an aircraft designer, he never feels able to trust her with full knowledge of the situation. Thus excluded, she is, in effect, marginalized from the status of citizen-investigator, and is left to succumb to the classic female malady of inappropriate desire. Christie's *N or M?* (1941), by contrast, seems to offer a more inclusive vision, suggesting women's capacity to evade the imputations of disloyalty and assert their citizenship via the back door. In a story about the "partners in crime" Tommy and Tuppence Beresford, Christie suggests that women *will* save the nation, whether men like it or not. Excluded from the offer of top-secret war work made to her husband, Tuppence uses her initiative, and such archetypally "feminine" skills as knitting and gossiping, to infiltrate a boarding house suspected of fifth-column activity. Her investigative triumph manages simultaneously to subvert and reassure. Tuppence is undoubtedly loyal to the nation, but she demonstrates this loyalty through a shameless display of deception and a disturbingly "natural" aptitude for espionage.

From the polemical to the popular, then, women writers engaged with the cultural constructions that problematized women's relationship to nation and war. They were also, as the work of writers such as Stevie Smith made clear, deeply concerned with the impact of war on the individual. Yet, as both writers at the time and subsequent critics have noted, the war resisted inscription, silencing many of those who had been vociferous commentators throughout the 1930s. "Its [sic] the unreality of force that muffles every thing [sic]," recorded Woolf in her diary on September 3, 1939, and the impact of this unreal reality on women's writing will be the focus of the next sections of this chapter.[28]

The impossibility of war writing I: looking outward

While writers such as Jameson continued to produce politically engaged fiction after the outbreak of war, others found themselves confronted by the difficulty of articulating the experience. In Woolf's *Between the Acts* (1941), for example, the war figures as an oblique presence, manifesting itself only in persistent, unsettling images of violence. Characters are bereft of words, unable to express themselves, and the relationship between writer and audience is depicted as the agonizing failure to "bring a common meaning to birth."[29] In Woolf's novel, moments of communication are fleeting and half-perceived, fragmentary triumphs over the instability and inadequacy of language. In its engagement with history, community, and nation, *Between the Acts* is undoubtedly a war novel, but it expresses nothing more clearly than the impossibility of writing about war.

Other writers were similarly changed by the conflict. The prolific Naomi Mitchison, who had produced a wealth of politically engaged fiction in the 1930s, confined herself to her diary during the war years. Her epic historical novel *The Bull Calves* (1947) was only completed after the end of the war, as was Bowen's *The Heat of the Day*. Smith, meanwhile, completed a wartime novel, but could not find a publisher and *The Holiday* only emerged in 1949, after she had replaced all war references with the nebulous concept of the "postwar." Reading the otherwise scarcely altered manuscript, it is perhaps not surprising that this account of post-traumatic stress and inchoate grief was judged unwelcome fare by wartime publishers: Smith's characters have moved beyond war-weariness to states of despair and suicidal melancholy. Yet Smith was unusual in her attempt to make explicit the pain of war. During the conflict itself the predominant tone of women's writing was one of almost clinical detachment: a written parallel to British cinema's discourse of documentary realism. In the age of Mass Observation, writers new and old observed their fellows and themselves with anthropological interest, adopting irony and comic commentary as practical methods for making sense of war.

Monica Dickens's *One Pair of Feet* (1942) typifies this mode of writing. Her account of a year spent training to be a nurse is characterized by a brisk detachment that refuses to dwell on the horrific reality of war, focusing instead on a grotesque depiction of the petty tyrannies of 1940s Britain. The opening passage sets the tone with its refusal of emotion and its acute recognition of what Adam Piette describes as the "fabricated communal feelings ... [that] aimed at transforming private imagination into public spirit":[30]

> One had got to be something; that was obvious. But what? It seemed that women, having been surplus for twenty years, were suddenly wanted in a hundred different places at once. You couldn't open a newspaper without

being told that you were wanted in the Army, the Navy or the Air Force; factory wheels would stop turning unless you rushed into overalls at once . . .

The Suffragettes could have saved themselves a lot of trouble if they had seen this coming. Men's jobs were open to women and trousers were selling like hot cakes in Kensington High Street.[31]

Dickens's comic hyperbole conveys a knowing acknowledgment of war's manipulative discourse, opening up a space for incisive criticism of the banal clichés of war. She never questions the necessity of patriotic duty, but her belief is pragmatic rather than emotive. For Dickens, as for Jan Struther's Mrs. Miniver, "one had to laugh,"[32] and this seemingly trite sentiment set the tone for responses to a war that, simply by coming second, could never generate the levels of outrage or, indeed, compassion that characterized the writing of the 1914–18 conflict.

Dickens was not the only writer to record the quotidian. Panter-Downes's regular "Letter from London" translated the chaos of war into cheery, businesslike reports for *New Yorker* readers, while in *Night Shift* (1941), Inez Holden's much admired reportage brought the voices of the working classes into the public domain. The value of recording the mundane in the face of exceptional circumstances is equally evident in the diaries of the period – and the detachment that characterizes much of this writing can be seen as a strategy of self-preservation, its distancing effect making safe the appalling experiences of bombing, displacement, and loss. This plain-speaking pragmatism is ironically euphemistic, determinedly avoiding what might be termed the emotional "reality" of war. The discourse of coping cannot simultaneously be a discourse that confronts trauma, and in this normalizing discourse – a form of writing as repression – there can only ever be an implicit acknowledgement of the unspeakable truth of war. For other writers, though, the psychological consequences of war became the crux of their writing, and their texts expose the impact of war on individual subjectivity.

The impossibility of war writing II: looking inward

"I wonder whether in a sense all wartime writing is not resistance writing?" asks Bowen in the preface to *The Demon Lover*.[33] Bowen's question resonates because it alerts us to the pervasiveness of war, its capacity to permeate the boundaries of individual subjectivity, to distort, disrupt, and displace the known parameters of self and society. It also reminds us that war can be as powerfully manifest as an implicit as an explicit presence within the text. Bowen's preface constructs war writing as a tentative and evasive concept in which the writer becomes a conduit for the "flying particles of something enormous and inchoate that had been going on."[34] In such a construction of the writer, both gender and war are complicated, and the right to write is no longer linked to a privileging of battlefront or Blitz experience. Rather, writing becomes a saving strategy, a reassembling of the self in the face of its threatened annihilation, a means of dealing with events that were "out of all proportion to our faculties for knowing, thinking and checking up":

> To survive, not only physically but spiritually, was essential. People whose homes had been blown up went to infinite lengths to assemble bits of themselves ... from the wreckage. In the same way, they assembled and checked themselves from stories and poems, from their memories, from one another's talk ... Every writer during this time was aware of the personal cry of the individual. And he was aware of the passionate attachment of men and women to every object or image or place or love or fragment of memory with which his or her destiny seemed to be identified.[35]

The patterns described by Bowen are equally the subject of the title story in Elizabeth Berridge's collection, *Tell It to a Stranger*. These stories, published in 1947, capture the necessity – and the difficulty – of wartime self-assembly. In "Tell It to a Stranger," Mrs. Hatfield is sanguine about the looting of her London house because she knows that this is an experience she can narrativize for the benefit of her wartime friends at the Belvedere, the hotel where she has sought refuge from the Blitz. As she travels back from inspecting the damage she rehearses her story, savoring the sensation of having "real" news to tell, of having an investment in the acts of war.[36] Her homecoming is devastated, however, by the discovery of the Belvedere bombed and on fire. Desperate to receive the reassurance of meaning guaranteed by her friends, she throws herself at the ruins, telling her story as if her life depended upon it, but when she is dragged from the flames she can say nothing to explain the meaning of her loss. Instead, the final words of the story – "My lovely wine glasses" – condense her trauma, displacing her real loss onto the meaningless property stolen from her London house.[37] In this succinct vignette, Berridge, like Bowen, presents an understanding of war writing in which the "particular" enables the allusive expression of a "general" that would otherwise be beyond articulation.[38] In some of Bowen's short stories, however, even this level of expression seems beyond the characters. Or rather – recognizing the risk of acknowledging the meaning of war – they choose to preserve their sanity through a refusal of the truth, describing their losses in tones reminiscent of the ironic detachment of the documentary realists.

In "Sunday Afternoon," Henry, visiting the neutral space of Ireland, attempts to answer his friends' questions about the bombing of London. The task defeats him, and he concludes that "as it does not connect with the rest of life, it is difficult, you know, to know what one feels. One's feelings seem to have no language for anything so preposterous."[39] In "Mysterious Kôr," by contrast, Pepita confronts the inarticulable logic of war's destruction with a regenerative logic of her own: "The war shows we've by no means come to the end. If you can blow whole places out of existence, you can blow whole places into it. I don't see why not."[40] Pepita's fantastical inversion enables her to take imaginative refuge in a space outside war, the magical city of Kôr, but the characters of "Careless Talk" are without such resources. In a bizarrely comic story, characters speak urgently in a dialogue without referents in which anything of substance – from evacuees to bombs – is dismissed as a "bore."[41] Bowen was not alone in her recognition of the unspeakable, as Elizabeth Taylor's *At Mrs Lippicote's* (1945) demonstrates. The novel deals on a thematic level with the alienated marriage of Julia and Roddy, their distance attributable in part to Julia's inability to admire her husband in an appropriately uncritical manner. However, in a bleak subplot the novel also depicts the extent to which dislocation destroys even the survivors of the Blitz. Mr. Taylor, who has lost his wife and his restaurant to the war, thinks back to the experience:

> "Bombed out" is a phrase the world was now used to. "But you were lucky," people would say, "not to have been sleeping there." "No, no one was hurt," he would say. It was like a game of tennis, that sort of conversation: the ball went back and forth, but no one was really involved, the expected replies were dealt and after the game had been kept up for a while, the other side tired and, feeling it had done well, changed the subject. But the truth had not been spoken.[42]

While Taylor suggests the destructiveness of such ritual conversations about the unspeakable, for many, emotional restraint was the only way to manage the excess of war. In a world in which "the overcharged subconsciousnesses of everybody overflowed and merged,"[43] and in which life became subject to unprecedented regulation, writing – even if it could not hope to express the totality of war's impact – became a vital mode of self-affirmation.

A (war) literature of their own?

As the previous sections indicate, the war did not produce a homogeneous literature. The responses of writers fluctuated in accordance with the changing phases of the conflict, and in response to their own experiences. Nancy Mitford's *Pigeon Pie* (1940) belongs, as she acknowledges, to the unreality of the so-called Phoney War, while *The Pursuit of Love* (1945) is emphatically a late war work, its blend of comedy and social comment acknowledging the weariness of a readership desperate for light relief. Struther's "Mrs. Miniver" stories (1939) face an unknowable future with cautious optimism; Holden's

It Was Different At the Time (1943) emerges from the bleakness of the "long haul" – the draining years of hard work and mundane sacrifice, when the first danger had receded but the end was nowhere in sight. The shifting character of women's responses continues into the war's aftermath. Panter-Downes's *One Fine Day* (1947) and Rose Macaulay's *The World My Wilderness* (1950) document the loss of direction characteristic of the postwar world, while Rebecca West's extended meditation on disloyalty, *The Meaning of Treason* (1947), is able to conduct an explicit analysis of national belonging that would have been impossible in the immediate context of conflict.

The literature of the Second World War is a vast body of writing whose relationship to conflict ranges from the immediate to the intangible. Within this body women wrote about the war, against the war, and in support of the war. They wrote in the war and they wrote themselves and their readers out of the war. They demonstrated, in the diversity of their production and the timescale over which it was produced, that war is a concept beyond combat, its impact far exceeding the customary parameters of 1939–45. For Lassner, British women's writing of this period "reaches beyond pleasing forms to shape an ethical/political aesthetic," while in contrast I have argued elsewhere that women writers' most effective engagement with war was at a remove, via strategies of displacement and absence.[44] The critical response to women writers and the war can be no more homogeneous than the work itself: indeed, much of the power of the writing lies in its capacity to suggest an excess of signification, permitting new generations to respond afresh to the nebulous complexity of living through and writing about war.

NOTES

1. Although much excellent historical work traces the impact of the war on the lives of American women, there has been less work on the literary output of the conflict. Exceptions include Susan Schweik's *A Gulf So Deeply Cut: American Women Poets and the Second World War* (Madison: University of Wisconsin Press, 1991), and a valuable overview of the gendered landscape of American writing about the war is provided by Susan Gubar, "This Is My Rifle, This Is My Gun: World War II and the Blitz on Women," in *Behind the Lines: Gender and the Two World Wars* ed. Margaret Randolph Higonnet, Jane Jenson, Sonya Michel, and Margaret Collins Weitz (New Haven: Yale University Press, 1987), pp. 227–59.

2. Phyllis Lassner, *British Women Writers of World War II: Battlegrounds of Their Own* (London: Macmillan, 1998), p. 2. See also Jenny Hartley, *Millions Like Us: British Women's Fiction of the Second World War* (London: Virago, 1997); Gill Plain, *Women's Fiction of the Second World War: Gender, Power and Resistance* (Edinburgh University Press, 1996), and Karen Schneider, *Loving Arms: British Women Writing the Second World War* (Lexington: University Press of Kentucky, 1997).

3. Annemarie Tröger, "German Women's Memories of World War II," in Higonnet *et al.*, *Behind the Lines*, p. 285.
4. See Adam Piette, *Imagination at War: British Fiction and Poetry 1939–1945* (London: Macmillan, 1995), pp. 1–7.
5. Elizabeth Bowen, "Preface" to *The Demon Lover*, in *The Mulberry Tree*, ed. Hermione Lee (New York: Harcourt Brace, 1986), p. 95.
6. Sonya O. Rose, *Which People's War? National Identity and Citizenship in Wartime Britain 1939–1945* (Oxford University Press, 2003), p. 122.
7. *Ibid.*, p. 128.
8. Mollie Panter-Downes, "Fin de Siècle," *Good Evening, Mrs Craven: The Wartime Stories of Mollie Panter-Downes* (London: Persephone Books, 1999), p. 68.
9. *Ibid.*, p. 71.
10. *Ibid.*, p. 69.
11. Hartley, *Millions Like Us*, p. 15.
12. *Ibid.*, p. 1.
13. Gubar, "This Is My Rifle," p. 240.
14. Virginia Woolf, *Three Guineas* (London: Hogarth, 1986), p. 90.
15. Elizabeth Bowen, *The Heat of the Day* (London: Penguin, 1962), p. 41.
16. Higonnet, *Behind the Lines*, p. 7.
17. Woolf, *Three Guineas*, p. 162.
18. *Ibid.*, pp. 121, 118.
19. *Ibid.*, p. 199.
20. *Ibid.*, p. 122.
21. *Ibid.*, p. 125.
22. *Ibid.*
23. Frances Partridge, *A Pacifist's War* (London: Phoenix, 1996), pp. 68, 35.
24. Betty Miller, *On the Side of the Angels*, (London: Virago, 1985), p. 141.
25. Wrenne Jarman, "Letter to Claudia," in *The Distaff Muse* ed. Clifford Bax and Meum Stewart (London: Hollis and Carter, 1949), p. 135. For a useful selection of women's poetry from the conflict see Catherine Reilly, ed., *Chaos of the Night: Women's Poetry and Verse of the Second World War* (London: Virago, 1984).
26. Stevie Smith, *Over the Frontier* (London: Virago, 1980), p. 197.
27. For a fuller account of Allingham, see Gill Plain, "'A Good Cry or a Nice Rape: Margery Allingham's Gender Agenda," *Critical Survey* 15, 2 (2003), 61–75; and for Christie's wartime writing see Plain, *Twentieth-Century Crime Fiction* (Edinburgh University Press, 2001), pp. 29–55.
28. Virginia Woolf, *The Diary of Virginia Woolf*, Vol. V: *1936–41*, ed. Anne Olivier Bell (London: Penguin, 1985), p. 234.
29. Virginia Woolf, *Between the Acts* (London: Grafton, 1978), p. 112.
30. Piette, *Imagination at War*, p. 2.
31. Monica Dickens, *One Pair of Feet* (London: Penguin, 1956), p. 7.
32. Jan Struther, *Mrs Miniver* (London: Virago, 1989), p. 63.
33. Bowen, "Preface," p. 97.
34. *Ibid.*, p. 95.
35. *Ibid.*, pp. 96, 97.
36. Elizabeth Berridge, "Tell it to a Stranger," *Tell It to A Stranger: Stories From the 1940s* (London: Persephone Books, 2000), p. 57.

37. *Ibid.*, p. 59.
38. Bowen, "Preface," p. 99.
39. Elizabeth Bowen, "Sunday Afternoon," *Collected Stories* (London: Penguin, 1983), p. 617.
40. Bowen, "Mysterious Kôr," *Collected Stories*, p. 730.
41. Bowen, "Careless Talk," *Collected Stories*, p. 669.
42. Elizabeth Taylor, *At Mrs Lippincote's* (London: Virago, 2006), p. 97.
43. Bowen, "Preface," p. 95.
44. Lassner, *British Women Writers*, p. 23; Plain, *Women's Fiction*, pp. 20–3, 191.

13

PHYLLIS LASSNER

Life writing and the Holocaust

Although the Holocaust (also known as *Shoah* in Hebrew and *Churban* in Yiddish) was an integral part of World War II, we rarely see their respective literatures shelved or catalogued together. On the one hand, distinguishing the Holocaust is historically justifiable: the intense focus on its planning and execution by the Nazis' Third Reich, the unprecedented extremes of its tortures, and the inconceivable suffering of its victims and survivors have required studying it as an event in its own right. On the other hand, this separation could be seen as mirroring the wartime neglect or even indifference to the Holocaust. The fate and rescue of the Jews and Hitler's other designated victims was not considered part of any Allied war aim. Indeed, the overarching response to reports of mass gassings and burnings was that the only way to save the victims was to win the war. Today, however, the justness of fighting the war, even in view of such misguided and horrific acts as the Allied firebombing of German cities, is predicated on acknowledging the necessity to defeat the power that would have perpetrated the Holocaust far beyond the murder of six million Jews and five million others.

The particularities of its civilian experience, what we can call its homeless front, raises urgent questions about the Holocaust that relate to debates not only about comparisons to other genocides. With certainty, its literature attests to the centrality of the Holocaust to any consideration of the war and to the horrific probabilities had the Allies been defeated. Moreover, while the production of Holocaust writing has created a canon of its own, its significance affects the criteria by which we define modern literature and its relation to the war and its memorialization. Running a full gamut of genres, including poetry, memoirs, diaries, short and long autobiographical and imagined fiction, meditative and critical essays, drama, and music, Holocaust creativity has become central to considerations of what we mean by modern cultural production. This chapter will provide overviews of the major ethical and aesthetic issues involved in the representation of the

Holocaust and their relation to its life writing, and then provide selected readings of sample memoirs and autobiographical fiction.

Although Hitler came to power in 1933 with deeply engrained anti-Semitic beliefs, official persecution of the Jews only began with the Nazis' Nuremberg Laws of 1934, which prohibited intermarriage and excluded Jews from the professions, state-supported education, and ownership of property and businesses. These laws set the stage for widespread but seemingly capricious acts of violence against Jews. As the vandalism, beatings, and murders escalated, however, it soon became apparent to the Jews of Germany and Austria that these were not signs of yet another albeit more extreme pogrom, but a meticulously orchestrated event that served as a prelude to the progression of the systematic destruction of the Jews and their culture. *Kristallnacht* ("night of broken glass"), on November 9, 1938, when synagogues, Jewish businesses and homes were attacked and burned, when Jewish men were beaten, arrested without charge, and sent to concentration camps, marked the moment when anti-Semitic attitudes were given legal sanction and transformed into the actions that would end the thousand-year-long continuous history of the Jews in Europe.

Once the Final Solution, a deadly euphemism for planned extermination, was implemented in 1942,[1] Jews all over Nazi-occupied Europe were rounded up and transported to their deaths by gas and incineration, beatings, shootings, starvation, and disease. The Holocaust only ended with liberation by American, British, and Soviet armies in 1945. Bounded by secrecy, barbed wire, and walled separation, the ghettos, forced labor, concentration, and death camps that we identify as the universe of the Final Solution constituted Hitler's *holy war* against the Jews. Though there were other designated victims, such as political dissidents, the Roma and Sinti, Jehovah's Witnesses, homosexuals, and the mentally and physically handicapped, the primary targets for extermination were the Jews. This war against the Jews, as the historian Lucy Dawidowicz denoted it, was one-sided; there were no mutual conflicts and no battlegrounds. In fact, German Jews were fully integrated citizen patriots, participating as much as they were permitted in the national culture and society as they did elsewhere in Europe. The shocks of being expelled from citizenship, schools, occupations, housing, recreational areas, and even the sidewalks, and then of being deported to the camps and ghettos, were designed to dehumanize and paralyze victims into passivity and silence, but instead, as a kind of resistance movement, the persecuted began to write.

In the Warsaw ghetto, for example, Emanuel Ringelblum, already a well-known writer, organized the *Oneg Shabbes* project, a group effort to keep individual diaries that would record daily occurrences for documentation and testimonial purposes. Buried in three milk cans, two of which were discovered after liberation, these writings, like the more anonymously voiced *Łódź Ghetto Chronicle*, have come to represent the persistence of Jewish culture even as it was being systematically obliterated. The individual and collective voices of the writers, including one hundred volumes of documentation and personal writing, testify not only to the ghettos' complicated power structure into which the Nazis coerced Jewish participation, the rampant starvation and disease, and the assemblage of corpses lining the streets, but also to the production of a literature that, in all its grotesque detail, is the measure of the critical creativity that resisted silence.

Because of the many unsettling moral quandaries seeping out of the Holocaust, such as the nature of complicity and responsibility, and although Holocaust writing comprises many narrative and expressive styles, its indebtedness to history takes precedence over many modern literary concerns that produced linguistic and formalistic experimentation for aesthetic purposes. In the context of modern literary history, even as modernist writers responded to crises of conscience and politics in the aftermath of World War I, historicity was subservient to imaginative interpretation. Such imaginative responses, as Inga Clendinnen asserts, "distilled and certified a transformation in a generation's understanding of what war, peace and politics mean. No comparable distillation of meanings has come out of the Holocaust, now more than [sixty] years past. It continues to defy assimilation."[2] Even totally imaginative Holocaust literature by those who were not there, who bear no personal losses or relation to the event, continues to be evaluated according to historical accuracy and in the service of testimony to an event whose meanings were negated by meaningless slaughter. Even as we agree that imaginative literature lends itself compellingly to subjective, psychological truths that cannot be captured in more dispassionate historical analyses, critics remain worried about transgressing the documentary, evidentiary warrants of Holocaust writing and about constructing meanings that universalize and therefore dilute attention to the actual atrocities. These concerns have shaped a major theme of Holocaust criticism coined by the eminent historian and survivor, Saul Friedländer: the limits of representation.[3] The question of limits of course suggests constraints or even censorship that may be externally imposed. But in its multivalent meanings, limits also highlight linguistic and lexical constraints for any writer struggling to find words and images to correspond with the unprecedented assembly-line machinery of the *extremis* of Nazi atrocities.

Survivors who struggle to represent their experiences accurately are also sensitive to how their accounts will be received, by family, by other survivors, and by those who weren't there and who may judge survivor behavior according to non-Holocaust social, moral, and narrative conventions. For example, Fanya Gottesfeld Heller waited until after her husband's death to write her memoir, *Strange and Unexpected Love*, suspecting all the while that her story transgressed expectations of women's survival strategies and Holocaust relationships. When her book was published she was castigated by members of her community for recounting the story of her love affair with the non-Jewish Ukrainian militiaman who saved her and her family. Even the supportive foreword by Rabbi Irving Greenberg is sensitive to the limits of social acceptance when he tells us that we "can appreciate the delicacy and tact of the account," that its emotional tenor lends "integrity and truth" in its "understated power."[4] Adding complexity to the term "limits," Geoffrey Hartman argues that

> even in the case of the Shoah there are no limits of representation, only limits of conceptualization. Though our technical capacity for depicting the extremest event is in place, it has outstripped the possibility of thinking conceptually or in terms of decorum about those representations, despite the growth of a literary and cultural criticism that wishes to overcome the intelligibility gap.[5]

For survivors, these conceptual, lexical, and social constraints combine with the complications of memory – traumatized, fragmented, interrupted, uncomprehending, and culturally shaped. Charlotte Delbo, French political prisoner and survivor of Auschwitz and author of the acclaimed memoir, *Auschwitz and After*, writes at the end of her life "*Expliquer l'inexplicable*" ("explain the inexplicable"). Though she felt that Auschwitz would always be part of her, she also reflected on the nature and vicissitudes of the lexical relationship to understanding and conveying the atrocities that comprised the camp experience. The first chapter of *Auschwitz and After*, "Arrivals, Departures," written in poetic form, prepares us for the non-linear method of a book that is as much about the workings of memory as it is about trying to invent a language of representing the horrors no one who endured them could understand as they were being perpetrated. And so the only fact she can pronounce with any certainty about the itinerary and conditions she shared with 230 Frenchwomen is, "They expect the worst – not the unthinkable."[6] How, she asks, can one translate that which is beyond precedent, imagination, and knowledge into language that persuades the speaker, not to mention the reader, that the place where the boxcars of prisoners have arrived is real when "They have no idea that this is the center of Europe. They look for the station's name. This is a station that has no name."[7]

No matter how many times Delbo repeats her simple declarations of uncertainty and disorientation of arrival at Auschwitz and no matter how many perspectives she represents, there is neither a history nor an analogy, neither tropes nor names that will even begin to approximate this "one-way street" called Auschwitz.[8] Years later when she writes her Holocaust past, she devotes a chapter to the contemplation of how ordinary words, that we assume correspond to such basic physical need as "thirst," fail. There is no correspondence between the word and the experience that "has no name" when "Lips try to speak but the mouth is paralyzed. A mouth cannot form words when it is dry, with no saliva."[9] In the camps, the lexical and situational limits of representing one's own experiences and responses were complicated by Nazi design when prisoners of different languages and cultural styles of communication were forced to share bunks and even standing room in the squalid, overcrowded wooden huts. Instead of producing communal sharing, whether of meager resources or knowledge, the only result of a cacophony of languages and needs was helplessness and then the struggle to live and die together, especially as the dead were quickly replaced by new conscripts to terror and bewilderment. As Primo Levi, another powerful Auschwitz memoirist, tells us in *Survival in Auschwitz* (originally translated *If This Is a Man*), one's ability to understand what was happening was thwarted by understanding neither the German orders nor the information one's bunkmate may have tried to share or withhold.

Delbo's reflections on language combine with those on memory to elucidate the dilemma of presenting the truth of that experience which may be unimaginable to the uninitiated but which she, like so many other survivors, feels compelled to recount. Memory, for Delbo, functions differently for ordinary times and experiences and for Auschwitz. Ordinary memory situates the terrors of Auschwitz in a past that one has survived and from which she can separate herself because it is a thinking and analytical memory. She can now think of herself as free in a present that is distinct from the Holocaust past. But unlike ordinary memory, deep memory is a sensory, physical experience, and remains so much a part of the self that there is no thinking or analyzing that will allow an escape from the past. Like Isaiah Spiegel, Ida Fink, and other Holocaust survivor writers, all of Delbo's writing combines these two memory activations with the language of graphic detail to bring us as close as she can to the horrors so that we are in a position where she can implore us to "Try to look. Just try and see."[10]

For Jewish survivors, the contingencies of memory-work resonate with Jewish traditions of historical consciousness and identity. For example, as the story of the Exodus from Egypt and the concomitant declaration of peoplehood are reclaimed by Jews everywhere reciting the story in annual rituals, a continuum of historical identity is created by reclaiming the ancient past as a memory that not only reaches the present but stretches into the future. And yet it is precisely because Jews have practiced their traditions in different languages and cultures, that for Holocaust survivors, as James

Young points out about ghetto diarists, this continuum is subject to translation, revision, and reinterpretation:

> In addition to time and place, the diarists' very language, tradition, and world view played crucial roles in the making of their literary witness. It may always be difficult to distinguish between the archetypal patterns the ghetto diarist has brought to events, those [that] are perceived in or inferred from them, and those that exist in his narrative. As raw as they may have been at the moment, the ghetto and camp experiences were immediately refined and organized by witnesses ... depending on [their] own historical past, religious paradigms, and ideological explanations.[11]

Young's analysis of the multifaceted strains of writing the Holocaust includes the reader for whom extant guides to reading literature are at best inadequate and more likely irrelevant. As many literary historians and critics of Holocaust writing explain, this is because its forms of expression do not accord with either traditional modes of rendering external realism or experimental narrative structures that express internal consciousness.

In these latter cases, even if the subject was the horrors of war or the abjection of individual characters, it has been assumed by readers and writers alike that imaginative access to these experiences could be made available in art and writing. For example, we use the term *Bildungsroman* to indicate a tradition of the novel of development and disillusionment, where we follow protagonists from childhood innocence through the journey to adult disenchantment, and regardless of whether the ending resolves conflict or leaves it open-ended, there is satisfaction in being able to identify with the themes embedded in great literature. In Holocaust literature there are no conflicts between good and evil, only a one-sided assault or imprisonment in what Primo Levi calls "the gray zone." Levi coined the term to highlight the macabre site of moral strangulation experienced by the Auschwitz *Sonderkommando*, the men who were commanded to keep order, brutally, if necessary, among those they led to the gas chambers, to clean up the excrement, blood, and other bodily fluids of the gassed, and to hoist the bodies and then shovel them into the crematorium ovens. While the *Sonderkommando* were given extra food and better living conditions, they also knew they would be killed and replaced within six months so that there would be no witnesses. The possibilities for choosing one's behavior in this "gray zone" were reduced to what Lawrence Langer calls "choiceless choices" – between ghastly and worst.[12] Commenting on the relation between those prisoners assigned to the gas chambers and those consigned to their gassing, Clendinnen notes that "[p]roduction-line killing allows small space for drama, while the huge contextual fact of the death of the multitude must trivialize the fate of the fortunate few."[13] None of these plot lines bears any possibilities for satisfying resolutions; there is neither an open-ended journey nor poetic justice. Even survivor stories betray our expectations of heroism, suspense, the resolve of the human spirit, and triumph over adversity.

In dramatic contrast, as poet Nelly Sachs warns, Holocaust literature requires that we read it as though it was written "with one eye ripped out."[14] Startling enough on its own, Sachs's image makes Delbo's plea to "just try and see" more chilling than its plaintive tone might suggest. Sachs is asking us to extend our imaginations far beyond what artistic realism, surrealism, or even postmodern hyperrealism could provide as clues. Sachs's demand cannot be fulfilled by recalling the Dadaist film *Un chien andalou*, with its image of a knife slicing an eye; Buñuel may be offering an absurdist vision of the relation between meaningless violence and the violence undergirding the construction of art or of an exposition of non-rational visual discourse. But the only parallel that can come to mind with Sachs's image is the all too real and rationally planned and executed tortures of the Nazis, atrocities that have no equivalent in artistic discourse before the Holocaust. Certainly, despite the immensity of the Holocaust's geographical reach and malevolent depths, despite its countless masses of victims, there are no grand literary themes that can inform or to which we can apply our reading of its twelve years of escalating and intensifying horrors. The oft-quoted remark of Jean Améry (born Hans Meyer), Auschwitz survivor, offers a glimpse into the fathomless chasm between artistic understanding and Auschwitz: "no bridge led from death in Auschwitz to *Death in Venice*."[15] If, as Langer posits, this statement represents "the *dis*continuity between culture and genocide during the years of the Third Reich," it also implies the question of what in our own cultural time and place prepares us to understand "such a doom."[16]

As writers of the Holocaust have grappled with how to create a bridge to readers' knowledge and understanding, they have produced a literature that not only defies conventional literary forms but its genre boundaries as well. As Hartman observes, this unconventional mixture of genres, incorporating both history and artistry, often makes works "hard to classify": as they "*supplement* an oral tradition in danger of dying out," younger artists, writers, and filmmakers reflect "on how to write it, a reflection on representation itself."[17] The question of audience is particularly fraught in the case of Holocaust diarists and memoirists. So many hoped that their writing would testify to the processes leading up to the atrocities as well as to the actual tortures and suffering, especially because they knew how inconceivable these would be to those on the outside. Thus the struggle to depict their experiences and observations had to find new forms of realism and epic writing, charged with gritty detail and repeated patterns of brutality that would take readers closer to the Holocaust than they might be able to tolerate. There is a double defiance in this testimonial writing, for not only did it resist conventions of lexical decorum, it rebelled against Himmler's grotesquely gleeful articulation of the Final Solution: that the Jews' disappearance would be mirrored in their "never-to-be-written page in history."[18] But this does not mean that diarists, particularly those of the ghetto experience, wrote without constraint. As Young reminds us, there was always the danger the diaries would be discovered and in the case of the *Oneg Shabbes* project, plans of the Warsaw uprising and other underground activities would lead to instant retaliation.[19] Given the combination of self-censorship and other subjective formations, whether the narrative forms Holocaust diarists and memoirists created could actually serve as documentary eyewitness evidence is a problem that historians and legal experts have wrestled with since the Nuremberg and other war crimes trials began their prosecution of perpetrators. Whatever their forms and constraints, however they would be understood, diaries remain testaments to the writers' efforts to retain their humanity and to sustain the production of Jewish culture and self-expression even as every effort was being made to strip them away.

Unlike the immediacy conveyed by diaries and even those memoirists writing shortly after liberation, memoirs written long afterward must address the lingering effects of their words not only on readers but on their relation to a present now so distant from the Holocaust that has already receded into the past. Ruth Kluger's highly acclaimed *Still Alive: A Holocaust Girlhood Remembered*, moves between past and present to show how the Holocaust past inflects the present and how her Holocaust story only achieves coherence when filtered through the adult consciousness shaped by her Auschwitz *Bildungsroman*. Similarly to the reception of Fanya Heller's memoir, Kluger's became controversial at the moment of publication for its emotional candor. Her memoir was seen as self-indulgent and disrespectful of her mother's suffering in their shared experience. This critical response reflects problems about sacralizing victims and survivors at the price of failing to accept the all too ordinary, humanly fraught, and tense relationships they carried into and out of the Holocaust. And so Kluger's revelations about her conflicted relationship with her mother before, during, and after Auschwitz defy readers' desires to find uplifting Holocaust stories of self-sacrifice and triumphs of the spirit. Instead, *Still Alive* challenges readers with its story of the triumph of anger. While some scholars claim that the act of writing the Holocaust can be cathartic and healing, Kluger's writing sustains its unyielding wrath, but not only at the perpetrators as we might expect. She also targets the self-righteousness of those, from the well-intentioned to defensive Germans, who would prefer that survivors put their memories to rest so audiences might be saved the pain of an ongoing confrontation with terror and loss.

Woven into her story of the Holocaust past are highly charged moments from her present, as when she interrupts the historical narrative to denounce an ongoing German reluctance about acknowledging guilt. A German woman Kluger names Gisela represents the "younger generation of Germans who couldn't be blamed for anything" and who "was determined to reduce the past until it fit into the box of a clean German conscience that won't cause her countrymen to lose any sleep . . . I am sure she resented that in warm weather I didn't wear long sleeves to cover up the Auschwitz number tattooed on my arm or try to hide it in some other way."[20] As though mirroring the Nazis' design of its deceptive façade at Theresienstadt, Gisela responds as follows to Kluger's experience at this concentration camp masquerading as a tolerably Spartan ghetto: "'Theresienstadt was a ghetto for old people and Jewish veterans', she says, reciting a bit of German folklore."[21] Mind you, Kluger's ire may focus on German self-deception but she does not neglect Americans who prefer to think that life in Theresienstadt had to be better than Vienna before deportation because such "subjective information" would require a makeover of "their inner museum of the Holocaust."[22] Such irony points not only to the experiential and cognitive distance between the survivor and her contemporary audience but to the dissonance created by a self-justifying need to situate the survivor into a non-Holocaust moral universe.

Kluger declares that she presents her "ongoing" story as moving "in circles," a technique that fits her efforts to make sense of the discordance between past and present as well as so many missing pieces, including her father's fate.[23] We see this circularity in her often unfathomable relationship with her mother, where it is sometimes difficult for her and for us to see where the subjectivity of one emerges from the other. This difficulty extended to the emotional honesty with which Kluger wished to depict their relationship. And so to save her mother the painful recognition of a critical portrait, Kluger did not publish her English language edition until after Alma Kluger died. And yet Ruth Kluger's portrait of Alma is no one-dimensional "Mommy dearest" act of vengeance. As with so much Holocaust writing, irony is Kluger's chosen tone to convey how the very paranoia that would isolate Alma from ordinary realities became a saving grace under Nazi domination. Her quicksilver intimations of danger so accurately mirrored the Nazi mindset that on several occasions her seemingly irrational decisions outsmarted the insidiously deceptive pathways to the gas chamber:

Selection, there was to be a selection. At a certain barracks at a certain time, women between the ages of fifteen and forty-five were to be chosen for a transport to a labor camp. Some argued that up to now every move had been for the worse, that one should therefore avoid the selection, stay away, try to remain here. My mother believed – and the world has since agreed with her – that Birkenau was the pits, and to get out was better than to stay. But the word *Selektion* was not a good word in Auschwitz, because it usually meant the gas chambers. One couldn't be sure that there really was a labor camp at the end of the process, though it seemed a reasonable assumption, given the parameters of the age group they were taking. But then, Auschwitz was not run on reasonable principles.[24]

Kluger's depictions of and reflections on her mother and their relationship recall Hartman's observation of a growing self-consciousness about narrating the Holocaust. Relating her mother's paranoia to the mentality and opera-tions of the Reich offers a dramatic reading of the difficulties of parsing and narrating the intricate psychological tortures designed to disorient prisoners and dislodge their intellectual capacities from every model of empirical think-ing they had ever learned or practiced. Given the masses of prisoners affected by this disorientation, a significant intervention performed by memoirs is the restoration of their individuality. And yet Kluger's narrative complicates this struggle for individuation as her story is so deeply entwined with her mother's. We can therefore read *Still Alive* as a dual struggle for subjectivity and distinctiveness: from the Nazis' ideological reduction of the Jews to collective subhumans and from the psychological or emotional bondage to her mother's domination. As Nancy K. Miller notes, "In *Still Alive*, the conundrum of survival is cast as a problem of narrative. How do you tell a survival story? ... And whose story is it?"[25]

Another form of Holocaust life writing is that of autobiographical fiction. In its many permutations, from the creation of a fictional first- or third-person narrator to imagined incidents and conflated or transformed time sequences, characters, and relationships, autobiographical fiction of Holocaust experi-ence reflects attempts to find or construct coherence around those missing pieces or to try to make sense of the Nazis' deceptive and disorienting death machinery. The boundaries between autobiography and autobiographical fiction are often blurred for readers because they generally assume that regardless of their unimaginable extremes, events occurred as depicted and that the protagonist's responses authentically represent the author who bears the same name. Like Kluger's memoir, which follows a jagged and circular movement between bewilderment at the Nazis' practices and her search for understanding of the person she became as a result, the stories of Ava Kadishson Schieber and Ida Fink construct bridges between moments of incomprehensible crisis and their memories. Schieber was hidden on a small farm in Serbia for four years from the age of fifteen. Being liberated into communist domination, she and her mother, her only surviving family member, escaped after another four years to Israel, the only place that would take them in. Many years later, after a successful career as a painter and set designer, she began to write autobiographical stories and poems and produced the volume *Soundless Roar*.

As Schieber reflects in her video testimony for the Facing History Project, in hiding, "Time stopped being meaningful – it became irrelevant. There was no time to be depressed or to indulge in rational thinking." Coursing back and forth between past and present and circling around an image, person, or incident from the past, her stories restore a moment in the past to present memory. Instead of producing an epiphany of understanding, however, the fused images only complicate questions about the chasm between historical and personal knowledge and memory. One can piece together the documentary evidence to shape a comprehensive narrative of the Nazi siege on the Jews, but as with her story "Ride into the City," what coherent story can we derive from the image of a mysterious man whose eyes meet those of an otherwise invisible narrator across their Belgrade street, but who disappears without speaking a word? In this story, the image of the man's face recurs for the narrator in that of a taxi driver whose resemblance incites the eruption of a memory in the form of an emotion out of the past: "Maybe I was projecting my feelings, which were becoming more intimate as I continued to experience long-buried emotions."[26] At the end, the taxi driver refuses Schieber's tip and instead thanks her for listening to his story. The knowledge that the driver's story sheds no light on the past ironically produces the meaning of her relationship with the nameless man of so long ago: "He did not turn toward me. I remained safe. That whole event probably took seconds; it hounded me for years."[27] Ava Schieber's dual consciousness of the past forever invading the present reveals how her combined acts of remembering and narrating a Holocaust experience will survive in her persistent but unanswerable questions.

Ida Fink introduces her collection *A Scrap of Time* with a proclamation about the inseparability of Holocaust memory and the structure of her stories:

> I want to talk about a certain time not measured in months and years. For so long I have wanted to talk about this time, and . . . not just about this one scrap of time. I wanted to, but I couldn't, I didn't know how. I was afraid, too, that this second time . . . had buried the other time under a layer of years, that this second time had crushed the first and destroyed it within me. But no. Today, digging around in the ruins of memory, I found it fresh and untouched by forgetfulness. This time was measured not in months but in a word.[28]

Like Delbo and Schieber, Fink finds it necessary to locate a scene or image both real and imagined from the Holocaust past that will convey the convergence of the two meanings they ascribe to time and memory. One is the excavation of an instance that dramatizes why there are no linguistic or other signs that might serve as guides to understanding the Nazis' highly structured but capricious and deceptive policies and acts of cruelty. The other is to mark an epiphany that despite its revelation of the realities created by the Nazis made no difference to a prisoner's fate. Fink's first-person narrator enters the fray of this effort to recapture an elusive past by persistently calling attention to her position at the sidelines of the events she recounts: "I should not have written 'we', for I was not standing in the ranks."[29] Instead of connoting a disconnect between herself and those who are being rounded up, betrayed, and otherwise disappearing, this distinction is part of a tension that suggests the narrator's tenuous position in relation to the victims and to the past: close yet distant, involved yet detached. Her retrospective ground is physically safe but vulnerable both to the vicissitudes of selective memory and the traumatic knowledge that her survival, like those who did not survive, was always subject to chance at any moment. The momentary and brief structure of the stories captures the sense of the dislodged lives of victims and survivors, a rupture she figures as the "fractured and broken" slabs on which the victims stand as they are being rounded up and which we also imagine as their gravestones.[30]

In particular, "The Key Game" illustrates how Fink's confluence of epiphany and unceasing terror shapes all her stories. As with the others, this drama of survival in the moment begins with a forecast of doom that neither characters nor reader can escape: "It was late, past ten o'clock. The day had long since ended."[31] Redolent with the abstraction of parables, this declaration tells us that the characters' time is not only up, but beyond over. Lacking names, the man, woman, and child are already on their way to dissolving into the exterminated mass. What is the point of knowing them by name, we are given to ask, if their individuality has disappeared even from the narrator's memory? With its foregone conclusion, the story is a memorial not only to the lost six million individuals but especially, in the figure of the child, to those who never had a chance to grow into their individuality. There can be no nurturing of a young self by parents whose only guidance consists of a lesson in futility. The key game is this lesson. A grim, inverted game of hide and seek, the idea is for the father to hide but not be found in the likely event that the Gestapo will come after him. While the story never depicts the Gestapo's appearance, the desperation with which the game is played portends an imminent invasion. Playing a pivotal role, the three-year-old boy must create a diversion by pretending to look for the keys to open the front door when the bell rings. The problem is not, as one might expect, that the three-year-old cannot master the part assigned to him, but rather that the father persistently fails.

In another significant reversal, the child is positioned by his parents as the "key" to their fate. Just as he must take his time looking for the keys to the front door, so he is the one who will deceive the enemy with his answers. In the compressed form of its three and a quarter pages, the story assigns multifaceted meanings to the word "key." And so we learn that the boy's blue eyes are the key to another diversion in suggesting an Aryan appearance. But as with the family's relentless rehearsals, the boy's genetic good fortune will work only if good luck prevails. A large part of the narrative's anxiety derives from its depiction of a father and son role reversal that is made to seem not only unnatural, but ontologically wrong, as though the very idea of the paternal has been destroyed in the reversal. Cast into the role of savior, the child both assumes the paternal role and loses his father who is portrayed as already dead with his pale face and clothes "streaked with lime and dust."[32] No amount of time or perfecting the child's performance can adjust the father's tiny hiding space, fit only for a small child. As the story ends with yet another rehearsal, the boy hesitates but is prodded to offer the answer that declares the loss of the game: "He's dead," a pronouncement affirmed by the narrator who tells us that the father "was already long dead to the people who would really ring the bell."[33]

As we have seen in this sampling of retrospective Holocaust life writing, the work of personal documentation is a work of memory in which the Holocaust past not only pervades the writing present but must be revisited imaginatively again and again to discover narrative coherence. Involved in this creative and critical effort are challenges for readers. As each memoir or story unfolds, in its circular movement always pulling the present back to the past, it warns us that if we are to gain any knowledge and strain toward understanding of the Holocaust, we cannot reach outside this circle, but join its endless and unanswerable questions. Among those questions is the one with which I began this essay. As Susan Suleiman asks: "Should memory of the Holocaust be considered as part of the memory of World War II? Or is it perhaps the other way around: Is memory of World War II part of the memory of the Holocaust?"[34] After weighing the differences and overlaps, Suleiman suggests that "If World War II was arguably the central event of the twentieth century, whose aftereffects and afterimages are still firmly lodged in public consciousness, it is in large part because the Holocaust was part of it."[35] Perhaps nowhere else is this part so dramatically apparent as in Holocaust life writing. In its intensely focused and personally drafted images this literature insists that the war cannot be understood without the historical consciousness that includes those who suffered the Holocaust.

NOTES

1. Although historians have found no written documentation of the decision to implement the Final Solution, it is generally agreed that it occurred at a meeting of Hitler's higher command at Wannsee, a Berlin suburb, in early 1942. The plan for more depersonalized, mechanized killing methods followed reports that the mass shootings had become inefficient because of damaging effects on the extermination squads. The plan was to kill all eleven million European Jews, including those in non-occupied countries.

2. Inga Clendinnen, *Reading the Holocaust* (Cambridge University Press, 1999), p. 164.

3. Elie Wiesel's essay "A Plea for the Dead" laments the proliferation of critical studies that impose abstract and anachronistic theories onto Holocaust writing. While he insists that his own memoir *Night* is not fiction, critics have noted its imaginative form that blurs genre boundaries. See Alan Rosen, *Approaches to Teaching Wiesel's Night* (New York: Modern Language Association, 2007).

4. Fanya Gottesfeld Heller, *Strange and Unexpected Love: A Teenage Girl's Holocaust Memoirs* (Hoboken: KTAV Publishing, 1993), p. xv.

5. Geoffrey Hartman, "The Book of the Destruction," in *Probing the Limits of Representation: Nazism and the Final Solution*, ed. Saul Friedlander (Cambridge, MA: Harvard University Press, 1992), p. 320.

6. Charlotte Delbo, *Auschwitz and After*, trans. Rosette C. Lamont (New Haven: Yale University Press, 1995), p. 4.

7. *Ibid.*, p. 5.

8. *Ibid.*, p. 7.

9. *Ibid.*, p. 70.

10. *Ibid.*, p. 84.

11. James Young, *Writing and Rewriting the Holocaust* (Bloomington: Indiana University Press, 1988), p. 26.

12. Lawrence Langer, *Admitting the Holocaust* (New York: Oxford University Press, 1995), p. 46.

13. Clendinnen, *Reading the Holocaust*, p. 168.

14. Quoted in Alvin Rosenfeld and Irving Greenberg, eds., *Confronting the Holocaust: The Impact of Elie Wiesel* (Bloomington: Indiana University Press, 1978), pp. 26–30. Young describes "an unmistakable resistance to overly theoretical readings of this literature," agreeing that theoretical constructs could very easily overwhelm "the horrible events at the heart of our inquiry" (*Writing*, p. 3).

15. Jean Améry, *At the Mind's Limits: Contemplations by a Survivor on Auschwitz and Its Realities*, trans. Sidney Rosenfeld and Stella Rosenfeld (Bloomington: Indiana University Press, 1980), p. 19.

16. Langer, *Admitting*, p. 55. Langer observes that Améry's sense that "[t]he culture of the past mocked the moral anarchy of the present" is not shared by all potential victims: for others, "[c]ultural traditions furnish a certain security and even sanctity to a life otherwise sundered from the normal props of existence. Few were able to endure on a diet of mere blank terror" (*Admitting*, p. 55).

17. Geoffrey Hartman, *The Longest Shadow: In the Aftermath of the Holocaust* (New York: Palgrave, 1996), p. 9. My emphasis.

18. Quoted in Young, *Writing*, p. 17.

19. *Ibid.*, p. 26.
20. Ruth Kluger, *Still Alive: A Holocaust Girlhood Remembered* (New York: The Feminist Press, 2001), p. 73.
21. *Ibid.*
22. *Ibid.*
23. *Ibid.*, pp. 39, 35.
24. *Ibid.*, p. 103.
25. Nancy K. Miller, "Ruth Kluger's *Still Alive: A Holocaust Girlhood Remembered*: An Unsentimental Education," in *Teaching the Representation of the Holocaust*, ed. Marianne Hirsch and Irene Kacandes (New York: Modern Language Association, 2004), p. 390.
26. Ava Kadishson Schieber, *Soundless Roar* (Evanston: Northwestern University Press, 2000), p. 90.
27. *Ibid.*, p. 93.
28. Ida Fink, "A Scrap of Time," *A Scrap of Time and Other Stories* (Evanston: Northwestern University Press, 1995), p. 3.
29. *Ibid.*, p. 4.
30. *Ibid.*
31. Fink, "The Key Game," *Scrap of Time*, p. 35.
32. *Ibid.*, p. 37.
33. *Ibid.*, p. 38.
34. Susan Rubin Suleiman, *Crises of Memory and the Second World War* (Cambridge, MA: Harvard University Press, 2006), p. 2.
35. *Ibid.*, p. 3.

14

LYNDSEY STONEBRIDGE

Theories of trauma

Amid a seemingly endless proliferation of images of wounded bodies, minds, cities, and states, today we might be forgiven for forgetting that the connection between war and trauma was forged only relatively recently. This is not to say that the Trojans didn't have their minds shattered by years of siege, or that the descendants of the Languedoc heretics didn't suffer with the memories of the burning bodies of their distant relatives. But the sense that war traumatizes, that it forces a crisis in what it means either to have a mind or to be able to remember what has happened in any straightforward way at all, is modern.

For psychoanalysis, trauma is what happens when thinking fails or can no longer take place. It is modern, because the experience of modernity makes thinking about and experiencing the world harder even as technology has supposedly made things easier. Modern war, the marriage of technology with barbarism as it was thought of by many in the middle of the twentieth century, has become the highly charged emblem of a moral, psychological, and existential paralysis of thought. "The mind ought to find a way out, but the mind has lost all capacity to so much as look outward," the philosopher Simone Weil wrote of the experience of being inside a war.[1] She was writing about Homer's war epic, and the model for all war stories to come, *The Iliad*. But the entrapment of which Weil writes so pressingly, the sense of being in the vice-like grip of an experience so intense that one cannot even think it, speaks directly to the year (1940) in which Weil was writing, and to her exile from a newly and devastatingly fallen France. The Second World War, perhaps more than any war before it, raises the question of how war can be held in the mind when the mind itself is under siege; of what it means to experience a trauma so unrelentingly forceful (Weil's essay is called "*The Iliad*, or the Poem of Force"), that it cannot be grasped consciously. This chapter is about how what was commonly thought of as a war on the mind by many progressive writers and thinkers in the First World War, became, by the Second, a war *in* the mind; and about how those mid-century trauma theories set the terms for contemporary literary theory's fascination with what, today, it is possible – or impossible – to think about that war, and about its most brutal and pernicious legacy, the Holocaust.

I

I want to start with three quite different examples of what we might now call trauma writing, taken from those darkest of years, 1938–41, the years of the *Anschluss*, the Munich Crisis, the Hitler–Stalin Pact, the fall of France and, by the summer of 1940, what looked like a very imminent threat to England. "[L]ovely, free, magnanimous England," wrote Sigmund Freud in June 1938 of his new home in exile, in a second Prefatory Note to the third part of his most strange, and most strained, late work, *Moses and Monotheism*; a text which not only contains Freud's final theory of trauma, but which is also deeply scarred with the historical and political wounds of the late 1930s. Indeed, it was a less than lovely England that greeted Freud, newly escaped from Nazi-occupied Vienna, with what he discreetly describes in the same Note as letters "concerned with the state of my soul, which pointed out to me the way of Christ and sought to enlighten me on the future of Israel."[2] These anti-Semitic letter-writers, Freud observes wryly, could not know him; could not know that this rationalist unbelieving Jew thought that all religion was a kind of illusion, or that his work on Moses was to argue that his own identity, that of a Jewish person, was founded not on divine truth, but on trauma.

For Freud's audacious argument in *Moses*, the argument that, he wrote, "tormented him" throughout the late 1930s "like an unlaid ghost," was that like the neurotic, Jewish monotheism took its identity from a series of revisions, distortions, historical truths, fantasies, and defenses all shaped in response to a traumatic kernel at the heart, Freud imagines, of the Moses story.[3] In Freud's "historical novel" (his subtitle) Moses was not a Jew, but an Egyptian: moreover, there was not one, but two Moses; just as Israel was forged not by one group of fleeing people, but two. There is a duality at the origin of monotheism, Freud argued on the eve of the war, and the trauma, the murder of Moses by his followers, an event that is both covered up and avowed in the Jewish tradition itself.

At the beginning of an event so traumatic that today it is impossible to even think about Jewish identity without it, Freud, then, not only restates his religious skepticism but, in what was to be his penultimate text about the science he originated, reaffirms psychoanalysis's starting point: that identity begins with a trauma, a wound in the psyche of which we cannot speak, but upon which we nonetheless fixate in our imperfect memories, fictions, repetitions, and compulsions. "We give the name of *traumas*," Freud writes in *Moses and Monotheism*, "to those impressions, experienced early and later forgotten, to which we attach such importance in the aetiology of the neurosis."[4] Note that the trauma lies not in the impression itself but, and this holds true for nearly all theories of trauma, in the *way* in which it gets into our heads (and out of them). Central to trauma theory is the idea that an impression can be both experienced *and* forgotten (sometimes in the same instant). Trauma thus divides the mind not only from itself, but also splits it in time: there's a lag, a snatch, in the experience of the traumatized that pulls them out of linear chronology.

Freud's model for this kind of latency in *Moses*, as elsewhere in his writing, is that of the accident. Pressing the analogy of the latency experienced by the traumatized individual with the forgetting of the murder of Moses in Jewish monotheism, he writes:

> It may happen that a man who has experienced some frightful accident – a railway collision for instance – leaves the scene of the event apparently uninjured. In the course of the next few weeks, however, he develops a number of severe psychical and motor symptoms which can only be traced to his shock, the concussion or whatever else it was. He now has a "traumatic neurosis."[5]

It was the new phenomenon of the railway accident, which left survivors physically unharmed but undeniably shocked, that had convinced not only Freud, but many others working with hysteria at the turn of the century, that the mind could live in two times at once. The only thing accidental about the experience of fighting in the trenches in the first war was that one managed to survive at all; nonetheless it was shell-shock that confirmed that the trauma of war, similarly, could obliterate the time of the mind (think of Septimus Warren Smith, Virginia Woolf's war-ravaged veteran in *Mrs. Dalloway*, as he tries to flee his dead comrade by throwing himself out of a window in peacetime London). What could be described as a traumatic temporality set the terms for much literary and cultural modernism in the first part of the twentieth century – as well as for what was to follow. Freud's originality was to insist that trauma not only had an effect on the mind, but that it constituted what we think of as human subjectivity itself, which is why, at the same time as he borrows from the model of the accident in *Moses and Monotheism*, Freud also argues, this time on an analogy that runs his narrative of human psychic *development* together with Jewish monotheism, that what cannot be assimilated in trauma is a shatteringly aggressive sexuality – the one that led the tribe to turn against Moses as its primal father, and the same drive that Freud elsewhere locates at the origin of culture and, most famously, in the Oedipus narrative.

While some later theorists have tended to sidestep the drive-invested nature of trauma in Freud, the point is important if we are to understand how for psychoanalysis the intensity of trauma is experienced at the very limits of the mind. Trace the development of the concept of trauma through Freud's thought and, on the one hand, it looks as if while Freud first conceptualized trauma in terms of sexuality, gradually his thinking became overshadowed by a second theory of trauma, this time modeled on the neurosis to which the war-ravaged foot soldiers of the first war, with their vacant gazes, tremors, paralyses, and Charlie Chaplin gaits, bore painful witness. With an eloquent narrative simplicity, the self-shattering of the subject of bourgeois hypocrisy gives way to the traumas of an increasingly atrocious century – as if the latter's consuming violence was the apotheosis of the former's alienation from itself. But it was also always clear to Freud that external events derive their traumatic force precisely because they activate fantasies and provoke the drives into actions and reactions. So, for the Freud of 1915, if not for others working with this new category of fatefully historicized hysteria, the shell-shocked veterans of the first war were not simply driven mad *by* the war; they were traumatized *because* the trauma of the war had undone their deepest fantasies of themselves as peacetime masculine subjects.[6] To encounter trauma for Freud, then, is also to encounter an alien part of ourselves; a "foreign body," as the rhetoric of his first studies on hysteria frequently has it, or as Freud finally describes it in *Moses*, with a loudly reverberating historical echo, "a State within a State, an inaccessible party; with which co-operation is impossible, but which may succeed in overcoming what is the normal party and forcing it into its service."[7]

Trauma does not simply describe the psychological effects of being invaded by history – as if the mind were some kind of island onto which history drops its load. Rather, it challenges us to think about the mind in a state (following Freud's freighting of the metaphor) of annexation to a history and politics that it experiences, but which it cannot always comprehend. It was Freud's description of this state in his famously complex *Beyond the Pleasure Principle* (1921) that attracted Walter Benjamin in what was to be one of his last writings published in his lifetime, "On Some Motifs in Baudelaire," part of his long fascination with the poet's articulation of modernity, which appeared in 1939, the same year as Freud's *Moses* was first published in English. In the repetitive nightmares of returning Great War veterans Freud had found evidence of how the psyche tried to master trauma retroactively by reliving unconsciously a catastrophe which could not be experienced fully first time around. The soldiers' dreams, like Baudelaire's lyrics as Benjamin reads them, are a way of organizing experience both after it has passed and in anticipation of its repetition. Both, in other words, register the effort of giving new form to an experience that throws one out of time and out of conscious experience. In a culture in which information has replaced narration, and in which sensation has become the norm, it is no longer possible to live experience in time, Benjamin argues. The question raised by Freud's theory of trauma is where experience goes when it can no longer be lived. Proust gave one answer when he reassembled the shattered fragments of modern experience into a new fictional logic in *À la recherche du temps perdu*. Baudelaire's poetry in which the shocks of modernity are parried with an energy which creates a world in which experience can be lived in what Benjamin calls the "after-image," gives another. By "shutting out" "the inhospitable, blinding age of big-scale industrialism," Benjamin writes, "the eye perceives an experience of a complementary nature in the form of its spontaneous after-image."[8] Thus in Baudelaire's Paris, city of many stimuli but little communication, it is not love at first sight, but love at last glance which brilliantly illuminates the night of the lone walker.

Even though its ostensible subject is the late nineteenth century, Benjamin's essay speaks as much as Freud's late work to the political despair of the 1930s. By 1939, the traumatophile modernism Benjamin describes so carefully was already exhausted by the modernity with which it had struggled so long; and his descriptions of how Baudelaire once fought ("duelled," "stabbed," "fenced") to wrest a new poetry from the fragmentation of a new epoch carry an acute historical pathos. Just as Freud made one last effort to uncover the fantasies and defenses of ideologies of race and identity, Benjamin gives us one last glimpse of a poet who, unlike others who made a "common cause with Fascism" by reinventing an age of myths, took the trauma of modern experience as his starting point.[9] Today, we can read these mid-century trauma writings as cut through with intimations of an immediate future which, both Freud and Benjamin seem to know, would threaten everything they had dared to think in the first decades of the century. And while they differ in their sense of where trauma comes from – Benjamin begins with the age of shock, while Freud begins with the individual – for both it is war that dramatizes most hideously the extent to which what Freud once described as the illusionary fantasies of western civilization foundered on a previously unthinkable barbarism.

In a remarkable passage commenting on how the first war had made it more, not less, difficult to narrate experience in his classic essay "The Storyteller" (1936), Benjamin writes:

> Never has experience been contradicted more thoroughly than strategic experience by tactical warfare, economic experience by inflation, bodily experience by mechanical warfare, moral experience by those in power. A generation that had gone to school on a horse-drawn streetcar now stood under the open sky in a countryside in which nothing remained unchanged but the clouds, and beneath these clouds, in a field of force of destructive torrents and explosions, was the tiny fragile human body.[10]

The power of that final sentence derives from a writing that knows that while war makes narrative communication inarticulate, the precision of one image can succeed in turning history into collective memory nonetheless. One way to describe trauma theory is as an effort to continue to attempt to represent the experience in some way – be it through the language of the unconscious or through the poetic fragment – of that tiny fragile human body as it is swept along, and frequently aside, by that field of force.

My third and final example of mid-century trauma writing comes from Virginia Woolf. Woolf, with her husband Leonard, was Freud's English publisher, and having resisted it for years, in 1939 was finally beginning to read Freud's writing – including *Moses and Monotheism*. Her final novel, *Between the Acts* (1941), with its piquant sense of the vertigo of national history-making and its appalled fascination with the imminent and catastrophic return of a primitive violence that lurks at the origins of a culture that fantasizes itself as civilized, can be read as Woolf's tribute to Freud's "historical novel." But it is in her unfinished memoir, "A Sketch of the Past," begun in April 1939 and written through the Battle of Britain and the fall of France, that Woolf most clearly develops her version of trauma writing. It is, writes Woolf, looking back at the origins of her creativity, her "shock-receiving capacity" that makes her a writer.[11] Her autobiographical sketch, thus, is not only about *what* she remembers of a childhood marked by the deaths of her mother, half-sister, and brother, sexual abuse by her half-brother and an adolescence suffocated by her dominating father, but also about *how* traumatic memory becomes a mode of writing. "I feel," Woolf echoes Proust, "that strong emotion must leave its trace; and it is only a question of discovering how we can get ourselves attached to it."[12] Believing by 1940 that the past was about to be swallowed up by a catastrophe that, at the very least, would send Woolf and her Jewish husband to their garage to kill themselves, in "Sketch" Woolf gathers those traces of emotions into a series of luminous metaphors that turn her lost past into a series of stunningly sensual memories – "scene making," Woolf calls it.[13]

But whereas an earlier tradition within modernism imagined the writer-as-memory-maker in terms of his creative ingenuity and aggression, Woolf's emphasis here is on a kind of passivity in the face of trauma – she "collapses." Many of the scenes Woolf remembers, she writes, "brought with them a peculiar horror and a physical collapse; they seemed dominant; myself passive."[14] This, then, is Woolf's 1939 version of the modern traumatophile, one who can only figure what she experiences at one remove, at least, from herself, "passive under some sledge-hammer blow."[15] While Woolf is writing about her Edwardian childhood, as France falls and the first bombs begin to fall on England, it is difficult not to read this passively traumatized figure in relation to Woolf's present, and its insistent, even energetic, repetition in her memoir as, perhaps, a way of warding off a final collapse (as Freud once remarked famously, it can take an awful lot of psychic activity to be truly passive). The very fragility of Woolf's figure of the writer as a young woman, in other words, can be read as a protest against a history which was becoming more, not less, traumatic. In an entry to "Sketch" dated July 19, 1939, Woolf suggests that to be a successful trauma writer, to reanimate the deadening modern present by reconnecting to the traces of the past through metaphor, or as she puts it "to feel the present sliding over the depths of the past," "peace is necessary."[16] Discontinuity, exile, moving, war "shallows; it turns the depths into hard thin splinters. As I say to L[eonard]: 'What's there real about this? Shall we ever live a real life again?'"[17]

Woolf didn't wait for the answer to her own question and took her own life in February 1941. She followed Benjamin, who had killed himself in September 1940 on the Franco-Spanish border. Freud had died in London almost exactly one year earlier. Working between psychoanalysis and late modernism, their final works can be read in terms of what could be described as a traumatic paradigm. Each writer asks us to think about what it really means for the mind to be possessed by an experience it cannot represent to itself. Each understands what it means to be inhabited by a lost past. And for all three, this conflict in the mind finds its most acute representation *and* realization in modern war. While Freud, as we will see, set the terms for much recent trauma theory, Benjamin reminds us about the modernity of trauma; a modernity with which we are still fatefully engaged, and with which the contemporary study of World War II is very much entangled. Woolf's energetic passivity in the face of trauma, in this later context, turns out to be a retrospectively prescient figure for a culture which can only connect with its traumatic past by imagining itself as some kind of receptive witness to an event it struggles to comprehend.

II

In a logic familiar to trauma theory these texts written early in the war provide many of the models for how contemporary theory was later to respond to the war itself. To say that the war was "traumatic" is a facile truism. Of course it was. Contemporary trauma theory begins with a more subtle point: that the unique forms that war took produced in their wake not only pained historical and emotional legacies, but also brought about what many have described as a kind of crisis of knowledge, particularly of historical knowledge. It was not the war itself that provoked this crisis. "War," wrote Primo Levi, "is always a terrible fact, to be deprecated, but it is in us, it has rationality, we 'understand' it."[18] What cannot be "understood" is what happened at Auschwitz. Responding to the same question that Freud was trying to address in *Moses and Monotheism* – how can one explain Nazi anti-Semitism? – in the Afterword to his classic *If This Is a Man*, Levi describes why understanding became a problem after Auschwitz:

> Let me explain: "understanding" a proposal or human behaviour means to "contain" it, contain its author, put oneself in his place, identify with him. Now, no normal human being will ever be able to identify with Hitler, Himmler, Goebbels, Eichmann, and endless others. This dismays us, and at the same time gives us a sense of relief, because perhaps it is desirable that their words (and also, unfortunately, their deeds) cannot be comprehensible to us. They are non-human words and deeds, really counter-human, without historic precedents, with difficulty comparable to the cruellest events of the biological struggle for existence. The war can be related to this struggle, but Auschwitz has nothing to do with war; it is neither an episode in it nor an extreme form of it.[19]

In 1948, Hannah Arendt had made a similar point. In its efforts to brutally demonstrate that absolutely anything was possible, she argued, the new totalitarianism flattened not only the European Diasporic Jewry, but also the moral and political categories by which its evil might even be comprehended. Arendt's response was to call for the political and philosophical re-invention of new categories of moral understanding.[20] The collapse of the political part of that hope was registered by the French filmmaker Claude Lanzmann, in 1990, who went so far as to put a moral taboo on historical comprehension when he spoke of the "obscenity of understanding" in relation to his ground-breaking film *Shoah* (1985).[21]

When contemporary trauma theorists write about an "incomprehensibility" at the heart of traumatic experience, then, they are not only repeating Freud's point about how we can never know our traumas consciously, but only live them through their after-effects (shell-shocked soldiers or the modernity of Baudelaire), they are also writing in a context in which categories of historical and moral understanding themselves are seen as absolutely problematic. Psychoanalysis becomes hugely significant in this context, not only because its starting premises are with what cannot be represented consciously – that is, with *unconscious* knowledge – but because its methodology works through the gaps in understanding; with what can be heard or said, for example, in the psychoanalytic exchange, or with a history which makes its presence felt, if not revealed explicitly, in the distortions of dreams, fantasies, and speech. It is this affinity with psychoanalysis which makes Lanzmann's film so important for trauma theory. At nine and a half hours long, *Shoah* eschews documentary footage and chronological historical narrative, in favor of a set of uniquely disturbing interviews between Lanzmann and survivors, bystanders, and perpetrators of the Holocaust. As the critic Shoshana Felman has pointed out, the dialogic form and cyclical structure of the film mirror the form and tempo of the psychoanalytic exchange.[22] In this way Lanzmann, as Felman also argues, is emphatically not trying to give the Holocaust a psychology; that would be to try to "contain" the event, or, in Levi's terms, to "understand" it. Rather the film, like psychoanalysis, deliberately works at the "limit of understanding," as Lanzmann's interviewees do not so much tell us about the past, as *repeat* the force of its trauma in a series of unnervingly poignant exchanges:

> How did it happen when the women came into the gas chamber?
>
> . . .
>
> I tell you something. To have a feeling about that . . . it was very hard to feel anything, because working there day and night, between dead people, between bodies, your feeling disappeared, you were dead. You had no feeling at all.[23]

What is revealed in these exchanges is the existence of a new traumatic "truth"; the French psychoanalyst Jacques Lacan might have called it an encounter with the real, in which the fantasies and narratives by which we ordinarily contain trauma collapse. With Lanzmann it is no longer possible to "remember" the Holocaust through a rhetoric of documentary footage, expert historical opinion, and pious silence (the sort of remembering, as trauma theory often has it, that we do culturally precisely in order to forget): rather one is compelled to recognize its continuing traumatic presence.

Crucial in all this is the figure of the witness and the emergence of a new type of historical testimony. "If the Greeks invented tragedy, the Romans the epistle and the Renaissance the sonnet," the Holocaust survivor Elie Wiesel has written famously, "our generation invented a new literature, that of testimony."[24] For contemporary trauma theory, the Holocaust provoked a crisis in witnessing for the same reason as it challenged our categories of understanding. Because it was, the psychoanalyst and survivor, Dori Laub, has argued, "an event without a witness," the Holocaust put a unique pressure on the ways in which it is possible to testify to it. "It was not only the reality of the situation and the lack of responsiveness of bystanders or the world that accounts for the fact that history was taking place with no witness," Laub writes:

> it was also the very circumstance of *being inside the event* that made unthinkable the very notion that a witness could exist, that is, someone who could step outside of the coercively totalitarian and dehumanizing frame of reference in which the event was taking place, and provide an independent frame of reference through which the event could be observed.[25]

"The mind ought to find a way out, but the mind has lost all capacity to so much as look outward," remember Simone Weil's words from 1940. There is no other to whom I can address my experience, writes Laub forty years later, no outside which would make that history, and thus myself, authentic.

To an extent, we can read today's trauma theorists as attempting to produce a critical discourse which is in some way adequate to the historical and epistemological dilemmas anticipated by Freud and Benjamin and made real by the Holocaust. It is perhaps not surprising, then, to find that the study of World War II has itself become something of a battleground for competing literary theories; as if finding a way of "reading" the war might somehow connect us to a history about which we superficially know so much, too much, but which somehow never seems real enough (both Benjamin and Freud would have read the sheer volume of World War II images and narratives as evidence, not of historical communication or the working through of the past, but of a profound kind of imaginative and psychical failure). On the one hand, the war asks us how it is possible to historicize an event whose very nature has set such a term on historical understanding itself. On the other, precisely because we continue to live the history of the war, not only in terms of its political legacies but also because the recent past has proved to be very bad about keeping its secrets, we forget the force of history to our frequently embarrassed moral cost.

For some critics, such as Cathy Caruth, one of its most influential proponents, trauma theory provides a way of reconciling the epistemological problems that follow in the wake of the Holocaust with a version of history, and so also of answering the charge that the focus on the materiality of language, associated with deconstruction, is negligently ahistorical. For Caruth, what is most significant about Freud's nightmare-stricken soldiers from *Beyond the Pleasure Principle* is the insistent return of what she terms "the literal" in their dreams: it is this returning literalness, she argues, "which thus constitutes trauma and points to its enigmatic core; the delay or incompletion in knowing, or even seeing, an overwhelming occurrence that then remains, in its insistent return, absolutely *true* to the event."[26] The historical truth of trauma, hence, is contained in its belatedness (what Freud called latency), as what is referenced by trauma is the moment, so to speak, when history is missed. History, thus, in its traumatic form, "can be grasped only in the very inaccessibility of its occurrence."[27] What war writing, in a very broad sense, does for Caruth is perform this inaccessibility so that it is in the paradoxes of language itself that we can rediscover the force of trauma and the imperative for a new form of historical witnessing. By "carrying that impossibility of knowing out of the empirical event itself," Caruth concludes her introduction to the widely influential collection *Trauma: Explorations in Memory*, "trauma opens up and challenges us to a new kind of listening, the witnessing, precisely, *of impossibility*."[28]

While some historians have embraced the idea that the experiences of World War II and, in particular, of the Holocaust, call for a kind of history writing that would be acutely sensitive to the challenge of representing traumatic forms of knowledge, others, not surprisingly, have been skeptical of a theory that turns to history only to announce its "impossibility."[29] Others still have questioned the extent to which what starts as a necessary acknowledgment of the unconscious legacies of the war in much trauma theory often slides into an unhelpful valorization of incomprehension itself.[30] Indeed, while it is one thing to say, with Levi, that the Holocaust puts a block on understanding the perpetrators of the event, it is another when trauma appears to engulf history itself. For even as trauma challenges us to respond to history by attempting to give form to what cannot be comprehended (this was Freud's legacy), the crisis in experience that accompanied modernity and found its apotheosis in World War II nonetheless still demands to be read historically (this is Benjamin's legacy). To succumb to historical incomprehension, it might be argued, is a counsel of despair. At such a moment, we could say, it is as if Benjamin's fragile human body is finally lost to the "field of force of destructive torrents and explosions," no longer able to even see that the "open sky" remains the same. "But it was not over," Woolf wrote of one of her early traumatic moments,

> for that night in the bath the dumb horror came over me. Again I had that hopeless sadness; that hammer blow; exposed to a whole avalanche of meaning that had heaped itself up and discharged itself upon me, unprotected with nothing to ward it off, so that I huddled up at the end of the bath, motionless. I could not explain it; I said nothing even to Nessa sponging herself at the other end.[31]

If this image from the early part of the war can still haunt us today, it is perhaps because of the way Woolf's passive vulnerability – her curiously charged inability to explain an event the force of which leaves her defenseless – speaks to the extent to which we are still in the paralyzed moral, existential, and psychological grip of the war. Freud taught us to be suspicious of those parts of our minds which were annexed to a history we could not comprehend. Benjamin understood how the unconscious could illuminate those parts of historical experience that were atrophied by modernity. In both we can read a challenge to describe, to imagine, and, possibly, to begin to comprehend the twentieth-century mind as one driven to the edge by the traumas of an atrocious history.

NOTES

1. Simone Weil, "The *Iliad* or the Poem of Force," *Simone Weil: An Anthology*, ed. Siân Miles (New York: Weidenfeld & Nicolson, 1986), p. 181.
2. Sigmund Freud, *Moses and Monotheism: Three Essays* (1939 [1934–38]), *Pelican Freud Library,* Vol. XIII: *The Origins of Religion*, trans. James Strachey, ed. James Strachey and Albert Dickson (Harmondsworth: Penguin, 1985), pp. 298–9.
3. *Ibid.*, p. 349.
4. *Ibid.*, p. 315.
5. *Ibid.*, p. 309.
6. Freud first developed his theories of sexual trauma with his work with hysterics at the turn of the century (see Freud and Breuer's *Studies in Hysteria* (*Pelican Freud Library,* Vol. III), and Freud's essay "The Aetiology of Hysteria" (1896), *The Standard Edition of the Complete Works of Sigmund Freud,* Vol. III). Freud quickly abandoned his original belief that hysterics suffered from the repressed memories of early sexual encounters (the so-called seduction theory), in favor of the idea that – while not discounting that such real events may actually have happened – it was fantasy that caused psychic disturbance. It was fantasy too, to Freud's mind, that made the trauma suffered by shell-shocked soldiers so unbearable precisely because what was shattered was the soldier's libidinal relation to themselves (their narcissism, as Freud put it). See Freud's "Introduction" to the Fifth International Psycho-Analytical Congress at Budapest, held in September 1918 (*Standard Edition*, Vol. XVII). For a useful introduction to these aspects of Freud's thinking in the context of contemporary trauma theory, see E. Ann Kaplan, "'Why Trauma Now?' Freud and Trauma Studies," *Trauma Culture: The Politics of Terror and Loss in Media and Literature* (New Brunswick: Rutgers University Press, 2005), pp. 24–41.
7. Freud, *Moses*, p. 319.
8. Walter Benjamin, "Some Motifs in Baudelaire" (1939), *Illuminations: Essays and Reflections*, ed. Hannah Arendt, trans. Harry Zorn (New York: Schocken Books, 1969), p. 157.
9. *Ibid.*, p. 156.
10. Benjamin, "The Storyteller," *Illuminations*, p. 84.
11. Virginia Woolf, "A Sketch of the Past," *Moments of Being*, ed. Jeanne Schulkind (San Diego, New York, and London: Harcourt, 1985), p. 72.
12. *Ibid.*, p. 67.
13. *Ibid.*, p. 142.
14. *Ibid.*, p. 72.
15. *Ibid.*, p. 78. Recalling the death of her half-sister, Stella, in a passage where she is clearly borrowing her metaphors from Freud, Woolf also describes her mind as a "substance": "a mind stuff and being stuff that was extraordinarily unprotected, unformed, unshielded, apprehensive, receptive, anticipatory" (*ibid.*, p. 124).
16. *Ibid.*, p. 98.
17. *Ibid.*
18. Primo Levi, "Afterword: The Author's Answers to His Readers' Questions," *If This Is a Man / The Truce*, trans. Stuart Woolf (London: Abacus, 1987), p. 395.
19. Levi, "Afterword," p. 395.

20. Hannah Arendt, *The Origins of Totalitarianism* (New York: Schocken Books, 2004), p. 624.
21. "It is enough to formulate the question in simplistic terms – Why have the Jews been killed? – for the question to reveal right away its obscenity. There is an absolute obscenity in the very project of understanding." Claude Lanzmann, "Hier ist kein Warum," *Au sujet de Shoah: Le film de Claude Lanzmann*, ed. Michel Deguy (Paris: Belin, 1990), p. 279.
22. Shoshana Felman, "Introduction" to "The Obscenity of Understanding: An Evening with Claude Lanzmann," in *Trauma: Explorations in Memory*, ed. Cathy Caruth (Baltimore and London: Johns Hopkins University Press, 1995), pp. 202–3.
23. Quoted in Shoshana Felman, "The Return of the Voice in Claude Lanzmann's *Shoah*," in Shoshana Felman and Dori Laub, *Testimony: Crises of Witnessing in Literature, Psychoanalysis, and History* (New York and London: Routledge, 1992), p. 219.
24. Elie Wiesel, "The Holocaust as a Literary Inspiration," in *Dimensions of the Holocaust* (Evanston: Northwestern University Press, 1977), p. 9. See also Lawrence L. Langer, *Holocaust Testimonies: The Ruins of Memory* (New Haven and London: Yale University Press, 1991).
25. Dori Laub, "An Event Without A Witness," in Felman and Laub, *Testimony*, p. 81.
26. Cathy Caruth, "Trauma and Experience: Introduction," in *Trauma: Explorations in Memory*, p. 5. See also Cathy Caruth, *Unclaimed Experience: Trauma, Narrative and History* (Baltimore and London: Johns Hopkins University Press, 1996) and her essay, "Parting Words: Trauma, Silence and Survival," in *Between the Psyche and the Polis: Refiguring History in Literature and Theory*, ed. Michael Rossington and Anne Whitehead (Aldershot: Ashgate, 2000), pp. 77–96.
27. Caruth, "Trauma and Experience," p. 8.
28. *Ibid.*, p. 10.
29. For a sense of the huge and important range of views on the question of the representation of the Holocaust, see the collection *Probing the Limits of Representation: Nazism and the "Final Solution*," ed. Saul Friedlander (Cambridge, MA: Harvard University Press, 1992). In his contribution, the historian Hayden White argues for a history writing which is awake to the demands of modernist representation. By contrast, and writing from the perspective of a historian of science, in *Trauma: A Genealogy* (Chicago and London: The University of Chicago Press, 2000), Ruth Leys offers a history of psychiatric and psychoanalytic theories of trauma which is highly critical of the extent to which contemporary trauma theory is blind not only to its historical precedents, but to its own contradictions.
30. See Dominick LaCapra, *History and Memory after Auschwitz* (Ithaca and London: Cornell University Press, 1998) for just such a critique. See especially the chapter "Lanzmann's *Shoah*: 'Here There Is No Why,'" pp. 95–138.
31. Woolf, "Sketch," p. 78.

15

PETRA RAU

The war in contemporary fiction

With very few exceptions, contemporary fiction dealing with World War II is produced by writers with no direct experience of the war. They do not remember it in any straightforward way but only know it at second or third hand through the memories, stories, and artifacts of earlier generations, and through popular war films, museum visits, pulp fiction, memoirs, TV documentaries, or history books. These sources may come to produce "prosthetic memories" for what is essentially a post-memorial generation.[1] Contemporary war writing therefore reimagines war in an often self-conscious postmodern translation for an audience whose interests and agendas might differ significantly from those of the wartime generation but whose "prosthetic memories" shape individual politics and identities. Certainly, since the fall of communism and the end of the Cold War in the 1990s, the return of the war to the agenda of writers and historians as a lucrative and award-winning topic allows us to reassess its legacies.

There is no doubt that the fight against Italian fascism, Japanese imperialism, and genocidal German Nazism was necessary, and that the world would be a very different place had these regimes not been destroyed. Yet in the light of continued postwar violence, new genocides, and new forms of imperialism, this moral certainty now seems strangely insufficient for the war to retain the cultural meanings it had previously. Not only have we become highly skeptical about our ability to heed moral imperatives and "learn from history," but literary writers in particular are also suspicious of History itself – History as a discursive practice that turns the past into a readable narrative – while still committed to our responsibilities towards historical accuracy and moral accountability. This ambivalent attitude continues some of the trends of wartime writing, which often set itself against myth-making, propaganda, and monumentalist historiography (in the Nietzschean sense of the narrative of a glorified past),[2] yet contemporary writing necessarily goes one step further. Not only does it debunk some of the popular myths about this war, it also examines why they came into being, how they have shaped the legacies of war, and how they have contributed to postwar identities.

Rewriting myth

Roland Barthes's essay on myth – highly influential for Angus Calder's analysis of British ways of reading the war in *The Myth of the Blitz* (1991) – defines the genre as follows:

> myth acts economically: it abolishes the complexity of human acts, it gives them the simplicity of essences, it does away with all dialectics, with any going back beyond what is immediately visible, it organizes a world which is without contradictions because it is without depth, a world wide open and wallowing in the evident, it establishes a blissful clarity: things appear to mean something by themselves.[3]

A simplified narrative impervious to truth or revision, myth captures a desirable emotional truth that guarantees its circulation and longevity *because* it creates meaning within a seemingly logical narrative of cause and effect without drawing attention to its retroactive constructedness. It is easy to see why myths have a limited shelf life while also retaining their currency in a particular culture. By the time they have lost their intended audience they have become commonplace. During the Blitz Londoners were credited with stoic resilience and undaunted spirit (despite considerable evidence to the contrary); in the terrorist attacks on July 7, 2005 that targeted the London public transport system, it was the mythologized Blitz that was evoked to indicate that this was and could be the only British response to a hostile act.

If in France, Britain, and Germany the literary imagination responds readily to renewed preoccupation with the war, this is because war remains a cornerstone of these nations' identities at home and abroad. In France, Marcel Ophüls's documentary *The Sorrow and the Pity* (1969) and Louis Malle's *Lacombe Lucien* (1974) had already shaken up complacent attitudes toward Gaullist myths about ubiquitous resistance, but it took the protractions surrounding the trial of the functionary Maurice Papon in the 1990s for a new generation to engage with the dilemmas of the Occupation and France's contribution to the Holocaust, as in Patrick Modiano's *The Search Warrant* (1996), Lydie Salvayare's *The Company of Ghosts* (1997), and, most spectacularly, Irène Némirovsky's posthumous fragment *Suite Française* (2004).

In American cultural memory, however, the Vietnam War would replace World War II as a more traumatic, more protracted, and far less morally clear-cut conflict. This is perhaps why the literary response to World War II seemed exhausted by the early 1970s, notwithstanding Thomas Pynchon's monumental *Gravity's Rainbow* (1973), which could not be more different from the anti-war novels about the horrors of combat by Heller, Jones, and Mailer. Yet for the literary historian Paul Fussell it is the highly censored war reportage and the remoteness of the Pacific and European battlefields from the US that limit the understanding and cultural relevance of the war in America.[4] If the war still features in large-scale Hollywood productions for a mass audience (*Saving Private Ryan*, *The English Patient*, *The Thin Red Line*, *The Longest Day*, *Pearl Harbor*, *Flags of Our Fathers*, *Letters from Iwo Jima*) this seems to suggest that aestheticized carnage and evil Nazis/imperial soldiers are acceptable as visual entertainment so long as this involves exotic romance or individual heroism – narrative constructions that retroactively lend meaning to arbitrary or systemic violence.

War films constantly interfere with the protagonist's experience and memory of "real war" in A. L. Kennedy's *Day* (2007) and J. G. Ballard's *Empire of the Sun* (1985): "Had his brain been damaged by too many war films?" asks Ballard's narrator.[5] Kennedy's protagonist, a former gunner in RAF Bomber Command (after Len Deighton's *Bomber*, this is only the second British novel to tackle the moral controversies surrounding the area bombing of Germany), and a "Kriegie" in a German camp, performs as an extra in a 1947 film production about a prisoner-of-war camp. Both ashamed and traumatized by his "real war," he recognizes that this "phoney" cinematic rendition invents digestible realities and acts of heroism for a postwar audience, just as a film like *The Great Escape* does not dwell on imprisonment nor *The Dam Busters* on civilian targets.[6] Films such as these constitute what Marianna Torgovnick has called the symptoms of a "war complex" – a cluster of clichés or myths that overwrite repressed feelings about killing and mass death.[7] This cluster has its roots in propaganda and official war reportage, suggests Ballard in *Empire of the Sun*: "layers of newsreels ... had imposed their own truth upon the war."[8]

The increasingly self-critical approach to the war reflects contemporary agendas in the humanities (postcolonial studies, gender and queer studies, memory and trauma studies). Avoiding any "wallowing in the evident," these novels often attempt to reinstate dialectics and contradictions, reintroduce little known or suppressed aspects of war, and attend more carefully to the experiences of a total war whose strategies redefined civilians as legitimate targets. It took *Empire of the Sun*, Anita Desai's *Baumgartner's Bombay* (1988), and Norbert Gstrein's *The English Years* (1999) to remind us of the ubiquitous practice of alien internment all over the globe. The psychological wounds resulting from rescue operations like the *Kindertransport* are at the heart of W. G. Sebald's *Austerlitz* (2001), while Rachel Seiffert's *The Dark Room* (2001) also focuses on children's disorientation more generally. Sarah

Waters's *The Night Watch* (2006), Kennedy's *Day*, and Peter Ho Davies's *The Welsh Girl* (2007) refuse to forget the situation of conscientious objectors, POWs, and exiles, and query the British myth of "national unity,"[9] while Ian McEwan's *Atonement* (2001) and Thomas Keneally's *The Widow and Her Hero* (2007) reinstate Dunkirk as a military disaster and the campaigns of Jaywick and Rimau as acts of sabotage. The moral complexity of representing perpetrators as victims informs *Day*, Günter Grass's *Crabwalk* (2002), and Stefan Chwin's *Death in Danzig* (1995).[10] There is also a clearer recognition of the psychological toll that waiting and lack of information take on those left on the "home front," on women and parents, and of the utter bleakness of wartime life and the austerity years that followed it. It is the cost of war, its traumatic nature rather than its ideological significance or its victories, that is highlighted in these books.

As Donna Coates implies above (Chapter 11), contemporary fiction recognizes more readily that imperial interests were at least as much at stake in the war as were high-flying notions of democratic freedom. We see this point being made as early as Olivia Manning's *Levant Trilogy* (1977–78). It is long overdue that the contribution of colonial troops to the defeat of Germany and Japan is fully recognized and that our gaze is redirected to non-European theatres of war. Biyi Bandele's *Burma Boy* (2007) depicts the experiences of Nigerian soldiers in Abyssinia and Burma, while Michael Ondaatje's *The English Patient* (1992) and Amitav Ghosh's epic *The Glass Palace* (2000) demonstrate the conflicts of loyalty for Indian soldiers in the service of the British Empire. These novels argue that colonial history makes it hard to define who or what the real enemy is, and they ask if the means by which the enemy is being fought do not render "us" like "them" – there's no blissful clarity of myth here.[11] Rigid class structures, domestic violence, racism, and intolerance rather than fascism are just as often cited as forces inimical to peace. In fact, contemporary fiction suggests something like an ideological vacuum that is only filled after the experience of loss – of a friend in combat, a parent, or a lover.

As in Homer and Herodotus, illicit love often stands at the beginning of conflict: "You had become the enemy not when you sided with Germany but when you began your affair with Katherine Clifton," comments Caravaggio, the Canadian thief-turned-spy in Ondaatje's *The English Patient*, on the adulterous affair between the English spy's wife and the Hungarian ethnographer-turned-collaborator, Count Ladislaus Almasy.[12] In Ondaatje's novel, both love and war "turn" everyone into something else, but rarely are national loyalties stronger than personal ones. There's hardly a decent war novel without its adulterous or illicit love affair, and these include homosexuality and "fraternization." But these liaisons are seldom celebrated as an exciting orgy amongst the ruins nor do they always provide the romantic relief from combat scenes; on the contrary, and as in much of the writing produced during the war, illicit sex can be a bleak, private form of war that mirrors social and ideological conflict in the real world and anticipates the difficult legacies of war: its betrayals, losses, and displacements.

History: disaster into epic

Historians have given war "a disgracefully good press," says a character in Penelope Lively's *Moon Tiger* (1987), suggesting that they have too often been in the service of dubious political ideologies to the point where myth and history are virtually indistinguishable.[13] This means that the very discipline supposed to guarantee our access to the past, historiography, is seen to obscure it. Frequent use of ironized, limited, or heavily mediated points of view, and disrupted or reverse chronology (as in, for example, *The English Patient*, *Austerlitz*, *The Night Watch*, and *Day*) are devices that enact futile, at best ambiguous, attempts to create out of the chaos and violence of war a meaningful narrative that might order events into the logic of cause and effect.

Historiography rationalizes retrospectively, according to the narrator of Philip Roth's *The Plot Against America* (2004):

> Turned wrong way round, the relentless unforeseen was what we schoolchildren studied as "History," harmless history, where everything unexpected in its own time is chronicled on the page as inevitable. The terror of the unforeseen is what the science of history hides, turning a disaster into an epic.[14]

This "terror of the unforeseen" which Roth masterfully reinstates in his alternate history[15] of an American anti-Semitic pogrom, is also something that the philosopher Hannah Arendt identified as the arbitrariness inherent in warfare: "nowhere does Fortuna, good or ill luck, play a more fateful role in human affairs than on the battlefield, and this intrusion of the utterly unexpected does not disappear when people call it a 'random event' and find it scientifically suspect; nor can it be eliminated by simulations, scenarios, game theories and the like."[16] There's no preparation for, and no justice in, death on the battlefield. It is noteworthy, however, that in imagining warfare even Arendt returns to the ancient notion of fate (or The Fates) that wreaks such havoc in Greek epic and yet, like divine intervention, orders the events into narratable form.

The first works of Western literature, Homer's epics *The Iliad* and *The Odyssey*, are perhaps already the first manifestation of myth as traumatic response – not merely a repetition of what (might have) happened but a translation of the "terror of the unforeseen," the chaos and arbitrariness of violence, into heroic epic that sediments a tradition of reading war and its aftermath. It is no coincidence that several recent novels reference Homer explicitly as the *Ur-text* for war writing, both template and revenant, when it comes to the uses of myth or mythology: "Mythology is much better stuff than history. It has form; logic; a message."[17] Yet in Louis de Bernières's *Captain Corelli's Mandolin* (1994), Bernhard Schlink's *Homecoming* (2006), Keneally's *The Widow and Her Hero*, and Kennedy's *Day*, the allusions to Homer also dismiss the concept of heroism as a war myth. As Calder has argued, heroism is not a natural product of conditions of violence but just another construction retrospectively imposed on events to give them meaning.[18] Let us remember that the hero Odysseus is not only cunning, persistent, and fearless, but also a liar, rapist, and thief. Achilles, highly sensitive to the loss of his comrade Patroclos, unleashes a degree of frenzied violence on his enemies that is beyond all proportion. For every valiant act of selfless bravery or foolish recklessness are countless others of cowardice, ineptitude, carelessness, and betrayal.

It is remarkable how many characters in these retrospective novels about the war read or produce written history themselves. Ondaatje's Count Almasy turns a copy of Herodotus's *Histories* into a personal-diary-cum-commonplace-book, adding marginalia and drawings. He supplements Herodotus's ethnographic observations and battle accounts while (literally) overwriting them with a more personal history of love and war. Both *Moon Tiger* and de Bernières's baroque, polyphonic *Captain Corelli's Mandolin* feature central characters who become irreverent historians, who first rewrite the official histories of their countries and times, assuming a feminist point-of-view or that of the colonized subject, before embarking on a global history of violence in which World War II features as a particularly gruesome conflict in a long chain of interconnected violence. Especially in fiction from the former Eastern Bloc, that chain links Stalinist purges, fascist occupation, civil war, and communist oppression, as in Nella Bielski's *The Year Is 42* (2004) and Chwin's *Death In Danzig*.

It is indicative that we repeatedly encounter characters for whom war has literally never ended or who are so traumatized that war remains a state of mind. In these fictional archeologies of belligerence we occasionally come across surreal repetitions and peculiar echoes of previous wars that read like tectonic rifts in the sedimented strata of war, as if "the passing of time was only an illusion":[19]

> This is a bang-up-to-date nineteen-forty-one medieval urban scene; a structured world in which you can see who everyone is. Those are two Sephardic Jewish ladies and that is a Sikh officer and there is a tribe of three from the home counties. That man knows how to fly an aeroplane and that one is trained to command tanks and that girl knows how to dress a wound.[20]

In this passage from *Moon Tiger* war demands readable identities, but the medieval urban scene is of course that of a pictorial *representation* – an icon, painting, or reredos – that *makes* the scene readable (and remember how confusing Kennedy's and Ballard's heroes found visual representations of "real war"). For Ondaatje, however, war creates a transhistorical synchronicity of barbarism:

> When the armies assembled at Sansepolcro, a town whose symbol is the crossbow, some soldiers acquired them and fired them silently at night over the walls of the untaken city. Field Marshal Kesselring of the retreating German army seriously considered the pouring of hot oil from battlements. Medieval scholars were pulled out of Oxford colleges and flown to Umbria. Their average age was sixty. They were billeted with the troops, and in meetings with strategic command they kept forgetting the invention of the airplane. They spoke of towns in terms of the art in them.[21]

Art historians as strategic advisors sounds absurd only if we forget that the medieval frescoes that appear to furnish a geography of art (as opposed to the maps of war) often depict the torture inflicted on saints or the violent encounters that assume center stage in ancient myth. Crossbows, airplanes, land mines, and (later in the novel) nuclear bombs: each age has turned its technological progress into strategic advances in warfare. Yet while there may be new ways of dying, the "terror of the unforeseen" remains the same, despite our access to representations of earlier forms of violence that should shake us out of our liberal complacency about human nature. In this bleak view of "progress" we are piling debris upon debris, like Walter Benjamin's angel of history:

> His face is turned towards the past. Where we perceive a chain of events, he sees one single catastrophe which keeps piling wreckage upon wreckage and hurls it in front of his feet. The angel would like to stay, awaken the dead, and make whole what has been smashed. But a storm is blowing from Paradise; it has got caught in his wings with such violence that the angel can no longer close them. This storm irresistibly propels him into the future to which his back is turned, while the pile of debris before him grows skyward. This storm is what we call progress.[22]

Benjamin's iconic representation of cataclysmic history in 1940 is perhaps the most well-known and melancholic response to the periodic accumulations of violence in human history, and its influence on contemporary writing about World War II is palpable.

Despite these layers, repetitions, and echoes that remind us of the universality of suffering, there remains a sense that official history is insufficient. The many unofficial, hidden, buried documents in these war novels suggest that the "real" stories of war never surface, remain outside circulation, are only transmitted through oral history, or have to compete against dangerous untruths. Truly brave acts remain obscure because those who commit them lead secret lives themselves, like the homosexual Carlo Guerico in *Captain Corelli* or the butch lesbian Kay in *The Night Watch*. Claudia's unorthodox world history in *Moon Tiger* remains unwritten. In Grass's *Crabwalk* a nasty Internet community proliferates neo-Nazi revisionist history. The penciled jottings on toilet paper in Keneally's novel are the literally disposable record of internment and officially unacknowledgeable sabotage. Letters are lost in flight (*Day*), and in Art Spiegelman's graphic novels *Maus* (1986) and *Maus II* (1991) memoirs are willfully destroyed.

Notwithstanding the postmodern suspicion of history as a grand narrative, many war novels eagerly acknowledge their debts to military and social history, archival documents in museums, and memoirs. Indeed both the intertextual and the historiographic references indicate that war writing requires poetic license. For better or worse, the impasse for the writer (and for the fictional writers and historians in war fiction) is to weigh between Clio and Calliope – the demands and satisfactions of history and aesthetics, truth and myth. The endings of *Atonement*, *Day*, and *The Widow and Her Hero* self-consciously point to their artificiality, to their yielding to the demands of fiction – or myth. In *Day*, Kennedy reunites her adulterous lovers albeit with the caveat of the bleak postwar years: "It will be complicated."[23] For the widow in Keneally's novel, a writer and poet in her own right, the gradual revelations about her husband's sabotage and execution stage the conflict between memory and myth on the one side and truth and justice on the other: "Since I was terrified that the more I heard, the more likely I was to find out some terrible indigestible reality, I felt a bad wife."[24] The abstract knowledge of war as an "indigestible reality" of chaos, blunder, brutality, and fear lies at the heart of our receptiveness to myth. Note the phrasing at the end of Keneally's novel: "*I prefer to believe* that it was for those men [twenty Malays accused of the sabotage Leo Waterhouse's crew committed unbeknownst to the Japanese] that Leo was ready to die rather than for some flatulent concept of military honour."[25] Keneally reads war backwards in order to demonstrate how we make it bearable: through a Penelopiad that overwrites *The Odyssey* which supersedes *The Iliad*: layers of myth over piles of debris.

McEwan's *Atonement* creates a similarly ironic layering of rewritings. On the surface, it is the story of Briony's betrayal of two lovers. The novel's middle section dramatizes the evacuation of the British Expeditionary Force at Dunkirk in 1940. On the one hand, these are conventional combat scenes; on the other, they offer a corrective to the finest hour version of the "Dunkirk spirit," a narrative that overwrites the debacle of that campaign with the "rescue by the little boats" that epitomizes the British spirit of resilience and national unity. At the end, however, Briony the writer not only admits to the painstaking historical research that allowed her as a non-combatant to write of the battlefield: "I love these little things, this pointillist approach to verisimilitude, the correction of detail that cumulatively gives such satisfaction."[26] The twist – the confession that gives this novel its meaning – is her admission that almost everything we have read so far is completely fictional, a novel within the novel:

> I no longer possess the courage of my pessimism. When I am dead ... and the novel is finally published, we will only exist as my inventions. Briony will be as much a fantasy as the lovers who shared a bed in Balham and enraged their landlady. No one will care what events and which individuals were misrepresented to make a novel. I know there's always a certain kind of reader who will be compelled to ask, But what *really* happened? The answer is simple: the lovers survive and flourish. As long as there is a single copy, a solitary typescript of my final draft, then my spontaneous, fortuitous sister and her medical prince survive to love.[27]

This paragraph unravels the text we have just read and throws us back to our own readerly desires for romance and closure. The Dunkirk section is the product of research: a corrective to the finest hour myth, it is nonetheless an "invention." The betrayed lovers' shabby bliss in wartime London is pure "fantasy" that undoes the arbitrariness of violent death at Dunkirk and in a bombing raid; her own fictionalized persona, a "misrepresentation." Briony's final draft with its happy ending is meant to be a fictional compensation for the "terror of the unforeseen," for "indigestible reality." Yet she knows that her revision of myth does not really constitute atonement – it is merely the license of the creator, as benevolent or vindictive as the Greek gods in the epics.

The exception to the current trend for historiographical skepticism and myth-debunking is clearly the Shoah. Juxtaposing "fiction" and "Holocaust" rings of Holocaust denial. More importantly, the discursive rules surrounding the representation of the Shoah privilege testimony. By no means an unproblematic genre, it can escape the charge of the aestheticization of horror more easily and need not claim, obscenely, to *make sense* of genocide, merely to record facts. Thomas Keneally adapted this strategy in *Schindler's Ark* (1982). Despite calling it a novel, he claimed in his preface, "I have attempted to avoid all fiction, though, since fiction would debase the record."[28] Sebald's heavily mediated account of deportation to Theresienstadt in *Austerlitz* has at its core a testimony, supplemented by intertextual literary references as well as extracts from the work of a notable Holocaust historian, and a photographically documented visit to the former camp and its museum. The bricolage of these media produces an uncategorizable work that therefore escapes the suspicion leveled at Holocaust fiction. As a work of post-memory, Spiegelman's *Maus* also manages to straddle witness account and fiction by visualizing testimony in graphic novel form, using defamiliarization, redrawn iconic photographs of the Shoah, and postmodern self-reflexivity about the problems of representation. As Andreas Huyssen argues, discursive rules may actually prevent us from finding a productive way of remembering the Shoah beyond frozen pious gestures: "The exclusive insistence on the true representation of the Holocaust in its uniqueness, unspeakability, and incommensurability may no longer do in the face of its multiple representations and functions as a ubiquitous trope in Western Culture."[29] Still, the few contemporary fictional accounts are often seen as controversial. Novels as different from one another as Imre Kertész's *Fatelessness* (1975) and Bernhard Schlink's *The Reader* (1995) therefore employ devices that distance the reader from familiar, comfortable attitudes towards the Holocaust, its victims and its perpetrators, be it a belated juridical enquiry that frames the postwar liaison of a teenage boy with a former concentration camp guard or the unfeeling facetiousness of Kertész's adolescent Kazetnik.

Post-memory: searching, reimagining, translating

Historiographical skepticism and representational impasses fuel post-memorial war writing rather than bring it to a halt, because we have realized that contemporary identities involve just as much myth-making on our part, however ironic or self-conscious this process may be. This is perhaps why writers like W. G. Sebald, Rachel Seiffert, and Jonathan Safran Foer literalize the trope of the quest for the past in their protagonists' journeys. Sebald's *Austerlitz*, Seiffert's *The Dark Room*, and Safran Foer's *Everything Is Illuminated* (2002) are concerned not just with the wartime events of expulsion and mass extermination but also with the ways in which these processes problematize postwar identities. It is no coincidence that their central characters are individuals who have constructed for themselves *ersatz* systems of meaning that are meant to compensate for a crucial narrative gap in their history, like symptoms of a (trans-)generational trauma: they are collectors (Safran Foer), architectural historians (Sebald), or teachers (Seiffert, Sebald).

These books focus on artifacts as custodians of lost identities: a ring, a piece of china, a photograph. Spectral metonymies, these melancholic objects stand for the desire to *fashion* out of those remnants stories of the past rather than merely *retrieve* what was lost as a result of war. They are "not so much an instrument of memory as an invention of it or a replacement," as Susan Sontag remarked on the contingent meanings of photographs.[30] In the following passage from *Austerlitz*, the Sebaldian narrator remembers Austerlitz remembering his Czech nanny Vera commenting on a stage photograph:

> Minutes went by, said Austerlitz ... before I heard Vera again, speaking of the mysterious quality peculiar to such photographs when they resurface from oblivion. One has the impression, she said, of something stirring in them, as if one caught small sighs of despair, *gémissements de désespoir* was her expression, said Austerlitz, as if the pictures had a memory of their own and remembered us, remembered the roles that we, the survivors, and those no longer among us had played in our former lives.[31]

In this heavily mediated passage (note the three narrators), the anthropomorphized photograph is ironized as well as made uncanny: it remembers us, not we it; it gives us meaning, not we it. Safran Foer's novel contains a similar passage about a ring archived, by a survivor of the razed shtetl Trachimbrod, in a cardboard box labeled REMAINS: "The ring does not exist for you. You exist for the ring. The ring is not in case of you. You are in case of the ring."[32] In this reversal of agency the "REMAINS" of history give us meaning rather than we, them.

Allusive intertextuality, ambiguous incorporation of photographic "documents," narrators who are fictional versions of their authors, self-consciously "periscopic" storytelling (refracted through several voices or perspectives that reveal otherwise unobtainable stories), and complicated syntax are the means through which these fictions caution us against reading the past in any straightforward way. Indeed, access to the experiences of wartime is literally and metaphorically a precarious translation project. Austerlitz, who has lost his mother tongue after the *Kindertransport* evacuation, finds peculiar fragments of Czech resurfacing as he retraces his Jewish family's wartime fate in Prague. Hanemann, the pathologist in Chwin's *Death in Danzig*, ekes out a living through giving German lessons in postwar Gdansk (Danzig) where all the street names have changed into Polish so that for its former inhabitants language, experience, and urban geography no longer match. The collaborator Kolesnik in Seiffert's *The Dark Room* can only speak of his war crimes in German, as if they are inadmissible in his native Belarusian. For the German Micha, who hopes that Kolesnik's story will lead him to the truth about his grandfather's genocidal activities on the Eastern Front, the translation problem extends to the correspondences between his grandfather as private individual and as soldier, between personal agency and historical responsibility. Abstract knowledge about the nation's Nazi past has to be married with private family history.

Much of the tragicomic effect of *Everything is Illuminated* stems from the Ukrainian translator-narrator Alex's imperfect English (of which the book's title is an example), distorted by literalizations, mixed registers, and the hapless use of a dictionary. Although the two narrators Jonathan and Alexander eventually trace their origin to the same shtetl, the curious idiom Alex adopts seems quite appropriate for communicating their diasporic lives and their dislocated identities. Safran Foer's *Extremely Loud and Incredibly Close* (2005) takes the event that launched the "war on terror" to dramatize the traumatic consequences of the arbitrariness of violence. But rather than Pearl Harbor, his historical reference point for the terrorist attacks on the World Trade Center in September 2001 is the bombardment of Dresden. This comparison underlines the commonality of suffering rather than subscribing to a mythologized precedence for retaliation. Like Benjamin's angel of history, we may be unable to "stay, awaken the dead, and make whole what has been smashed" (although Safran Foer includes a flipbook attempt), but we really need to understand and reflect critically on the cultural meanings, the prosthetic memories we have given the Second World War if we want to harbor any liberal hopes that the sky-high pile of debris at the angel's feet might at one point stop increasing.

NOTES

1. Alison Landsberg, *Prosthetic Memory: The Transformation of American Remembrance in the Age of Mass Culture* (New York: Columbia University Press, 2004). Marianne Hirsch uses the term "post-memory" for "the relationship of children of survivors of cultural or collective trauma to the experiences of their parents." Marianne Hirsch, "Surviving Images: Holocaust Photographs and the work of Postmemory," in *Visual Culture and the Holocaust,* ed. Barbie Zelizer (London: Athlone, 2001), p. 218.
2. In his essay on the burden of historical consciousness "On the Uses and Disadvantages of History for Life" (1874), Friedrich Nietzsche distinguishes between the monumentalist, antiquarian, and critical attitudes to history. Friedrich Nietzsche, *Untimely Meditations*, ed. Daniel Breazeale, trans. R. J. Hollingdale (Cambridge University Press, 1997), pp. 67ff.
3. Roland Barthes, *Mythologies* trans. Annette Lavers (London: Vintage, 1993), p. 143.
4. Paul Fussell, *Wartime: Understanding and Behavior in the Second World War* (Oxford University Press, 1989), p. 268.
5. J. G. Ballard, *Empire of the Sun* (London: Panther 1984), p. 14.
6. A. L. Kennedy, *Day* (London: Jonathan Cape, 2007), p. 34. See S. P. Mackenzie, *The Colditz Myth: British and Commonwealth Prisoners of War in Nazi Germany* (Oxford University Press, 2004).
7. Marianna Torgovnick, *The War Complex: World War II in Our Time* (University of Chicago Press, 2005).
8. Ballard, *Empire*, p. 346.

9. For critical accounts of "the people's war," see Angus Calder, *The People's War* (London: Jonathan Cape, 1969) and Sonya O. Rose's *Which People's War? National Identity and Citizenship in Wartime Britain, 1939–1945* (Oxford University Press, 2003).

10. On this issue see Bill Niven, ed., *Germans as Victims: Remembering the Past in Contemporary Germany* (Houndmills: Palgrave, 2006).

11. The popular thrillers of Len Deighton, Frank Harris, Sebastian Faulks, Alan Furst, Robert Wilson, and Josef Kanon use this genre to dramatize some of the murkier sides of wartime strategies and their long legacies.

12. Michael Ondaatje, *The English Patient* (London: Picador 1992), p. 254.

13. Penelope Lively, *Moon Tiger* (Harmondsworth: Penguin, 1988), p. 102.

14. Philip Roth, *The Plot Against America* (London: Jonathan Cape, 2004), pp. 113.

15. Even for the Allies, victory incorporates the haunting possibility of what did *not* happen, which over the years has grown into an entire (bestselling) subgenre of alternate history. With the exception of Harry Mulisch's *The Future of Yesteryear* (1972), Christoph Ransmayr's *The Dog King* (1995), and Philip Roth's *The Plot Against America*, these anxieties remain within the remit of popular fiction. See Gavriel D. Rosenfeld, *The World Hitler Never Made: Alternate History and the Memory of Nazism* (Oxford University Press, 2005).

16. Hannah Arendt, *On Violence* (New York: Harcourt Brace, 1969), p. 3.

17. Lively, *Moon Tiger*, p. 7.

18. Angus Calder, *Disasters and Heroes: On War, Memory and Representation* (Cardiff: University of Wales Press, 2004), p. 122.

19. Stefan Chwin, *Death In Danzig*, trans. Philip Boehm (London: Secker & Warburg, 2004), p. 113.

20. Lively, *Moon Tiger*, p. 69.

21. Ondaatje, *The English Patient*, p 69.

22. Walter Benjamin, "Theses on the Philosophy of History," *Illuminations*, ed. Hannah Arendt, trans. Harry Zorn (London: Pimlico, 1999), p. 249.

23. A. L. Kennedy, *Day* (London: Jonathan Cape, 2007), p. 273.

24. Thomas Keneally, *The Widow and Her Hero* (London: Sceptre, 2007), p. 154.

25. *Ibid.*, p. 258 (emphasis added).

26. Ian McEwan, *Atonement* (London: Jonathan Cape, 2001), p. 359.

27. *Ibid.*, p. 371.

28. Thomas Keneally, *Schindler's Ark* (London: Book Club Associates, 1983), p. 10. For a useful reading of Keneally's novel against Steven Spielberg's adaptation *Schindler's List* see Margot Norris, *Writing War in the Twentieth Century* (Charlottesville: University of Virginia Press, 2000), pp. 99–143.

29. Andreas Huyssen, *Twilight Memories: Marking Time in a Culture of Amnesia* (London: Routledge, 1995), p. 256.

30. Susan Sontag, *On Photography* (Harmondsworth: Penguin, 1979), p. 165.

31. W. G. Sebald, *Austerlitz*, trans. Anthea Bell (Harmondsworth: Penguin, 2001), p. 258.

32. Jonathan Safran Foer, *Everything Is Illuminated* (Harmondsworth: Penguin, 2002), p. 192.

Military history

Addison, Paul, and Jeremy A. Crang, eds. *Firestorm: The Bombing of Dresden*, 1945. London: Pimlico, 2006.

Bartov, Omer. *Hitler's Army: Soldiers, Nazis, and War in the Third Reich*. New York: Oxford University Press, 1991.

Beaufre, André. *1940: The Fall of France*. Trans. Desmond Flower. London: Cassell, 1967.

Beevor, Antony, *Stalingrad*. New York: Viking, 1998.

Bellamy, Chris. *Absolute War: Soviet Russia in the Second World War*. New York: Knopf, 2007.

Black, Jeremy. *World War Two: A Military History*. London: Routledge, 2003.

Calvocoressi, Peter, Guy Wint, and John Pritchard. *The Penguin History of the Second World War*. London: Penguin, 1999.

Churchill, Winston. *The Second World War*. 6 vols. London: Cassell, 1948–54.

Davies, Norman. *No Simple Victory: World War II in Europe, 1939–1945*. New York: Viking, 2007.

Dear, Ian, and M. R. D. Foot, eds. *The Oxford Companion to World War II*. Oxford University Press, 1995.

Erickson, John. *The Road to Stalingrad*. London: Weidenfeld & Nicolson, 1975. *The Road to Berlin*. London: Granada, 1983.

Frank, Richard B. *Downfall: The End of the Imperial Japanese Empire*. New York: Random House, 1999.

French, David. *Raising Churchill's Army: The British Army and the War Against Germany 1919–1945*. Oxford University Press, 2000.

Friedrich, Jörg. *The Fire: The Bombing of Germany 1940–1945*. Trans. Allison Brown. New York: Columbia University Press, 2006.

Fritz, Stephen G. *Frontsoldaten: The German Soldier in World War II*. Lexington: University Press of Kentucky, 1995. *Endkampf: Soldiers, Civilians, and the Death of the Third Reich*. Lexington: University Press of Kentucky, 2004.

Gilbert, Martin. *The Second World War: A Complete History*. London: Chatto & Windus, 1970.

Grayling, A. C. *Among the Dead Cities: Is the Targeting of Civilians in War Ever Justified?* London: Bloomsbury, 2007.

Hastings, Max. *Armageddon: The Battle For Germany, 1944–1945*. New York: Knopf, 2004.

Keegan, John, *The Second World War*. London: Hutchinson, 1989.

Knox, MacGregor. *Hitler's Italian Allies: Royal Armed Forces, Fascist Regime, and the War of 1940–43*. Cambridge University Press, 2000.

Liddell Hart, B. H. *History of the Second World War*. London: Cassell, 1970.

Lowe, Keith. *Inferno: The Fiery Destruction of Hamburg, 1943*. New York: Scribner, 2007.

Lucas, James. *Last Days of the Third Reich: The Collapse of Nazi Germany, May 1945*. London: Cassell, 2000.

Lyons, Michael J. *World War II: A Short History*. 4th edn. Prentice Hall, 2003.

Maddox, Robert James. *The United States and World War II*. Boulder, CO: Westview Press, 1992.

Merridale, Catherine. *Ivan's War: Life and Death in the Red Army, 1939–1945*. New York: Holt, 2006.

Michel, Henri. *The Second World War*. Trans. Douglas Parmee. New York: Praeger, 1974.

Miller, Donald L., and Henry Steele Commager. *The Story of World War II*. New York: Simon & Schuster, 2001.

Murray, Williamson, and Allan R. Millett. *A War To Be Won: Fighting the Second World War*. Cambridge, MA: Harvard University Press, 2000.

Overy, Richard. *Why The Allies Won*. New York: Norton, 1996.

    Russia's War: A History of the Soviet Effort, 1941–1945. Harmondsworth: Penguin, 1998.

Parker, R. A. C. *Struggle For Survival: The History of the Second World War*. Oxford University Press, 1989.

    The Second World War: A Short History. Oxford University Press, 1997.

Pitt, Barrie. *The Military History of World War II*. New York: The Military Press, 1986.

Ray, John. *The Second World War: A Narrative History*. London: Cassell, 1999.

Rees, Laurence. *Horror in the East: Japan and the Atrocities of World War II*. New York: Da Capo Press, 2002.

Schom, Alan. *The Eagle and the Rising Sun: The Japanese-American War, 1941–1943*. New York: Norton, 2004.

Stokesbury, James L. *A Short History of World War II*. New York: Morrow, 1980.

Tucker, Spencer C. *The Second World War*. New York: Palgrave Macmillan, 2004.

Weinberg, Gerhard L. *A World At Arms: A Global History of World War II*. Cambridge University Press, 1994.

Political history

Bell, P. M. H. *The Origins of the Second World War in Europe*. Harlow: Longman, 2007.

Christofferson, Thomas R., with Michael S. Christofferson. *France during World War II: From Defeat to Liberation*. New York: Fordham University Press, 2006.

Davies, Peter. *France and the Second World War: Occupation, Collaboration, and Resistance*. London: Routledge, 2001.

Duggan, Christopher. *The Force of Destiny: A History of Italy since 1796*. London: Allen Lane, 2007.

Jackson, Julian. *France: The Dark Years, 1940–1944*. Oxford University Press, 2001.

Judt, Tony. *Resistance and Revolution in Mediterranean Europe, 1939–1948*. London: Routledge, 1989.

  Postwar: A History of Europe Since 1945. New York: Penguin, 2005.

Kershaw, Ian. *Fateful Choices: Ten Decisions That Changed The World, 1940–1941*. London: Penguin, 2007.

Lamb, Margaret, and Nicholas Tarling. *From Versailles to Pearl Harbor: The Origins of the Second World War in Europe and Asia*. Basingstoke: Palgrave, 2001.

Knox, MacGregor. *Common Destiny: Dictatorship, Foreign Policy and War in Fascist Italy and Nazi Germany*. Cambridge University Press, 2000.

Morgan, Philip. *The Fall of Mussolini: Italians and the War, 1940–1945*. Oxford University Press, 2007.

Murphy, David E. *What Stalin Knew: The Enigma of Barbarossa*. New Haven, CT: Yale University Press, 2005.

Plowright, John. *The Causes, Course and Outcomes of World War II*. Basingstoke: Palgrave Macmillan, 2007.

Ponting, Clive. *1940: Myth and Reality*. London: Hamish Hamilton, 1990.

Rothwell, Victor. *War Aims in the Second World War: The War Aims of the Major Belligerents, 1939–1945*. Edinburgh University Press, 2005.

Sainsbury, Keith. *Churchill and Roosevelt at War: The War They Fought and The Peace They Hoped To Make*. Houndmills: Macmillan, 1994.

Shirer, William L. *The Rise and Fall of the Third Reich*. New York: Simon & Schuster, 1960.

Stoler, Mark A. *Allies in War: Britain and America Against the Axis Powers*. London: Hodder Arnold, 2005.

Taylor, A. J. P. *The Origins of the Second World War*. London: Hamish Hamilton, 1961.

Toland, John. *The Rising Sun: The Decline and Fall of the Japanese Empire, 1936–1945*. New York: Random House, 1970.

Cultural and social history

Adams, Michael C. C. *The Best War Ever: America and World War II*. Baltimore: Johns Hopkins University Press, 1993.

Barnouw, Dagmar. *Germany 1945: Views of War and Violence*. Bloomington: Indiana University Press, 1997.

  The War in the Empty Air: Victims, Perpetrators, and Postwar Germans. Bloomington: Indiana University Press, 2005.

Bosworth, R. J. B. *Mussolini's Italy: Life under the Fascist Dictatorship, 1915–1945*. London: Penguin, 2007.

Bourke, Joanna. *The Second World War: A People's History*. Oxford University Press, 2001.

Burrin, Philippe. *France under the Germans: Collaboration and Compromise*. Trans. Janet Lloyd. New York: The New Press, 1997.

Calder, Angus. *The People's War: Britain, 1939–1945*. New York: Pantheon, 1969.

  The Myth of the Blitz. London: Jonathan Cape, 1991.

Campbell, John, ed. *The Experience of World War II*. New York: Oxford University Press, 1989.

Connelly, Mark. *We Can Take It! Britain and the Memory of the Second World War*. Harlow: Longman Pearson, 2004.

Diamond, Hanna. *Women and the Second World War in France, 1939–1948: Choices and Constraints*. London: Longman, 1999.

Donnelly, Mark. *Britain in the Second World War*. London: Routledge, 1999.

Dowling, Timothy C., ed. *Personal Perspectives: World War II*. Santa Barbara: ABC-CLIO, 2005.

Fussell, Paul. *Wartime: Understanding and Behavior in the Second World War*. New York: Oxford University Press, 1989.

Gildea, Robert. *Marianne in Chains: Everyday Life in the French Heartland under the German Occupation*. New York: Metropolitan Books, 2003.

Harrisson, Tom. *Living Through The Blitz*. London: Collins, 1976.

Lingeman, Richard R. *Don't You Know There's a War On? The American Home Front, 1941–1945*. Rev. edn. New York: Nation Books, 2003.

Mackay, Robert. *The Test of War: Inside Britain 1939–1945*. London: UCL Press, 1999. *Half the Battle: Civilian Morale in Britain during the Second World War*. Manchester University Press, 2002.

Marwick, Arthur. *The Home Front: The British and the Second World War*. London: Thames & Hudson, 1976.

The New Yorker Book of War Pieces: London, 1939 to Hiroshima, 1945. New York: Schocken, 1988.

Paris, Erna. *Long Shadows: Truth, Lies and History*. London: Bloomsbury, 2000.

Rose, Sonya O. *Which People's War? National Identity and Citizenship in Wartime Britain*. Oxford University Press, 2004.

Rousso, Henry. *The Vichy Syndrome: History and Memory in France since 1944*. Trans. Arthur Goldhammer. Cambridge, MA and London: Harvard University Press, 1991.

Smith, Harold, ed. *Britain in the Second World War: A Social History*. Manchester University Press, 1996.

Smith, Malcolm. *Britain and 1940: History, Myth and Popular Memory*. London: Routledge, 2000.

Terkel, Studs. *The Good War: An Oral History of World War Two*. New York: Pantheon, 1984.

Vinen, Richard. *The Unfree French: Life under the Occupation*. New Haven: Yale University Press, 2006.

Winkler, Allan M. *Home Front USA: America during World War II*. 2nd edn. Wheeling, IL: Harlan Davidson, 2000.

Yellin, Emily. *Our Mothers' War: American Women at Home and at the Front during World War II*. New York: Free Press, 2004.

Holocaust history and representation

Bergen, Doris L. *War and Genocide: A Concise History of the Holocaust*. Lanham: Rowman and Littlefield, 2003.

Bernard-Donals, Michael, and Richard Glejzer. *Between Witness and Testimony: The Holocaust and the Limits of Representation*. Albany: State University of New York Press, 2001.

Clendinnen, Inga. *Reading the Holocaust*. Cambridge University Press, 1999.

Epstein, Julia, and Lori H. Lefkovitz, eds. *Shaping Losses: Cultural Memory and the Holocaust.* Urbana: University of Illinois Press, 2001.

Friedlander, Saul, ed. *Probing the Limits of Representation: Nazism and the Final Solution.* Cambridge, MA: Harvard University Press, 1992.

Hilberg, Raul. *The Destruction of the European Jews.* Rev. edn. New York: Holmes & Meier, 1985.

Hornstein, Shelley, and Florence Jacobowitz, eds. *Image and Remembrance: Representation and the Holocaust.* Bloomington: Indiana University Press, 2003.

Horowitz, Sara. *Voicing the Void: Muteness and Memory in Holocaust Fiction.* Albany: State University of New York Press, 1997.

Kremer, Lilian S. *Women's Holocaust Writing.* Lincoln: University of Nebraska Press, 1999.

Lang, Berel, ed. *Writing and the Holocaust.* New York: Holmes & Meier, 1988.

Niewyck, Donald L. *The Holocaust: Problems and Perspectives of Interpretation.* 3rd edn. Boston: Houghton Mifflin, 2003.

Rees, Laurence. *Auschwitz: A New History.* New York: Public Affairs, 2005.

Rosenfeld, Alvin. *A Double Dying: Reflections on Holocaust Literature.* Bloomington: Indiana University Press, 1980.

Roskies, David. *The Literature of Destruction: Jewish Responses to Catastrophe.* Philadelphia: The Jewish Publication Society, 1988.

Rothberg, Michael. *Traumatic Realism: The Demands of Holocaust Representation.* Minneapolis: University of Minnesota Press, 2000.

Sicher, Ephraim, ed. *Breaking Crystal: Writing and Memory after Auschwitz.* Urbana: University of Illinois Press, 1998.

Van Alphen, Ernst. *Caught by History: Holocaust Effects in Contemporary Art, Literature, and Theory.* Stanford University Press, 1997.

Vice, Sue. *Holocaust Fiction.* London: Routledge, 2000.

Literary criticism

Aldridge, John. *After The Lost Generation: A Critical Study of the Writers of Two Wars.* New York: Arbor House, 1985.

Atack, Margaret. *Literature and the French Resistance: Cultural Politics and Narrative Forms, 1940–1950.* Manchester University Press, 1989.

Bergonzi, Bernard. *Wartime and Aftermath: English Literature and its Background, 1939–1960.* Oxford University Press, 1993.

Bevan, David, ed. *Literature and War.* Amsterdam: Rodopi, 1990.

Byles, Joanne Montgomery. *War, Women, and Poetry, 1914–1945: British and German Writers and Activists.* Newark: University of Delaware Press, 1995.

Calder, Robert. *Beware the British Serpent: The Role of Writers in British Propaganda in the United States,1939–1945.* Montreal: McGill-Queen's University Press, 2004.

Cloonan, William J. *The Writing of War: French and German Fiction and World War II.* Gainesville: University Press of Florida, 1999.

Davidson, Mildred. *The Poetry is in the Pity.* London: Chatto & Windus, 1972.

Dawes, James. *The Language of War: Literature and Culture in the U.S. from the Civil War through World War II.* Cambridge, MA: Harvard University Press, 2002.

Estrin, Barbara L. *The American Love Lyric After Auschwitz and Hiroshima.* New York: Palgrave, 2001.

Fussell, Paul, ed. *The Norton Book of Modern War*. New York: Norton, 1991.

Gallagher, Jean. *The World Wars through the Female Gaze*. Carbondale: Southern Illinois University Press, 1998.

Gerster, Robin. *Big-Noting: The Heroic Theme in Australian War Writing*. Melbourne University Press, 1987.

Goldensohn, Lorrie. *Dismantling Glory: Twentieth-Century Soldier Poetry*. New York: Columbia University Press, 2003.

Gubar, Susan. *Poetry After Auschwitz: Remembering What One Never Knew*. Bloomington: Indiana University Press, 2003.

Harris, Frederick J. *Encounters With Darkness: French and German Writers on World War II*. New York: Oxford University Press, 1983.

Hartley, Jenny. *Millions Like Us: British Women's Fiction of the Second World War*. London: Virago, 1997.

Harvey, A. D. *A Muse of Fire: Literature, Art and War*. London: Hambledon, 1998.

Hewison, Robert. *Under Siege: Literary Life in London, 1939–1945*. London: Weidenfeld & Nicolson, 1977.

Higgins, Ian, ed. *The Second World War in Literature: Eight Essays*. Edinburgh: Scottish Academic Press, 1986.

Hodgson, Katharine. *Written with the Bayonet: Soviet Russian Poetry of World War Two*. Liverpool University Press, 1996.

Holsinger, M. Paul, and Mary Anne Schofield. *Visions of War: World War II in Popular Literature and Culture*. Bowling Green State University Popular Press, 1992.

Klein, Holger, with John Flower and Eric Homberger. *The Second World War in Fiction*. London: Macmillan, 1984.

Knowles, Sebastian D. G. *A Purgatorial Flame: Seven British Writers in the Second World War*. Philadelphia: University of Pennsylvania Press, 1990.

Lassner, Phyllis. *British Women Writers of World War II: Battlegrounds of Their Own*. Basingstoke and London: Macmillan, 1998.

Limon, John. *Writing After War: American War Fiction from Realism to Postmodernism*. New York: Oxford University Press, 1994.

Longley, Edna. *Poetry in the Wars*. Newark: University of Delaware Press, 1987.

Lyon, Philippa. *Twentieth-Century War Poetry*. Basingstoke: Palgrave Macmillan, 2005.

MacKay, Marina. *Modernism and World War II*. Cambridge University Press, 2007.

Mengham, Rod, and N. H. Reeve. *The Fiction of the 1940s: Stories of Survival*. Basingstoke: Palgrave, 2001.

Mole, Gary D. *Beyond the Limit-Experience: French Poetry of the Deportation, 1940–1945*. New York: Peter Lang, 2002.

Munton, Alan. *English Fiction of the Second World War*. London: Faber, 1989.

Norris, Margot. *Writing War in the Twentieth Century*. Charlottesville: University of Virginia Press, 2000.

Novak, Dagmar. *A Dubious Glory: War and the Canadian Novel*. New York: Peter Lang, 2000.

Oostdijk, Diederik, and Markha G. Valenta, eds. *Tales of the Great American Victory*. Amsterdam: VU University Press, 2006.

Peitsch, Helmut, Charles Burdett, and Claire Gorrara, eds. *European Memories of the Second World War*. New York: Berghahn Books, 1999.

Piette, Adam. *Imagination at War: British Fiction and Poetry 1939–1945*. Basingstoke: Macmillan, 1995.

Plain, Gill. *Women's Fiction of the Second World War: Gender, Power and Resistance*. Edinburgh University Press, 1996.

Phillips, Kathy J. *Manipulating Masculinity: War and Gender in Modern British and American Literature*. New York: Palgrave Macmillan, 2006.

Rawlinson, Mark. *British Writing of the Second World War*. Oxford: Clarendon Press, 2000.

Reilly, Catherine, ed. *Chaos of the Night: Women's Poetry and Verse of the Second World War*. London: Virago, 1984.

Ryan, Judith. *The Uncompleted Past: Postwar German Novels and the Third Reich*. Detroit: Wayne State University Press, 1983.

Scannell, Vernon. *Not Without Glory: Poets of the Second World War*. London: Woburn Press, 1976.

Schneider, Karen. *Loving Arms: British Women Writing the Second World War*. Lexington: University Press of Kentucky, 1997.

Schweik, Susan M. *A Gulf So Deeply Cut: American Women Poets and the Second World War*. Madison: University of Wisconsin Press, 1991.

Sebald, W. G. *On the Natural History of Destruction*. New York: Random House, 2003.

Shires, Linda M. *British Poetry of the Second World War*. New York: St. Martin's Press, 1985.

Stewart, Victoria. *Women's Autobiography: War and Trauma*. Basingstoke: Palgrave Macmillan, 2003.
  Narratives of Memory: British Writing of the 1940s. Basingstoke: Palgrave Macmillan, 2006.

Stonebridge, Lyndsey. *The Writing of Anxiety: Imagining Wartime in Mid-Century British Culture*. Basingstoke: Palgrave Macmillan, 2007.

Stout, Janis P. *Coming Out of War: Poetry, Grieving, and the Culture of the World Wars*. Tuscaloosa: University of Alabama Press, 2005.

Suleiman, Susan Rubin. *Crises of Memory and the Second World War*. Cambridge, MA: Harvard University Press, 2006.

Tachibana, Reiko. *Narrative as Counter-Memory: A Half-Century of Postwar Writing in Germany and Japan*. Albany: State University of New York Press, 1998.

Tate, Trudi. *War Literature in the Twentieth Century*. Oxford: Blackwell, 2007.

Torgovnick, Marianna. *The War Complex: World War II in Our Time*. University of Chicago Press, 2005.

Vees-Gulani, Susanne. *Trauma and Guilt: Literature of Wartime Bombing in Germany*. Berlin: W. de Gruyter, 2003.

Waldmeir, Joseph J. *American Novels of the Second World War*. The Hague: Mouton, 1969.

Walsh, Jeffrey. *American War Literature, 1914 to Vietnam*. New York: St. Martin's, 1982.

Whittier Treat, John. *Writing Ground Zero: Japanese Literature and the Atomic Bomb*. University of Chicago Press, 1995.

Wilms, Wilfried, and William Rasch, eds. *Bombs Away! Representing the Air War over Europe and Japan*. Amsterdam: Rodopi, 2006.

INDEX

Cambridge Companions to ...

AUTHORS

TOPICS